Enlightening
the
Constitutional
Debate

THE ROYAL
SOCIETY
OF EDINBURGH

BRITISH
ACADEMY
for the humanities and social sciences

Reports: Elizabeth Hemsley and Peter Barr

Illustrations © Iain McIntosh

Design: Emma Quinn

Secretariat: Jenny Liddell

Printed in Scotland by 21 Colour Ltd.

Contents

Foreword

One of the most important peacetime issues facing the United Kingdom will be decided in the Referendum on Scottish Independence on 18 September 2014. The decision reached by the people of Scotland will also be of vital importance to the other nations of the United Kingdom.

Because of the significance of the Referendum and its outcome, the Royal Society of Edinburgh and the British Academy commissioned a series of events to examine the key questions and issues that surround the complex question of Scotland's constitutional future.

The series of events began in early 2012 with discussion seminars in London and Edinburgh, in which a range of academic and policy experts scoped out the issues facing Scotland and the UK, including looking at evidence from other countries where major constitutional change has taken place.

We then followed this up over the last year with events in Edinburgh, London, Glasgow and Aberdeen, involving experts in a range of fields. Each event has sought to analyse the effect of constitutional change on a particular policy area: Scotland & the EU; taxation & spending; defence & international relations; the real economy; currency, banking & financial services; culture & broadcasting; borders, immigration and citizenship; science & higher education; welfare & public services; and historical, legal and constitutional issues.

This book, which is a record of these events, is intended to contribute to an informed debate around the critical areas that will shape the future of Scotland and the United Kingdom. It is also intended to be part of a record of the issues that have been central to the debate about whether Scotland becomes independent or remains part of the United Kingdom. The Royal Society of Edinburgh and the British Academy are both independent organisations and take no position on the debate about Scotland's constitutional position and the future of the United Kingdom.

The publication of this report is not intended to influence the outcome of the Referendum in a particular way. Our hope is that it will help to bring the highly informed analysis that characterised the joint series of events to as wide an audience as possible.

We hope that people will read the information and views contained within these pages, or watch the debates available online, to consider the broad range of views that exist on the question of the UK's constitutional future. The analyses that inform the reports in this book illustrate vividly the issues that will shape the future relationship between Scotland and the other nations of the United Kingdom, whatever decision is made in September.

Sir John Arbuthnott MRIA PRSE
President, The Royal Society of Edinburgh

Lord Stern of Brentford PBA
President, British Academy

Introduction

by Alan Alexander and Iain McLean

The origins of this book

The Scottish National Party (SNP) formed a minority administration after the Scottish Parliament election of 2007. They announced that they planned to hold an independence Referendum. But in that parliament they did not control sufficient votes to legislate for one. In 2011, they won more than half the seats in the Scottish Parliament that will sit until 2016. Their manifesto had reiterated the promise to hold a Referendum if they won. They therefore took this commitment forward, negotiating with the UK Government to ensure that the result would be legal, binding, and recognised by both governments. This agreement was signed in Edinburgh by First Minister Alex Salmond and Prime Minister David Cameron on 15 October 2012.

Until then, interest in the Referendum outcome had been muted in Scotland and non-existent in the rest of the UK (rUK). Commentators then awoke to the fact that Scotland could decide in 2014 to become an independent state. The Referendum date was later set for 18 September 2014. The Scottish Government plans that, if the vote then is *Yes*, Independence Day will follow in March 2016, and the Scottish Parliament already due to be elected in May 2016 will be the first parliament of an independent Scotland. Scottish MPs will depart from the House of Commons during this process. In the period between the Referendum and Independence Day, detailed negotiations would take place between the two governments on the process and specifics of separation.

Now, never a day goes past without a commentator weighing in on TV or on the editorial pages to give the world the benefit of their views. But these views are often not based on evidence. However, even before the Edinburgh Agreement, the two sponsoring national academies had decided to run a joint series of expert seminars, in order to bring evidence to the table.

The British Academy was established in 1902. It is an independent national academy of Fellows elected for their eminence in research and publication. It is the UK's expert body that supports and speaks for the humanities and social sciences. The Royal Society of Edinburgh is the senior body by more than a century, being an enduring memorial to the Scottish Enlightenment of the 18th Century. It was established in 1783 by Royal Charter for "the advancement of learning and useful knowledge". Its Founding Fellows included Adam Smith, Benjamin Franklin, the chemist Joseph Black, and the geologist James Hutton. Whereas the British Academy covers only humanities and social sciences, leaving natural sciences, medicine and engineering to the Royal Society and other national academies, the RSE represents all academic subjects, as well as the arts, culture, business and enterprise.

In 2012, the two academies set up a joint committee to plan the events reported in this book. We held a total of eleven seminars, three in London and eight in Scotland. Some of the events were invitation-only; but most were open. A record was taken of all of them – both of the presentations and the points raised in discussion – and it was planned from the outset that the record should be published as the two academies' contribution to Enlightening the Constitutional Debate.

We emphasise that we are not taking sides. We do not argue for *Yes* or *No*. The aim of this book is to offer evidence, not to persuade.

What our experts found

Our experts started the series by warning against the 'false legal certainty' that was being claimed about Scotland's admission, readmission, or continuation in the European Union. The Scottish Government was making claims about the process that were being contradicted by officials in the UK Government and the EU. As there has never been a comparable secession within an EU member state, nobody knows for sure what EU law would require. This remains one of the 'known unknowns' that we discuss on the following pages.

Introduction

Our session on tax and spending examined how governments would balance the budget in Scotland after both a *Yes* and a *No* vote. After a *Yes*, the risks identified were the current downward trend of North Sea Oil revenue, and Scotland's unfavourable old-age dependency ratio (that is, ratio of the population over 65 to population of working age). The first would put downward pressure on tax receipts; the second, upward pressure on social protection entitlement spending. After a *No*, there would be pressure to reform the current 'Barnett' Formula for block grant to Wales, Scotland and Northern Ireland. This is being led from Wales, where policy makers believe that a needs assessment would be more appropriate. Therefore, relative block grant to Scotland may decline, or be reshaped, following a *No* vote.

On defence and international relations, our experts began by outlining the tasks of a defence force. This question should be resolved, for an independent Scotland, before the question of how much to spend on defence. Too often, the discussion proceeds in the opposite direction: deciding a budget first, and what to buy afterwards. On the Trident submarines currently based at Faslane, it was noted that the UK's policy of refusing to "pre-negotiate", as it puts it, for the contingency of a 'Yes' vote, makes it particularly hard to predict how the issue will be resolved. But Trident like-for-like replacement policy may cease to be the consensus policy of all UK parties that it currently is. The question was also raised as to whether the decommissioning of Trident could be achieved within the Referendum-to-Independence-Day timetable suggested by the Scottish Government.

Our experts on the real economy examined the business case for and against independence. Scotland's brand risked contamination from anti-EU sentiment in England, which was not shared by the leading Scottish political parties. An independent Scotland would be a small, open economy, highly dependent on revenues and employment from the North Sea, accounting for up to 20% of Scottish GDP. As oil is a depleting resource, there is a strong case for an oil fund to invest against the day it run out; but oil revenue cannot at the same time be spent to maintain the current level of public services.

We held two expert sessions on currency and banking, one in London and one in Edinburgh. The Edinburgh session was particularly topical, as it took place a few hours after the Governor of the Bank of England, Mark Carney, spoke in Edinburgh on the requirements for a currency union to succeed, mentioned below. Of the various currency options open to an independent Scotland, our experts discarded two as impractical: namely, joining the Euro, and 'sterlingisation' (*viz.*, using the pound sterling as Scotland's currency without formal institutions to support it, such as an independent central bank or an agreed currency area with the rest of the UK). The remaining viable options included a formal monetary union (the Scottish Government's preferred option); an independent currency pegged to another, as in Denmark or Hong Kong; or an independent currency allowed to float across a wider range of values. Each of these options carries significant risks. One risk is of speculative pressure against the Scottish currency. Such pressure destroyed the Czech–Slovak monetary union of 1993 within weeks of its creation.

Our experts on culture and broadcasting discussed how (or whether) the role of the BBC should be fulfilled in an independent Scotland. However, the case for new TV channels in Scotland could be made whether the Referendum vote was 'Yes' or 'No'. There was a question to be answered as to the conditions upon which a Scottish Broadcasting Service, in the event of independence, would have access to content produced by the BBC, which would then be an institution of rUK.

On immigration and citizenship, our experts noted that the issue would be more urgent now than when the Irish Free State was created in 1922; then taking a leisurely thirteen years to draw up its nationality rules. The Scottish Government is comfortable with Scots having dual citizenship after independence, but one of our experts warned of the risks of Scottish policy then being "hollowed out" as a result of decisions taken in other jurisdictions with many dual citizens. Our experts noted that the Scottish Government plans a more liberal immigration policy than the current UK, for good reasons of labour force strengthening; but they wondered how such policies would be consistent with maintaining the Common Travel Area with the rest of the UK, Ireland, the Channel Islands and the Isle of Man.

Introduction

On science and higher education policy, our experts explored what one of them called the "delicate ecology" of higher education and research funding in Scotland. Opposing views were expressed: that the present system of funding via the UK Research Councils should be maintained if Scotland votes 'Yes', and that "small is beautiful" when it comes to research and innovation. The calibre of Scotland's universities was celebrated. Options for future funding of Scottish, English and EU students are unclear in the event of either a 'Yes' or a 'No' vote.

On welfare and public services, our experts warned that social protection expenditure would be under severe pressure in Scotland whether the vote is 'Yes' or 'No', because of the need to bring the budget closer to balance in either case. The people want welfare expenditure to be controlled from Scotland, which might be a good idea in any case, even with a 'No' vote, because of the close link with the NHS and local authority spending, which are already devolved. This would require hard thinking about the purposes and structure of tax to pay for the welfare state. One possibility would be to make National Insurance a more real (as opposed to notional) social insurance tax.

On the historical, legal and constitutional aspects of the debate, our experts looked at the future of the Union in terms of changing understandings of sovereignty, shifting patterns of national identity, and uncertainty over the course of post-Referendum constitutional politics. It was noted that neither side in the debate sought to emphasise a classically strong conception of sovereignty as the 'prize' of a 'Yes' or 'No' vote. On the nationalist side, the retention of various historical aspects of Union post-independence – monarchy, currency, social etc., – is stressed. On the Unionist side there is acceptance in principle that levels of fiscal and legislative autonomy beyond the enhancements to the devolution settlement already provided for under the Scotland Act 2012 are constitutionally viable. If this suggests that the constitutional options are situated on a spectrum rather than offering a clear binary choice, the question of political identity, too, is fuzzy. The vast majority of Scots profess a Scottish identity, but today this takes a predominantly civic rather than ethnic form. Also, many combine their Scottishness with a more or less strong British identity. Identity, then, can be no simple predictor of allegiance in the constitutional debate and, given the prominence of Scottish identity, the form and strength of supplementary British identity may be the more significant variable.

In these shifting constitutional sands, it is unlikely that the September Referendum will offer a definitive resolution. Certain matters may be predicted with some confidence, including the international legal standing of rUK as the 'continuator'[1] state and the treatment of an independent Scotland as a new state. As the vote draws nearer, however, its long-term significance remains shrouded in doubt. A 'Yes' vote will be the cue for complex negotiations with the EU and rUK alike, A 'No' vote is also likely to be the prelude to a new constitutional accommodation, in which any extension of devolved powers to Scotland is likely to engage the other nations of the United Kingdom much more than previous rounds of Scottish constitutional reform have done.

Some known unknowns

The Scottish Government's White Paper *Scotland's Future*[2] and the UK Government's *Scotland Analysis* series[3] confirm the finding of our own experts that there are some things that cannot be settled by unilateral action. As we know that we do not know what will happen, we use former US Defense Secretary Donald Rumsfeld's useful phrase and label them 'known unknowns'. Many relate to negotiations after a *Yes* vote; some to political developments after a *No* vote.

If the Scots vote 'Yes'…

… then the Scottish negotiators must enter discussions with several other bodies. As these bodies ('counterparties') will bring their own policies and priorities to the table, we do not know what will happen. In some of these cases, the Scottish Government's counterparty has already stated its position. We disregard these statements for two reasons:

1 *Possible time inconsistency.* A counterparty may make a statement now of how it would react in the event of negotiations with Scotland after a 'Yes' vote. But that 'Yes' will in itself change the context, to the extent that the counterparty's intention then may be different from its stated intention now.

---

1 In the inelegant jargon of international lawyers.
2 http://www.scotland.gov.uk/Publications/2013/11/9348
3 https://www.gov.uk/government/collections/scotland-analysis

Introduction

2 *Future elections.* A UK General Election will take place on 7 May 2015 (or possibly earlier). A European Parliament election will take place on 22 May 2014. The policy of the European Council / Council of Ministers of the European Union is set by its member-state governments. There are 28 of these; therefore an average of about seven will hold a general election each year. NATO's policy is set by its Council, the North Atlantic Council, which explains:

"Decisions are agreed upon on the basis of unanimity and common accord. There is no voting or decision by majority. This means that policies decided upon by the North Atlantic Council (NAC) are supported by and are the expression of the collective will of all the sovereign states that are members of the Alliance and are accepted by all of them."[4]

Hence, as with the EU, the policy of NATO will change in response to general elections in its member states, but at a slower rate because of the unanimity requirement.

The main known unknowns relate to the European Union, NATO and the rest of the United Kingdom (rUK).

The European Union

The Scottish Government has stated that it is 'appropriate … that Scotland's transition to full membership is secured under the general provisions of Article 48 [of the Treaty of European Union, which] … provides for a Treaty amendment to be agreed by common accord on the part of the representatives of the governments of the member states'. The alternative route, Article 49, 'provides the legal basis, and defines the procedure, for a conventional enlargement where the candidate country is seeking membership from outside the EU'. The Scottish Government prefers the Article 48 route, but recognises that the decision is the counterparty's: 'it will be for the EU member states … to take forward the most appropriate procedure under which an independent Scotland will become a signatory to the EU Treaties'.

4 http://www.nato.int/cps/en/natolive/topics_49763.htm?, consulted 28.01.2014

EU law specialists have doubted whether Article 48 is appropriate[5]. However, we consider both options. Under Article 48, the party negotiating on Scotland's behalf would not be the Scottish Government, but the UK Government. The UK Government in office on 19 September 2014 (i.e., the Conservative–Lib Dem Coalition Government) would start; and, if the negotiations were not complete by May 2015, the successor UK Government would continue. The Coalition Government may itself wish to put other Treaty amendments into the discussion. If the UK Government elected in 2015 is Conservative, then Prime Minister Cameron has promised an in-out referendum on revised terms which he promises will have been negotiated: so these matters will certainly be added to the Article 48 agenda. The Scottish Government, in short, will have no control over either the content or the outcome of negotiations under Article 48.

Under Article 49, it would be in control of its own application. Its White Paper says that it "will approach EU membership negotiations on the principle of *continuity of effect*". Scotland, of course, is currently a full member of the EU and accepts what Eurocrats call the *acquis communautaire*: i.e., the accumulated legislation, legal acts and court decisions which constitute the body of European Union law. But it would not automatically inherit the various opt-outs and rebates that the current UK has secured from the EU: e.g., a contributions rebate and an opt-out from the Schengen common travel area. The outcome of those will emerge from the negotiations with a counterparty (the European Council) whose composition is currently unknown.

NATO

The Scottish Government states that it "will notify NATO of our intention to join the alliance... the basic premise of NATO is that all members must make an active commitment to the alliance and Scotland would recognise and play our full part in building collective security and capability". However, the White Paper also states that "The Scottish Government is committed to securing the complete withdrawal of Trident from an independent Scotland as quickly as can be both safely and responsibly achieved". We cannot say how NATO's Council will respond to these two commitments. But, as the Council acts by unanimity, we can say that its position will be determined by whichever member state is both most hostile to Scotland's proposals and prepared to threaten a veto.

---

5 e.g., Prof. Kenneth Armstrong, evidence to Scottish Affairs Committee, House of Commons, 15.01.2014, at http://www.publications.parliament.uk/pa/cm201314/cmselect/cmscotaf/uc140-xiii/uc14001.htm

Introduction

rUK

The Scottish Government acknowledges that after a 'Yes' vote, there will have to be negotiations with representatives of rUK over a huge range of issues. They will include:

> Splitting of UK assets and liabilities;

> Sharing some existing UK services, including overseas embassies and consulates, the Driver and Vehicle Licensing Authority (DVLA) and the BBC;

> The future employment situation of public and military employees of the UK in Scotland, and of Scottish public and military employees in rUK;

> The Common Travel Area currently comprising the UK, Ireland, the Channel Islands and the Isle of Man (this negotiation will also involve the other counterparty governments);

> Sterling and the Bank of England;

> The nuclear submarine base at Faslane and the armed warhead store at Coulport, which are the main components of what is currently Her Majesty's Naval Base (HMNB) Clyde.

For many of these negotiations, international law offers a default position. Were the parties, after failing to agree, to submit their dispute to arbitration, there are principles of international law that determine which party gets what. Unlike in a divorce, we do not think it is remotely likely that Scotland and rUK will have to go to arbitration on any of these issues. But the common knowledge of what would probably happen if they *did* go to arbitration will limit the range of creative suggestions that might otherwise be made. On other matters – most obviously Faslane and Coulport – principles of international law will not help the negotiators. On those, a purely political bargain must be struck.

Splitting immovable assets – land and buildings – is easy. Those located in Scotland go to Scotland. Those located in rUK go to rUK. This would doubtless be followed by some agreed swaps, as one country ended up with assets that both agreed would better serve the needs of the other. Immovable assets located outside the present UK would fall to the rUK as the 'continuator' state, although the Scottish Government has stated that it would like to negotiate an agreement for the shared use of some UK diplomatic premises.

Movable, tangible assets such as tanks and computers would be assigned according to their purpose rather than their location. In most cases, this would have the same consequence as a split by location, but in some cases (e.g., military equipment; equipment relating to UK government functions currently carried out in Scotland) it would not.

Splitting liabilities could be more controversial. In relation to the UK's existing stock of government bonds on issue, HM Treasury has stated that

"the continuing UK Government would in all circumstances honour the contractual terms of the debt issued by the UK Government. An independent Scottish state would become responsible for a fair and proportionate share of the UK's current liabilities.

An entirely separate contract between the continuing UK Government and an independent Scottish state's Government would need to be established. The respective shares of debt and the terms of repayment would be subject to negotiation."[6]

Because this statement is addressed to the markets rather than the electorate, it does not suffer from the problems of time-inconsistency and political change mentioned above. It is, in practice, inconceivable that a future (r)UK Government would renege on it. The consequences would be too awful to contemplate.

Various principles for apportioning liabilities between Scotland and rUK have been suggested. The Scottish Government says:

"The national debt could be apportioned by reference to the historic contribution made to the UK's public finances by Scotland, or on the basis of our population share. We may choose to offset Scotland's share of the value of UK assets against our inherited debt."

The problem with the 'historic contribution' proposal is that there is no agreed starting date. Should it be 1707? Data are scanty for the first 200 years or so of the Union. But any later starting date may be seen as arbitrary and chosen to maximise bargaining advantage. As there is no default position in international law for the 'historic contribution' apportionment, we predict that for most liabilities the choice will be between 'population share' and 'relative GDP'.

---

6   14 January 2014, at
    https://www.gov.uk/government/publications/uk-debt-and-the-scotland-independence-referendum, consulted 28.01.14

Introduction

Population share is simple and an obvious default. Considerations of ability to repay may, however, push the parties towards an apportionment based on relative GDP. The Scottish Government repeatedly states that, once North Sea activity and tax receipts are assigned to Scotland, Scottish GDP per head will be higher than that of rUK on Independence Day. A relative GDP assignment of liabilities would in that case be less favourable to Scotland than a population share assignment.

For the liabilities and contingent liabilities arising from the UK bailout of failing banks in 2008–09 – including RBS and the then Bank of Scotland group – we are not aware of any agreed principles of international law that may be applicable. Pension liabilities should be easier. There are two main liabilities – state pension entitlements of people living in Scotland or wishing to claim state pension in Scotland; and the liabilities of unfunded and under-funded schemes for public employees. For the latter:

> "the Scottish Government proposes taking our fair share of pension liabilities based on responsibilities for meeting the pension entitlements of pensioners who live in Scotland."

The bargaining position of rUK is unknown.

Shared services should not be difficult, so long as the distinction between assets and institutions is borne in mind. As recently explained by Adam Tomkins, John Millar Professor of Public Law at Glasgow University:

> "international law shows you that, in the context of a state succession of this nature, there is every difference between institutions and assets. Institutions of the UK become institutions of the rest of the UK, but assets of those institutions fall to be apportioned equitably." [7]

For example, the assets of the DVLA and the BBC – studios, computer systems, vans... – will fall to be apportioned equitably. But as *institutions*, they will be institutions of the rUK after independence. It is only common sense that Scotland should then to seek to buy some services from them, but that will be a matter of contractual agreement.

7   Scottish Affairs Select Committee, 15.01.2014, oral evidence, Q4181

Arrangements for public servants should be a matter of common sense and good human resources management. Though there may be difficulties in the Armed Services, because the Scottish Government's plan for less expensive defence may mean fewer jobs for service personnel, in most areas, and it is probable that mutual goodwill would produce a solution that is acceptable to both governments and at least to the vast majority of affected public servants. Until independence, civil servants working for the Scottish Government remain part of the UK's unified civil service. This would facilitate moves between the UK and Scottish services around the time of Independence Day.

The *Common Travel Area* should be easy, on two conditions: (i) that the EU does not insist on Scotland joining the Schengen Area, which would normally be part of the *acquis*; and (ii) that Scotland is willing to coordinate its policy on migration with the rUK, Ireland, the Isle of Man and the Channel Islands. Condition (i) is a matter of common sense, which we hope will prevail. Condition (ii) may be more problematic if the Scottish Government after independence maintains the current Scottish Government's wish to

> "take forward a points-based approach targeted at particular Scottish requirements … [and] a new model of asylum services separate from immigration." (WP pp 270–71)

An immigrant to one member of a common travel area is an immigrant to all of them. Therefore, negotiations to remain in the CTA will have as counterparties all five of the other parties to it. All five will have to approve Scotland's migration policy.

We have left the two most difficult areas to the last. The Scottish Government insists that Scotland will remain in the sterling area, and will seek membership of the Monetary Policy Committee of the Bank of England. It argues that that is in the interests of rUK as well as of Scotland, because the present UK is what economists label an optimum currency area. The current UK Government insists that the rUK Government would be very unlikely to agree to that. Although we discount these statements for the reasons given above (time inconsistency and possible change of government), they point to a real problem. Sterling is an institution, not an asset. Therefore, after independence, it becomes an institution of the continuator state, namely rUK. Its negotiators will consider whether admitting Scotland to a currency union is indeed in the interests of rUK.

Introduction

The 'optimal currency area' argument should have some traction; but so too will arguments which conclude that the near-collapse of the Eurozone from 2009 onwards occurred, among other reasons, because some Eurozone members were fiscally undisciplined. It is predictable, therefore, that rUK will insist that if it admits Scotland to a common currency area, Scotland will have to agree to harsh rules caping its maximum public debt and deficit. In a noteworthy speech in Edinburgh on January 29 2014, Mark Carney, Governor of the Bank of England, said:

"Any arrangement to retain sterling in an independent Scotland would need to be negotiated between the Westminster and Scottish Parliaments. The Bank of England would implement whatever monetary arrangements were put in place."

He went on to point out that a monetary union requires close cooperation between its member states on budgeting and bank regulation. On bank regulation, for instance:

"the European process illustrates the difficulty of building the institutional arrangements for a common insurance scheme across sovereign states. This is unsurprising, since mutualised deposit guarantee schemes imply a pooling of risk and loss of sovereignty. All member states must be persuaded that they won't simply be left with the bill for the mistakes of others."[8]

Whereas on currency and banking Scotland's position appears weak, on Faslane and Coulport it appears strong. The Scottish Government states that an independent Scotland does not wish to be a nuclear weapons state. Indeed it cannot be, because the Nuclear Non-proliferation Treaty (NPT) of 1970, which Scotland would presumably sign, states that "the NPT non-nuclear-weapon states agree never to acquire nuclear weapons". Therefore it is proper for Scotland to give notice to rUK, as it already has done, that the nuclear-armed submarines and warheads must be removed from Scottish soil. What is unclear is how the rUK will respond. Quite independently of the Faslane question, the UK political parties and the armed services are in the middle of arguments about how, or whether, to replace the present Trident deterrent force.

8   Mark Carney, Speech to Scottish Council (Development and Industry), at
    http://www.bankofengland.co.uk/publications/Documents/speeches/2014/speech706.pdf, accessed 30.01.2014

These arguments cut across parties (and Services). We cannot predict the stance to be taken by the UK Government which will be elected in 2015. Even if negotiations are started by the current Coalition Government, its position on Trident and Faslane may be altered by the new Government. Apart from the terms of the NPT, international law is no help here. The outcome, whatever it is, will be intrinsically political.

We also predict that deals on these difficult issues will be linked, even though they are conceptually separate. There is no logical connection between Scotland's currency and rUK's nuclear-armed submarines, but there will certainly be a political connection. We do not know how this most important pair of known unknowns will end up.

If the Scots vote 'No'...

... then the Scotland Act 2012 will be brought into operation. How this will work was explained above. Its key feature is that the UK will withdraw from 10p in the pound of income tax, which will require the Scottish Parliament to set a rate of Scottish income tax. It cannot sit on its hands. This change will increase the fiscal responsibility of the Parliament, because it will have to weigh the last pound of tax it receives against the last pound it spends, and decide whether it would prefer to tax more or to spend less.

However, all the main Unionist parties in Scotland have signalled that they wish to go beyond the "Calman" scheme embodied in the Act of 2012. We do not have any of the details as this book goes to press. All of them would like to devolve more spending powers to the Scottish Parliament. That must require devolving more tax powers. But this raises difficulties. For instance, rates of VAT may not normally be varied within a single EU member state. An independent Scotland can choose its VAT rate. A devolved Scotland cannot. It can vary rates of Corporation Tax, but recent worries and parliamentary inquiries into the tax affairs of multinational companies suggest that this would not be a wise move for either Scotland or rUK. The only taxes of any consequence that are left are the rest of income tax, and National Insurance. We await the Unionist parties' detailed proposals. It is somewhat disappointing that no detail has been produced by either the Conservative or the Labour Parties as we go to press.

Scotland
and the EU

Scotland and the EU

13 March 2013, at the Royal Society of Edinburgh

INTRODUCTION

The purpose of this seminar was to examine in the context of a Referendum vote in favour of independence, issues relating to Scotland's accession to, and membership of, the European Union. This seminar was the first in a series of eleven, organised by the Royal Society of Edinburgh in partnership with the British Academy, with the objective of Enlightening the Constitutional Debate.

The subject of Scotland and the EU was addressed by a panel of three expert speakers:

> **Neil Walker FBA FRSE,** Regius Professor of Public Law and the Law of Nature and Nations, University of Edinburgh;

> **Graham Avery,** St. Antony's College, University of Oxford and European Policy Centre, Brussels;

> **Diana Panke,** Professor of Political Science, University of Freiburg.

This seminar was conducted as an open, public discussion seminar. This report provides a summary of the positions outlined by the speakers, and of the subsequent public discussion.

PROFESSOR NEIL WALKER FBA FRSE,
REGIUS PROFESSOR OF PUBLIC LAW AND THE LAW
OF NATURE AND NATIONS, UNIVERSITY OF EDINBURGH

Professor Walker began by analysing the nature of the argument about Scotland's possible accession to the EU in the event of an independence vote. He suggested that this argument had so far represented 'false certainties' about the legality of Scotland's accession to the EU, and that, given the absence of legal certainty, the argument would be more a political than a legal one.

Coining the phrase 'false legal certainty', Professor Walker explained that both sides of the debate on the possibility of Scotland's accession to the EU have relied upon an assumed position of legal certainty which does not exist. The SNP's position has been characterised by an assumption that Scotland will automatically become a member of the EU upon achieving independence, while the position of the UK Government has been characterised by an assumption that Scotland will have to go through a full accession process if it wishes to become an EU member state. Although both sides of the debate have asserted the correctness of their positions, a resolution has not been reached. This demonstrates the genuine difficulty of the question and the absence of a clear legal position.

Elucidating the absence of legal certainty, Professor Walker referred to the lack of legal precedent for a situation in which an EU member state splits and both sides wish to remain EU members. He suggested that Greenland's position with regard to Denmark offers only an indirect analogy, because Greenland has not sought membership of the EU. In response to the lack of clear legal precedent, both sides of the debate on Scotland's EU membership have had to draw inferences. According to normal rules of state succession, only one state succeeds; this being the position relied upon by the UK Government. The SNP position is that there is no precedent for five million citizens being thrown out of the EU. By this interpretation the EU is a constitutional entity and the burden of proof as to why citizens should be made to leave lies with those insisting that they do so.

Professor Walker indicated that further uncertainty exists in the question of whether this debate should take place within, and be guided by, international or EU law. Beginning with the premise that the EU is simply an international organization 'with frills', Professor Walker suggested that normal international law rules of state continuity would apply. This being the case, the favour lies with the UK (excluding Scotland) remaining an EU member and Scotland re-applying.

Scotland and the EU

This is on the basis that the UK has a larger population than Scotland, is more likely to receive recognition by third parties, and that Scotland is the party initiating the split. However, Professor Walker went on to suggest that the position offered by international law is not definitive, and that it may be unhelpful to follow the international law position when we have European law to refer to. European case law, he pointed out, famously refers to the EU as a distinctive legal order, meaning that we need not assume that normal rules of accession necessarily apply. If we look at the treaties and purposes of the EU as a whole, including its focus on respect for minorities and inter-state cooperation, then we can assume that there is some guidance for all EU member states to cooperate in ensuring that Scotland is able to remain an EU member state. If the EU is a 'constitutional club', then member citizens cannot simply be ejected; citizens are held to be members just as much as states are, and their rights as members will be taken seriously. This interpretation will require that Scotland is enabled to fast-track its accession to the EU, or that amendment is made to existing EU treaties to ensure Scotland's continued membership.

Having highlighted the possible opposition between the international law and the European law positions, Professor Walker posed the question, 'which of these streams of law should prevail in deciding the question of an independent Scotland's membership of the EU?' Professor Walker argued that international law has no real standing to answer the question about Scotland's EU membership. He acknowledged, however, that even in the European context, it is not easy to see how this question might be answered. The EU has no written constitution informing us who makes these types of decisions; the European Court of Justice has no obvious standing or advisory jurisdiction; the European Commission is just an executive body; and the Council of Ministers, whilst being an authoritative body, provides no certainty as to who should make decisions in cases of dispute. In the absence of legal certainty, the question about Scotland's EU membership becomes as much about politics as it does about legality.

Professor Walker acknowledged the importance of bringing the best legal arguments to the table in deciding the question of Scotland's EU membership, and referred to the moral authority of the law. He stated that in the event of Scotland's independence, there would need to be either an accession treaty or an amendment treaty to enable EU membership, but identified that whatever legal process was undertaken, the debate would be a largely political one.

Referring to the politics of the question, Professor Walker acknowledged the possible reluctance of other European member states to allow separatist nations to accede to the EU with ease. He identified Spain as one state which may have fears over the precedent this might set with regard to Catalonia. In response, Professor Walker raised two points. The first was that these states must be required to act in the context of public reason; i.e., they must give a good public reason against Scotland's accession to the EU, which makes sense as part of the history of the European Union. He felt that these states would struggle to make this case. The second point was that Scotland's position vis-à-vis the UK is unique in the context of other separatist movements in Europe, because if Scotland did secede from the UK, it would not be contra the constitutional process. Rather, it would be consensual. As distinct from other national minorities seeking independence, Scottish independence, should it be realised, would have constitutional legitimacy.

MR GRAHAM AVERY,
ST. ANTONY'S COLLEGE, UNIVERSITY OF OXFORD
& EUROPEAN POLICY CENTRE, BRUSSELS

Following Professor Walker's analysis of the legal and political arguments about Scotland's accession to the EU, Mr Avery spoke about what the process of Scotland's accession might look like. Mr Avery called it 'absurd and unlikely' that an independent Scotland would have to go through the same EU accession process as a non-member state, and proposed to outline a 'common sense approach' to Scotland's accession to the EU. Mr Avery set out to explain what the traditional procedure for accession looks like, why this procedure would not be suitable for Scotland, and finally what a common sense approach would look like.

According to traditional procedure, accession to the EU is a lengthy process, requiring a lengthy opinion by the European Commission on whether the applicant is able to comply with the conditions of membership; a thirty-five-chapter negotiation with the applicant country; and a reporting process on the applicant country's progress towards meeting the conditions of membership. The entire procedure can take up to ten years. Mr Avery asserted that this procedure would not be appropriate for Scotland, which is already an EU member and has been for the last 40 years. He acknowledged that there is no precedent for an existing member state acceding to the EU, and no article stating the procedure for this. The case of Scotland's accession to the EU would not even count as a case of EU enlargement, but uniquely as accession without enlargement.

Scotland and the EU

Mr Avery declared that it would not be in the interest of any EU member states for Scotland to be made to leave and re-apply for membership. During any such interim period, Scotland would cease to pay into the EU budget, its territorial waters would lie outwith the jurisdiction of the EU, and customs controls would have to be established between Scotland and other EU member states. A common sense approach would therefore suggest using the date between the referendum on Scotland's constitutional future and the date of its (hypothetical) independence to put in place the necessary treaty amendments to ensure that Scotland could be an EU member from the date of its independence. Professor Avery suggested that a simplified procedure could be created for this, as in the case of German reunification, the distinction being that treaties would have to be amended to take account of Scotland as an independent state.

Mr Avery also referred to the separatist movement in Catalonia, and the possibility of Spain taking a hard line on the question of Scottish independence. Like Professor Walker, Mr Avery felt that this hard line would not stand the 'test of reality'. He suggested that it would not be in the interests of any national ministries, in particular Fisheries or Finance ministries, to force Scotland to leave the EU.

Having set out the argument for a 'common sense approach' to Scotland's accession, Mr Avery proceeded to discuss what might be the terms of Scotland's EU membership. With regard to the Eurozone, Mr Avery asked whether Scotland was likely to want to stay outside the Euro, and whether it would be obliged to eventually join the Euro. He suggested that because new EU members are not initially permitted to join the Euro, Scotland would be able to opt into the Euro if it felt this was in the national interest, but would be under no immediate obligation to do so. With regard to the necessary changes in secondary legislation, Mr Avery suggested that Scotland would need to wait until it was a full, independent EU member before commencing negotiations, most prominently about the budget and about the fisheries situation. He suggested that there would be a difficult negotiation for Scotland regarding the budget. On the subject of Scotland's relationship with the rest of the UK throughout this process, Mr Avery suggested that in the pre-independence period, before Scotland becomes an EU member state, it would need the support and cooperation of Britain's EU representatives. He felt it was likely that Britain would support Scotland during this process, and support Scotland's accelerated accession, because an independent Scotland outside the EU would be problematic for Britain. Mr Avery ended by acknowledging that a decision by Britain to leave the EU in 2017 would complicate the Scottish position.

Professor Diana Panke,
Professor of Political Science, University of Freiburg

Professor Panke spoke about the influence small states within the EU can have in the negotiation of EU Directives, with a view to understanding how an independent Scotland might operate within the EU and what levels of influence it might expect to hold. Professor Panke based her exploration of this question upon two hypothetical conditions:

1   That the 2014 Referendum results in Scottish independence; and

2   That an independent Scotland accedes to the European Union

On the basis of these two assumptions, Professor Panke asked the questions:

a   What are the challenges faced by small states (as members of the EU)?

b   What can be learned from the activities of small states within the EU about how these states can 'punch above their weight' in negotiations?

The central point raised by Professor Panke was that the levels of influence held by different states in the EU cannot be straightforwardly attributed to their size. States of similar sizes, she pointed out, have been observed to hold different levels of influence, and some small states are more active and engaged than others. The question, then, is how this can be explained and what Scotland, as a small state, can learn from this. Professor Panke proceeded to discuss the levels of involvement smaller states can have within the EU in reference to their levels of activity and their levels of influence.

In relation to activity levels, the point was made that low levels of activity by smaller states often occur not as a result of a lack of willingness to be proactive in negotiation, but due to a lack of capacity. For small member states, this lack of capacity does not lie in Brussels, with a Permanent Representative, but at home with national Ministries. National Ministries are responsible for formulating the decisions to be taken back to the negotiating table in Brussels, so low capacity at Ministerial level can mean that instructions are slow to reach Brussels and may not arrive until negotiations are already well underway. It can also mean that the instructions sent to Brussels are vague and do not contain enough information to be useful in having an impact upon debate and negotiation.

Scotland and the EU

On the matter of the influence small states can expect to have on proceedings and negotiations, Professor Panke explained that levels of activity and levels of influence are closely connected, and again not attributable to size alone. Small states with active diplomats are more likely to influence EU directives than states with less active diplomats.

It is important for diplomats to participate in negotiations from the early stages, and to use the resources at their disposal effectively. Where a small state has some bargaining power or negotiating tool at hand, it should be aware of this and able to use it to its own advantage.

Professor Panke gave some consideration as to how her observations about the activity and influence of small states in the EU might be applied by Scotland so as to maximise its own levels of influence as a small EU member state. Professor Panke identified several challenges that would be faced by Scotland as a small member state, should it accede to the EU. These included the system of weighted voting, which would see Scotland in possession of a lower number of votes and less leverage than larger states, and the fact that Scotland's national Ministries would be smaller than those of many other member states, and might struggle to produce national positions on issues being debated in Brussels. With these challenges in mind, Professor Panke posed the hypothetical question; How would Scotland manage to make the most of EU membership with limited national capacities?

A central point was that Scotland, as a small state, would be unable to negotiate on all issues discussed in Brussels; it would therefore need to have a very clear strategy and priority list. It would be essential for the national Ministry to have knowledge of EU issues, and to be willing to dedicate time to working on these issues ahead of national ones. Professor Panke also noted that there would be a need for diplomats to be proactive in ensuring they got support for priority issues before these were brought to the negotiating table. High levels of institutional knowledge about the EU would also be advantageous.

With reference to Scotland's hypothetical position as a new, independent EU member state, Professor Panke observed that Scotland would have the advantage of already being English speaking, and of already having some Scottish diplomats with knowledge of the EU and how it works. Scotland, she observed, would not be starting from zero as an EU member.

QUESTIONS AND ANSWERS

The Q&A commenced with a question about the treaty amendment process and the possible influence of UK voters on this. The question referred to legislation which provides that treaty changes in Brussels directly affecting the UK must be put to a referendum of UK voters before they can be adopted. The question posed was whether this legislation was likely to affect negotiations around Scotland's accession to the EU; for example if the UK population decided to reject a treaty change providing for Scottish accession. Mr Avery responded to this question by clarifying that the legislation referred to provides for a referendum only in the instance that powers are passed from the UK to Brussels, concluding that this legislation would not be applicable in the instance of a treaty amendment enabling Scotland's accession to the EU.

Mr Avery's response was followed by a question about the role of the European Parliament throughout any such accession process. It was posited that if the process of Scotland's accession is likely to be political rather than legal, then European Parliamentarians would be very much involved. Neil Walker responded to this point by concurring that Parliamentarians would play a role in this process, and suggesting that there is certainly a role for the European Parliament in the process of treaty amendment. He also indicated that there would need to be some process which generated European opinion on this matter, and that this might be found with the European Parliament.

A question was posed about the time scale for the accession process, in reference to the Scottish Government intention that there would be 18 months between a 'yes' vote in the referendum and Scottish independence. Given that accession to the EU usually requires laws to be put in place and institutions to be established, the question was whether Scotland would be ready to accede to the EU by the date of independence, and whether the process of becoming ready could be fast-tracked. Mr Avery responded that Scotland, as a member of the EU within the UK, should already be fulfilling a lot of EU treaty obligations. He suggested that some secondary legislation would need to be addressed, but that the vast majority of it would already be in place. Peter Jones added that while a lot of secondary legislation would be in place already, a lot of EU trade law would not be in place in Scotland, because this is not a devolved matter. There would therefore need to be some process for reporting on and implementing these laws into Scots law.

Scotland and the EU

The general assumption that Scotland would want to join the EU was questioned, and the idea that there are clear advantages to Scotland remaining outside the EU was raised. Professor Walker suggested that while a small minority of the SNP are not pro-Europe, this did not amount to a strong core, and there is little evidence at present of a move in that direction. He added that this position might be reconsidered if a lot of obstacles to Scotland's accession were put in place. Peter Jones referred to a poll taken by *The Times* newspaper, which indicated that while 58% of Scots thought there should be a referendum on EU membership, 60% were in support of EU membership.

The question of political economy was raised, and speakers were asked to give an indication of the figures they thought would be involved in the enlargement of bureaucracy required for Scotland to 'punch above its weight' in the manner described by Professor Panke. A figure on how much Scotland would need to pay was invited. Speakers were unable to comment or speculate on precise figures; however, Mr Avery suggested that Scotland could simply draw on resources currently deployed in London to deal with issues in Europe. He suggested that Scotland would need a Ministry and a Foreign Service, but that there were many talented Scots in Brussels and in the UK Foreign Office who might decide to work in a Scottish equivalent institution, if one existed.

Referring to the subject of Scotland's membership of the Eurozone, it was suggested that some experts believe Scotland would be obliged to join the Euro, should it accede to the EU. Speakers were asked to comment on whether this position was correct and, if so, what the financial implications for Scotland might be. Mr Avery responded by acknowledging that different opinions have been expressed on the question of the Euro. He pointed out that Sweden is not in the Euro, and that in practice member states only join the Euro once the criteria for doing so have been met. He suggested that meeting those criteria is optional, but added that in the next twenty years the Eurozone is likely to increase in importance. He suggested that Scotland needs to consider the long-term national interest of joining the Euro. Professor Walker replied by suggesting that we should not place too much emphasis on the Swedish analogy, indicating that new members joining the EU have done so on the basis that they will seek to join the Euro. Peter Jones argued that new member states do give a commitment to joining the Euro, but that the EU has no means of compelling them to join.

Professor Walker cautioned that there may be a stronger sense of political obligation for new states joining the EU to take the Euro than there has been for those states which joined before the Euro was introduced. He suggested that the commitment to join the Euro might not be a 'paper commitment', but could be taken very seriously.

Peter Jones referred to the European Convention on Human Rights and suggested that this would be an important Convention in determining whether Scotland is able to join the EU and how it is treated during the process. Professor Walker added that a condition of Scotland's accession would be that it met the Copenhagen Agreement, and that the Scottish constitution would have a commitment to treat EU rights as a minimum standard.

A question was raised as to what the effect on Scotland might be of Britain deciding to leave the EU in 2017. Peter Jones responded that the referendum on Scottish independence is set for 2014, and the 18-month timescale to independence would see Scotland independent by 2016, before the UK referendum on Europe. Assuming a 'fast-track' accession process is implemented to enable Scotland to be a full EU member by the date of independence, Scotland should not be directly affected by the UK decision on Europe. Professor Walker interjected that if this timetable slips, the situation could become difficult. However, he pointed out that the UK Government is committed to honouring the Scottish referendum and its outcome. Therefore, if the timetable were to slip, the UK Government would presumably have to make adjustments to avoid undermining the results of the Scottish referendum.

Mr Avery spoke of the UK approach to Europe and Britain's frequent desire to opt out of EU initiatives, and suggested that it would be to Scotland's advantage if it did not display such exceptionalism. Professor Walker indicated that the most difficult period for Scotland would be the time between a 'yes' vote and independence. He suggested that there would need to be a constitutional platform up and running on independence day, and argued that this approach dovetails with the common sense argument on Scotland's accession. He suggested that prior negotiations would be crucial to get everything in place by the date of independence.

It was asked what the impact of Scottish independence might be on the UK's negotiating position within Europe. Peter Jones suggested that the UK rebate would not survive any new negotiations. He argued that the rebate annoys other states, and that it is hard to see how this could be retained in the renegotiations and reconfigurations that would take place in the event of Scottish independence.

Scotland and the EU

Mr Avery suggested that Scotland would not necessarily be unhelpful to the UK, and could be a useful partner on some things. He also argued that in the event of Scotland's accession, the other EU member states would not want to see old issues and negotiations which have already been settled opened up and revisited. Professor Panke suggested that where Scotland and the UK shared interests, it would be useful to both for Scotland to be an independent EU member state, since they would have more leverage as two states than as one. Mr Avery suggested that what a state pays into the EU depends upon its GDP, so Scotland joining the EU should not cause the EU to spend any more or less. He therefore argued that there would be no reason for Scotland's accession to lead to the reopening of budgetary issues. The point was raised by an audience member that the press tends to highlight areas of disagreement between Scotland and the UK; it was argued that where there are areas of common interest, Scotland and the UK take a constructive approach and would continue to do so in the event of Scottish independence.

The issue of the tight time frame for accession was raised again. It was pointed out that Scotland's accession would involve a three-stage process of the referendum itself; agreement being reached with Westminster regarding independence; and accession being agreed with Brussels.

The question was posed as to what Scotland's status would be from early 2017 if we had only reached stage two of this process by the date of independence. How realistic is it that accession would be achieved in 18 months? Professor Walker suggested that under a normal case of accession, a state would be commencing the process from a 'ground zero' position, with no prior history of membership. He suggested that in the Scottish instance there are two viable possibilities – accession with a conditional transition period; or a transition pact which ensured that rights and obligations held by Scotland under EU treaty continued to apply in the Scottish context until negotiations were concluded. He argued that the alternative to this was unthinkable, and would amount to a legal 'no man's land' in which Portuguese fishermen could not fish in Scottish waters, for example, and all students from outside Scotland would be considered as international students.

A point was raised about the difficulty of making a decision on how to vote in the 2014 referendum with only theory and assumption about Scotland's position regarding the EU to go on, and it was asked whether it is likely that voters will get a definitive position on this ahead of the referendum.

Peter Jones suggested that the UK Government was unlikely to pre-negotiate and that the EU won't consider a country's possible membership until it has had a formal application to join, so the chances of knowing Scotland's position with regard to EU membership prior to the referendum are remote.

Professor Walker offered the definitive answer that yes, Scotland can join the EU in principle. The devil, he observed, is in the detail – in particular with relation to what the terms of Scotland's accession would be. He added that uncertainty over future membership of the EU is not an issue unique to Scotland, observing that the UK Government is currently committed to the repatriation of powers from Brussels to the UK and a referendum on the UK's future membership of Europe.

Mr Avery suggested that EU membership is just one of the many issues which voters will need to consider when weighing up what Scotland's future might be.

A question was raised about the EU acquis (the 31-chapter body of European Union Law accumulated through legislation, Acts and court decisions). It was posited that with regard to the acquis, a one-section statute could be created to say that, from the date of independence, the Acts and regulations incorporated by the acquis would continue in force in Scotland. It was asked whether this procedure would suffice for Scotland's continued EU membership, and pointed out that this is what has happened in Ireland, where UK Acts, including the Bill of Rights, still apply. It was also asked whether it was necessary to have ratification of any amendment allowing Scotland's continued EU membership. It was observed that Croatia's accession treaty required ratification, but that the subsequent amendments to EU treaty did not; those amendments being subjected instead to a simplified revision procedure.

On this basis, the question was raised as to whether it is clear that the ratification of treaty amendments would be required. Mr Avery suggested that the minimum essential in the instance of treaty amendment would be institutional changes which affected each member state, and indicated his inclination that ratification would be required. With regard to how long this process of ratification would take, he suggested it could take any amount of time, but argued that if the amendments were uncontroversial, there would be no reason that ratification could not be concluded rapidly. Professor Walker examined the idea that a simplified revision procedure might be applied, in place of ratification. He suggested that it was not obvious that a simplified revision procedure would apply, but concluded that the question remained an open one.

Scotland and the EU

Peter Jones referred speakers back to the first part of the question, on the idea of one legislative Act listing all of the laws and regulations to be incorporated into Scottish law. He asked whether it is the case that in the process of accession, many countries become bogged down by Parliamentarians wanting to go through every line of the acquis and to maximise advantage where possible. Mr Avery responded that with regard to his proposed common sense procedure for accession, although Scotland would not be a direct party to the treaty amendments because it would not yet be an EU member state, it would be of capital importance for the Scottish Parliament to have a voice on the techniques adopted for implementation of the acquis in Scotland.

Professor Walker suggested that a one-line statute could do the job, and argued that it would not be in the interest of the Scottish political class, insofar as they desire independence, to make the process a difficult one. He suggested that there might be aspects of the process which Scotland could revisit, possibly including its continuing negotiations with the rest of the UK, but emphasised that it is possible to achieve 'in principle' agreements even where detailed agreements are still to be put in place.

Peter Jones suggested that a key complaint made about EU membership is that EU law often has to be formally incorporated into national law, and that this process is seen by some as very burdensome. He asked whether we might expect to see pressure from lobby groups for Scotland to take the opportunity to re-visit this process and make it less burdensome. Professor Walker responded that this might be the case, but highlighted the need for a clear distinction between the formality of transposition on the one hand and the opening up of substantive questions on the other.

It was asked whether there are any potentially adverse affects on Scottish commerce as a result of the uncertainty around Scotland's future ahead of the referendum. Peter Jones suggested that uncertainty has not been a dominant factor so far. He suggested that foreign property sales might possibly be affected, but observed that in Quebec, uncertainty only became an issue when opinion polls began indicating that a 'Yes' vote (to EU membership) was likely.

It was suggested that the process of Scotland's accession is subject to huge debate, and observed that the UK Government has commissioned research suggesting that Scotland would have to undergo a full accession process. However, if Scotland were able to fast-track its EU membership, the issue of opt-outs would still remain, and would be very important. It was questioned whether Scotland would be able to negotiate all the current opt-outs that it enjoys as part of the UK, especially given the limited timetable it has to negotiate EU membership. It was also observed that when voting within the Council of the EU, a system of qualified majority voting applies, assigning higher numbers of votes to member states with larger populations. Under this system, the UK currently has 29 votes in the Council, whereas countries of a similar population size to Scotland, for example Denmark, Ireland and Finland, currently have only around seven. On this basis, it was suggested that Scotland could expect less influence in the Council of the EU as a small independent member state than as part of the UK.

Taking the latter part of the question, Professor Panke advised that the Lisbon Treaty has changed the voting mechanism in the Council of Ministers so that it no longer relies upon states having a straightforward number of votes. Instead, voting occurs in two rounds. In the first round of voting each state is counted once, and 55% of states must vote in favour. If this threshold is reached, the states which voted in favour are then looked at to see whether they represent 65% of the population. Professor Panke described this as a compromise between the 'one state, one vote' and the 'one citizen, one vote' principles and indicated that the old system of each state having a clear number of votes no longer exists. She advised that this new mechanism would be optional from 2014 and compulsory from 2017.

Professor Walker responded to the first part of the question by suggesting that there are grounds for thinking that Scotland would require a full accession process, but that there is no reason to believe that this would need to be as lengthy or complex as for other states. He observed that the difference between an accession treaty and an amendment treaty would not be as significant for Scotland as it would be for a country starting from scratch with an application for EU membership. He conceded, however, that it would be difficult for Scotland to negotiate its position with regard to many of the issues discussed throughout this session.

Scotland and the EU

CONCLUDING REMARKS

The discussion seminar concluded after just over two hours, due to constraints of time rather than exhaustion of the discussion.

The debate proved rich and informative, with a broad range of issues under the heading of 'Scotland and the EU' covered. The purpose of the seminar was to facilitate and inform public debate on the question of Scotland's constitutional future, in the context of EU membership. In support of this objective, the speaking panel provided insightful introductions to central, and in some instances unexplored, aspects of this debate.

The discussion yielded as many questions as it did answers, but the exploration of these questions and the acknowledgement of areas of uncertainty proved as informative as any of the definitive answers that were available. Mr Avery's reminder that decisions about Scotland's constitutional future will not rest on the EU question alone might provide some relief to those overwhelmed by the number of uncertainties surrounding this particular question. It also serves as a useful reminder that there are a host of topics yet to be explored and elucidated as part of the effort to Enlighten the Constitutional Debate.

Tax and Spending

ENLIGHTENING THE CONSTITUTIONAL DEBATE

Tax and Spending
17 April 2013, at the British Academy

INTRODUCTION

This was the second seminar in the series, and consisted of presentations by three speakers followed by a round-table discussion forum. It took place at the British Academy in London and was conducted under the Chatham House Rule, which encourages frank exchanges by not attributing comments to named participants. Each speaker presentation was followed by a Question and Answer session, and the seminar concluded with an open, roundtable discussion.

Chair: **Professor Lord Paul Bew**

Speakers:

> **Paul Johnson**, Institute for Fiscal Studies

> **Gerald Holtham**, former Chair of the Independent Commission on Funding and Finance for Wales [Professor Holtham was unable to attend the seminar; his contributions were presented by Professor Iain McLean]

> **Paul Doyle**, HM Treasury

This chapter also covers discussion held at a related public discussion seminar in the series on Currency, Banking and Taxation (the tenth in the series), which was held at the Royal Society of Edinburgh on 29 January 2014. The discussion held at this event is summarised at the end of this chapter, with speaker contributions attributed to named speakers.

UK Government's Scotland Analysis Programme

A programme of work is currently being run by the UK Government with the aim of examining Scotland's place within the UK and how this might be affected by different constitutional options, including an independent Scotland. This programme will look at and analyse Scotland's existing arrangements as part of the UK, covering topics including the constitution; the economy; public finance; taxation; defence; energy; and welfare. Where possible and appropriate, the programme will also explore the potential implications of Scottish independence for each of these areas. It was observed that the UK Government has been keen to engage with and gather evidence from third parties including academics, think-tanks and other experts, especially those based in Scotland. Some of the key, cross-cutting themes that will be examined as part of this programme of work were identified as being:

> The opportunity for Scotland to pool risks with the rest of the UK, for example in relation to military or security threats, or economic challenges;

> The scale of the UK, particularly in relation to its ability to access a larger single, domestic market in which firms from key sectors conduct the majority of their trade;

> The potential influence of the UK on Scotland's behalf in international institutions;

> The levels of integration reached by Scotland and the rest of the UK, including institutions which are shared across the UK.

It was observed that uncertainty remained around how these functions would be replaced in an independent Scotland.

Debate to date has largely been based around Government revenue and expenditure statistics produced by the Scottish Government (Government Expenditure and Revenue Scotland – GERS). It was acknowledged that this is an important set of statistics for analysing fiscal issues in Scotland. However, it was also pointed out that these statistics are viewed by the UK Government as a set of sub-national accounts, which is implicit in the fact that they break down UK-level data into a Scottish component. The position of the UK Government is that there is difficulty around an assumption that these figures represent the likely fiscal position of a future, independent Scotland.

Tax and Spending

This difficulty is exacerbated by the fact that the figures are backward looking, and cannot be reliably used to predict the fiscal situation for a future Scotland. It was suggested that there is a clear need for a reliable set of predictions on what this future fiscal situation might be. It was noted that GERS does provide useful evidence on the status of Scotland's public finances as part of the UK.

Referring to charts made available on the day, it was observed that, at an aggregate level, Scotland has enjoyed consistently high levels of public spending, around 10% higher than the rest of the UK, with relatively similar onshore tax revenues. This means that the gap between onshore tax and spend is bigger in Scotland than in the rest of the UK. It was acknowledged that this analysis does not give the full picture however, since it does not take into account North Sea Oil revenues. North Sea Oil revenue offsets Scotland's higher public spending to some degree, and it was suggested that this fact demonstrates the importance of the North Sea Oil revenue to Scotland's fiscal situation and to the debate on Scotland's fiscal future. The volatility of North Sea Oil revenues was referred to, and it was suggested that while this volatility can be managed quite well at the UK level – where North Sea Oil receipts account for between 1% and 2% of overall receipts – at the Scottish level, where these receipts constitute around 10% to 20% of overall receipts, the impact of this volatility is likely to be much greater.

Having discussed Scotland's fiscal situation based on past data provided by GERS, attention was turned to current financial issues facing HM Treasury and the Scottish Government, with funding reform and accountability identified as key. It was observed that the Scotland Act (2012) represents the biggest transfer of fiscal powers in 300 years, giving the Scottish Government powers over income tax, stamp duty land tax and land-fill tax, along with borrowing powers which enable it to vary the levels of tax and spending in Scotland. It was also observed that the Scotland Act (2012) will increase the amount of self-financing in the Scottish budget, from around 15% as things stand at the moment to around one-third once the powers afforded by the Act are fully introduced, from 2016/2017. It was pointed out that enacting these new powers is merely the start, and that the process of fiscal devolution represents new and complex territory for both the Scottish and UK Governments.

With regard to Scotland's future, it was pointed out that a feature of almost all developed economies is that they will experience long-term fiscal pressures of one form or another. The most common of these are an ageing population and declining resources, both of which apply to the UK and Scotland. It was suggested that these pressures are likely to be felt more acutely in Scotland than by the UK as a whole. Two pressures particularly likely to impact upon Scotland in the future were identified: a decline in oil and gas revenues: and a high dependency ratio within the Scottish population. These two pressures were discussed in turn.

Declining oil and gas revenues: A chart produced by the Office for Budget Responsibility (OBR) was referred to, demonstrating a long-term decline in oil revenues for the UK as a whole. Referring to the earlier chart demonstrating Scotland's heavier reliance on oil revenues compared with the rest of the UK, it was pointed out that the impact of this on Scotland's public finances could be profound. The OBR forecast indicates that by 2016/17 oil receipts will reduce by half, compared with recent years. The question was raised as to how this gap in revenue would be funded going forward, particularly in an independent Scotland.

Demographic pressures and the dependency ratio: A chart showing the dependency ratio (which was described by the speaker as being the ratio of persons aged 65 and over to persons aged 15 to 65) for the UK and Scotland was referred to. It was observed that Scotland and the UK are currently in a similar position, but that the forecast shows a divergence, with Scotland's dependency ratio increasing more significantly than that of the UK. The point was raised that this demographic trend, representing a decline in the working age population, is likely to impact upon Scotland's tax base, and also upon money available for public services.

Taking the identified fiscal pressures facing a future Scotland, and the GERS analysis discussed earlier, the question was posed: *What does the future fiscal position of Scotland look like?* It was observed that there are very few estimates of this available at the moment, and even fewer which extend beyond the medium and into the long term. A fiscal forecast produced by the Centre for Public Policy for Regions (CPPR)[1] at the University of Glasgow was referred to as providing the most up-to-date estimate currently available. This forecast uses the GERS and the OBR data, and predicts that while UK and Scottish fiscal situations are currently very similar, there will be a divergence towards 2017/18, with the UK fiscal position improving more rapidly, but with both countries remaining in deficit. It was suggested that many more estimates like this one are needed to help inform the debate about Scotland's fiscal future.

1 http://www.gla.ac.uk/schools/socialpolitical/cppr/currentpublications/

Tax and Spending

PRINCIPLES FOR DISTRIBUTING A BLOCK GRANT AROUND THE UK

The question of how the arrangement for a block grant might be reformed in the light of possible constitutional change in Scotland is an example of an issue pertinent to England, Northern Ireland and Wales, as well as to Scotland.

There are two main components of identifiable public spending, these being *formula spend* and *entitlement spend*. Entitlement spend refers to expenditure which is based purely on entitlement, for example welfare benefits, and which goes to those who are entitled to it, wherever they may be geographically. It was explained that the UK currently operates on a system of *formula funding*, according to which locally delivered services are funded on the basis of complex formulae which calculate the spending need of Local Authorities in different policy areas, on the basis of relevant characteristics of the local population. A formula-based system also underlies the allocation of funding by HM Treasury to the four regions of the UK – England, Scotland, Wales and Northern Ireland – by means of the *Barnett Formula*. This formula dates from the 1970s, and adjusts the amount of public expenditure allocated to the devolved regions of the UK in accordance with changes to public expenditure in England.

It was pointed out that the system employed by HM Treasury for the allocation of block grants to the four regions of the UK represents an *expenditure*-based system, with expenditures in England on those policy areas devolved to the territories in question forming the basis for the block grant to each territory. This expenditure-based system also underlies the formulae applied by each region of the UK when allocating revenue support grants for Local Authorities. It was explained that these formulae are typically based upon an index of need for each Local Authority, which is driven by relevant demographic indicators such as morbidity and mortality for each area. It was pointed out that these formulae are slightly different, and take into account slightly different indicators, in each of the four regions of the UK.

The expenditure-based model differs from a revenue-based model, which would start by looking at the taxing capacity of each region or each Local Authority. It was suggested that although the tax-raising capacity of Local Authorities does enter into the formulae of the four regions of the UK, this in no way forms a central part of formula funding across the UK. The UK formula system cannot therefore be considered revenue based, except in the most trivial sense.

Scrutinising the current, expenditure-based model, a piece of research undertaken by Stirling University, found that if the formulae used by England were to be applied to Scottish Local Authorities, and the formulae used by Scotland were to be applied to English Local Authorities, the results would be completely different. This was observed to raise some concern over the use of expenditure-based systems. A report produced by the Independent Commission on Funding and Finance for Wales (ICFFW)[2] analysed how funding to Wales would look if Wales was treated as a region of England. Instead of directly re-running the English formulae, this piece of research looked at the results of the block grant allocations to each region of England and attempted to identify and explain what the main indicators determining allocations to each Local Authority in England are. The research showed that 95% of variations in funding can be attributed to four variable factors: poverty; cost (which is heavily affected by sparsity); dependency; and sickness. By applying the revealed preferences of the English formulae to Wales, it was revealed that Wales would get the same in block transfers as it does at present, as would Northern Ireland. Scotland, however, would get less. In terms of how we might proceed after the referendum, it was suggested that an expenditure-based system applied across the rest of the UK is feasible, and could be an option if Scotland chooses independence. It is difficult to make this sort of system work if Scotland remains within the union however, and in that event the problem of how block grants should be allocated in the future remains to be solved.

The default position for Scotland in the event of a 'No' vote in the Referendum is the full implementation of the Scotland Act (2012), which will entail a change in the way Scotland is currently financed. The default position in the event of a 'Yes' vote is Scottish independence, which does not remove the question of how a block grant for the rest of the UK should be distributed between Northern Ireland, Wales and the regions of England.

2 http://wales.gov.uk/funding/financereform/report/?lang=en

Tax and Spending

THE POTENTIAL FISCAL SITUATION IN THE EVENT OF SCOTTISH INDEPENDENCE

It is important when looking at Scottish independence to examine not only Scotland's potential fiscal position in comparison with the UK, but also to examine what the absolute fiscal positions of Scotland and the UK will be, both at the Referendum and beyond. It was observed that the overall fiscal positions of both Scotland and the UK are unlikely to be 'happy'. The annual deficit in 2014 will still be very large, and will continue to be significant in 2016 and 2017, and the context of the short-term fiscal situation in the UK will be one of dramatic spending cuts. It was observed that the levels of outstanding national debt will continue to rise through 2014, 2015 and 2016. High levels of national debt will put the UK and Scotland in the top bracket of OECD countries on levels of debt, and will make Scotland in particular one of the only countries of its size and population to have such high debt.

It was suggested that the relative fiscal context of Scotland is, in the short term, very straightforward, with Scottish income and tax per head being very similar to the rest of the UK and spending per head around 10% to 12% higher. Ignoring North Sea Oil revenues, the Scottish deficit is higher than that of the UK, and taking account of oil revenues it is roughly the same, although volatility is increased. Given the impact of North Sea Oil revenues, an important question going forward was highlighted as being *what will happen to oil revenues in the short and medium term?* If CPPR and OBR forecasts are correct, this will draw Scotland into a worse fiscal position than the rest of the UK over the next few years, although it was acknowledged that there is huge uncertainty around the future of oil revenues.

The question was posed as to what kind of fiscal architecture an independent Scotland might want to put in place; would Scotland, for example, want to put in place something like the OBR? A further question was posed around how an independent Scotland might account for volatile and diminishing oil revenues when thinking about what its fiscal rules ought to look like. It was suggested that cautious medium-term fiscal rules would remove oil revenues from the fiscal balance, so that over a protracted period a fiscal balance excluding oil revenues would be sought. It was suggested that this approach is a possible equivalent to building up an 'oil fund'.

An independent Scotland would have many more tax choices. Scotland would be inheriting a tax system that is not optimal, and would have the opportunity to move towards a more rational and neutral tax system, should it so choose. It was suggested that there will be some questions in relation to the tax system which will be different for countries which are smaller and more open than the UK as a whole, for example:

> How to structure corporation tax – especially in a country which will remain very integrated with the rest of the UK;

> How to take account of cross-border issues in indirect taxes, and;

> How to think about whether there are differences in the responsiveness of labour supply and avoidance behaviour to rates of income tax and corporate tax.

The example of the taxation of alcohol was raised. It was observed that Scotland has introduced minimum pricing for alcohol rather than levying a higher tax on alcohol, and suggested that an independent Scotland would be able to tax alcohol as it chose to, subject to EU rules.

It was further suggested that an independent Scotland would have many more choices available around spending; at present spending in Scotland is higher than the rest of the UK across every single devolved sector, not simply in relation to higher education, social welfare or health. Choices are available as to how Scotland manages its future spending.

Recognition was given to the earlier point that long-term fiscal issues in Scotland will probably look similar to those in the UK and other developed nations; for example regarding the ageing population and the associated pressure on health care, plus increased fiscal challenges as a result of these factors. Initial analysis indicates the possibility of greater pressure as a result of these factors in Scotland, however, due to a faster ageing population coupled with the structure of social care funding. Qualitatively, the fiscal challenges facing Scotland will not be dissimilar to those facing the rest of the UK, but it was suggested that quantitatively, Scotland's fiscal pressures may be more challenging than those faced by the rest of the UK.

Tax and Spending

QUESTIONS & ANSWERS

Division of National Debt

A question was posed regarding the division of national debt should Scotland become independent. The Scottish Government was referenced as suggesting that Scotland takes a 'population share' of the national debt, and HM Treasury as also believing that a population share could be used to divide and allocate the national debt. The advantage of a population share is that it is easily understood and readily acceptable. It was pointed out, however, that there is a complication with this idea, which derives from the fact that the markets also have a say and an interest in the issue of the national debt. The primary concern of the market relates to ability to pay; if Scotland were to become independent, it would accrue around 10% of GDP and roughly the same proportion of tax-raising power. A population share of national debt would be based on Scotland's 8.4% of the UK population. It was suggested that an allocation of national debt based on Scotland's population share was likely to be rejected by the markets on the basis that it would place a greater burden of the national debt on the UK, and Scotland would be seen as getting off lightly. The market interest is predominantly in maintaining stability in the repayment of debt. It was pointed out that the UK Government has a commitment to not pre-negotiating the terms of independence, and that UK Government Ministers do not have a negotiating position to adopt on this issue as yet. It was observed that there are a number of methods for dividing the national debt, based for example on population share, or on GDP. All of these methods produce quite high numbers, but it is not yet possible to comment upon what the preferred method might be. The biggest challenge will be how to put any division of national debt into practice.

Social Welfare

A point was raised about social welfare. It was observed that there will be a seminar on Welfare & Public Service as part of the Enlightening the Constitutional Debate series, and suggested that this is a key issue which takes us to the heart of the social union. A report produced by Sheffield Hallam University was referred to[3], which examines the consequences for Scotland of the reform of welfare. It was suggested that if Scotland were to become independent it would be possible to devise a system of social welfare very different from the existing one.

3 http://www.scottish.parliament.uk/S4_Welfare_Reform_Committee/Reports/wrR-13-02w.pdf

It was further suggested that the issue of social welfare is one which lies at the centre of the case for the social union. Closely related to this is the question around state and public sector pension provision, the regulation of pensions in an independent Scotland, and the transition of pensions between states, for example the possibility of accruing pension entitlements in state A and receiving payments in state B. It was suggested that these issues are all central to the continuity of the social union.

It was suggested that with regard to the welfare debate, the issue for the UK Government is two-fold; there is one issue relating to affordability, which is about reducing the welfare bill, and a second issue around providing the right incentives to get people back into work. It was acknowledged that the pension questions are very tricky, particularly with regard to the transfer of entitlements across national boundaries and the continuation of entitlements already accrued in the event of independence. It was suggested that there is a large amount of uncertainty in this area.

Controls on Funding

An observation was made about the controls that will be applied to funds allocated to Scotland from the UK budget. While much of the discussion so far has focused upon the different approaches that might be applied to the allocation of funds, for example expenditure based or revenue based systems, it was suggested that a further consideration is around what sorts of controls will be applied to any money allocated to Scotland. The point was raised that when the 1998 Scotland Act was passed and the block grant was being discussed, the money allocated to Scotland came with very few strings. It was pointed out that gradually restrictions have been applied so that there are now rigid controls and far less flexibility. The point was made that when budgets are tight, there is a tendency to operate in the margins, so anything which affects these becomes very important. There is a lot of UK central control over policy decisions that can be made in Scotland.

Speakers recognised that there has been a tightening up of the regulations and restrictions applied to the funds allocated to Scotland, but suggested that these controls are put in place to ensure that the credibility HM Treasury has within global markets is maintained. It was suggested that the tightening of controls has been part of a move towards an overall strategy to reduce the deficit.

Tax and Spending

Revenue Data

A question was raised about revenue, and it was suggested that there are certain revenue figures on which we don't currently have clarity; in particular, corporation tax. It was pointed out that just two or three percentage points, when dealing with large fiscal deficits, can make a huge difference, and yet these figures are not fully understood. The question was posed as to whether there are any proposals for HM Revenue and Customs to try and deal with this issue.

Quite a lot of data on spending is geographic, but with some areas of taxation this is more difficult. With corporation tax, for example, a lot of data raised is based on where the company is headquartered and not where the tax itself is accrued. Getting a more detailed picture of these areas is therefore likely to be a challenge. It was suggested that it would be useful to examine the way tax receipts break down across the UK and that this is something the UK Government will want to look into.

Fiscal Rules

A question was raised relating to fiscal rules, and what currency arrangements will be assumed when looking at these. It was pointed out that fiscal policy within a monetary union is wholly different to having a floating currency. A comment was also made on the position of non-pre-negotiation on Scotland's constitutional future taken by UK Minsters. It was indicated that while pre-negotiation is not expected, it would be helpful to have a statement from the UK Government about principles that might be applied, for example in relation to the separation of the national debt. It was suggested that refusal to provide this is more of a political tactic than something which is assisting open and fair debate, and the refusal of the UK Government to pre-negotiate on Scotland's constitutional future was contrasted with the position taken by the UK Government on Europe and UK membership of the EU.

It was pointed out that if Scotland becomes part of the EU it will be bound by the fiscal rules set by the Eurozone, however if it was part of a sterling zone then consideration would need to be given to the fiscal rules that would be applied. It was observed that the implications of different currency arrangements will be very different and that UK fiscal rules are far less binding than EU fiscal rules would be.

Division of National Debt

The earlier point regarding the division of the national debt was returned to. It was observed that in relation to the Quebec referendum, which was conducted in 1995 at a time when Canada was suffering a sovereign debt crisis, the lack of clarity around issues such as the division of this debt caused an enormous amount of uncertainty, which was reflected in the markets. It was further observed that when opinion polls began to demonstrate that there could be a 'Yes' vote in the Referendum, there was a fall in the value of the Canadian dollar and a spike in interest rates because of 'capital flight' – the flow of assets and money out of the country. It was suggested that the reluctance of the UK Government to open up pre-negotiation could raise the possibility of uncertainty and economic disruption across the whole of the UK.

A point was made regarding the GERS figures referred to in the speaker presentations. It was suggested that as members of the public, we are asked to make choices effectively on this one source of data. The majority of tax data in GERS is extrapolated from UK figures, and no separate sampling or stress testing of GERS data is undertaken. The point was made that by using a different method for calculating corporation tax, different conclusions are reached, and that even if GERS is only 5% or 10% out, in real terms this amounts to around half a billion pounds. HMRC and the UK Government should acknowledge that GERS is not as robust as it has been thought to be.

Fiscal Autonomy

A further point was made in relation to Scotland's fiscal autonomy. It was pointed out that the Scottish Parliament has always had the ability to raise additional levies, but politically it has never chosen to do so for a number of reasons.

In response to this point, it was suggested that the examples given of tax and spend decisions taken (or not taken) by the Scottish Government, illustrate the issues about having an expenditure-based rather than a revenue-based system. The Scottish Parliament has always had revenue options; from the Scotland Act (1998) until the full implementation of the Scotland Act (2012) it has had the power to vary income and property tax, and has shown no interest in doing anything with this power other than to freeze council tax. It was suggested that the consultation held by the current Scottish Government on stamp duty land tax perhaps demonstrates that the Scottish Government are beginning to think about what a rational tax package might look like, however it was observed that a more robust and responsive tax system is difficult to achieve within the current expenditure based system.

At this point the Q & A session was drawn to a close and more open discussion invited.

Tax and Spending

DISCUSSION

Opening the discussion, a point was made that in the current debate around currency and fiscal choices, we are frequently constrained by the fact that our analysis and tools are based on the world as it was pre-2007, when in fact the world has changed quite considerably since 2007. A further concern was expressed about the longevity of work being done at the moment. It was observed that new fiscal rules and policies may need to last up to 300 years, and will therefore need to be robust. It was also observed that issues of fiscal policy are wider than Scotland and the UK, and have relevance throughout Europe. It was therefore suggested that we need to think more broadly about how certain types of risk sharing can be done, and how fiscal unions across borders might work and what this means for nationalism in the broader sense.

The issue of risk sharing was discussed in further detail, and the question of which risks are shared at which level was identified as important. It was suggested that prominent risks to consider are those which we have traditionally sought to insure against with the welfare state; for example, through old age pensions, unemployment insurance, and sickness benefits. It was observed that in the European context, there is no automatic assumption that German tax-payers pay Greek pensions, for example, whereas there is an assumption within the UK that UK tax-payers will pool resources in order to pay UK pensions and social security benefits, even where this involves transfers across subnational boundaries. It was observed that there is a purely nationalist view identifiable in relation to discourse in Scotland, which argues that the sharing community for this purpose should be Scotland, and that Scotland and Scottish people would be better off under this arrangement because of North Sea Oil revenues. It was further observed that an 'undeveloped' argument in the opposite direction holds that once state boundaries have been set, that is the area within which you share. The unionist side of the Scottish debate has not successfully unpacked that argument yet. With regard to public expenditure distribution, discussion tends to focus on block grants, but the biggest element of public spending is social security. There was thought to be an interesting question around whether there is any possibility for a devolved Scottish-only solution to the distribution of public expenditure, as opposed to an independent Scottish-only solution, i.e. *is there a system under which we can decentralise social security?*

On the subject of welfare, it was suggested that it is possible to imagine a settlement whereby Scotland has control over the main elements of redistribution, but agrees risk sharing with other jurisdictions. It was pointed out that this does happen in some federations; in the Canadian context, for example, there is a social union which does not depend upon the notion of a shared national identity. The notion of social risk is changing to take account of new social risks, many of which are being dealt with at the sub-state level, because they involve linking social interventions with active labour market and economic policy. It was suggested that this is the area of the welfare state where a lot of innovation is taking place. The observation was made that in the UK, the focus is more on passive support than active support, and it was suggested that this needs to change. A change from passive to more active support will have implications for how services will be delivered, and undermines the idea that everything should be delivered at the level of the nation state. Looking at particular examples, like getting people into work, it was observed that passive support is delivered at the national level and that more active support is devolved to the local level, and that this does not provide good incentives for getting people back into work. Different philosophies for how people can be encouraged and supported into work do exist at the local level; Scotland for example is seen as having less sympathy for punitive measures designed to get people into work than England. It was suggested that there is a tendency to look at the welfare state of ten years ago when discussing these issues, instead of the welfare state of the future. In thinking about the welfare state of the future, it is important to consider policy issues first and taxation after. A final point was made about fiscal equalisation and sharing; there are no obvious examples of states that have succeeded in arriving at a permanent method for sharing resources. Instead, most European countries deal with the question sequentially, one problem/barrier at a time. This was referred to as 'fixing the squeaky wheel', and it was suggested that there is no solution to that because there is a 'messy' political reality which drives these things.

In response to this comment, it was suggested that Ireland was a 'squeaky wheel' for the British Government from the time formula funding started, and that funding for Northern Ireland and Scotland has also been problematic. Wales, however, has never been a 'squeaky wheel', and nor have most regions of England. It was observed that there has to be a more robust way of managing things than simply 'oiling squeaky wheels' or dealing with problems sequentially. It was suggested that the report referred to earlier, by the ICFFW, provides a set of proposals which could be the basis for a coherent, UK-wide expenditure-based system. It was also pointed out that there are revenue-based systems available too.

Tax and Spending

Bringing the discussion back round to the forthcoming Referendum on Scottish independence, it was pointed out that, regardless of the outcome of the Referendum, the *status quo* will not be an option in Scotland. There will be three political parties in Scotland offering three different ways of implementing the full scope of the Scotland Act, or another offering to implement full Scottish independence. The issue therefore is how sustainable what comes after the Referendum will be, and how long-lasting. It was observed that people in Scotland equate having their own Parliament with creating their own laws, but they don't typically equate it with fiscal issues. There is no tangible link, because taxes are currently handed over to the UK Government. Knowledge of the link between the Scottish Government and the management of fiscal issues is something that is missing in the lead up to the Referendum. It was suggested that plans and proposals for fiscal devolution should be developed and communicated to the Scottish people now, ahead of the Referendum, so that voters have a clear view of what is on offer. If this is left until after the Referendum, the public will have less engagement with the process.

Echoing the point that there will be no status quo after the Referendum, it was observed that whatever the outcome, the Scottish Referendum will be 'transformatory'. The union sought by Scottish people, it was suggested, is very different from the union that exists at present, in that Scottish people appear to want extensive self-government. The first question, therefore, is whether the union can adapt to what Scottish voters appear to want. The second question is: *What are the implications of this likely to be for those who live in the rest of the UK?* It was argued that if the union is to survive it will have to remake itself, and will have to find a way of balancing all interests across the union. The union need not necessarily be the sort of union we have been used to, which provides for relatively homogenous living across the UK, instead there will be a need to reconcile unity with diversity.

Responding to this point, it was acknowledged that Scottish opinion appears to be focused on wanting greater devolution; however, it was also observed that when Scottish people have been asked service by service what they want, for the majority of reserved policy areas people want things to be the same in Scotland as they are across the rest of the UK. A majority of people in Scotland, therefore, appear to want things to remain the same as they are for the rest of the UK, but also to want greater devolution.

This was referred to as the devolution paradox, and it was suggested that if further devolution takes place, the likely outcome is that very similar outcomes will be achieved in each devolved area. People tend to have strong attachments to the idea of being able to make their own decisions about things, but also to have attachments to the same substantive outcomes.

The question of national identity was raised, and it was suggested that this would be central in the event of a 'No' vote in the Referendum, and would guide the question: *What is the nature of the union you want to have?* It was observed that Scotland and the UK may want different types of union. Union has always, in the Scottish case, meant decentralised power. From 1707, Scotland's union with the UK has entailed Scottish exceptionalism; the Scottish church was something that really mattered in 1707, and this remained resolutely separate. The Scottish legal system was also fairly distinct from and alien to the English legal system. By the end of the 20th Century, Scotland's devolution had become based around a series of administrative departments, so that around 50% of public spending in Scotland was devolved. This incremental process was crystallised by the creation of the Scottish Parliament, but the big questions of representation and taxation were not addressed, and they need to be addressed now. This will involve some mixture between a revenue-based and an expenditure-based system, and between now and 2014 there needs to be a cohesive and stable offering for Scotland which is also appropriate for the rest of the UK.

On the basis of the suggestion that the *status quo* will not survive the Referendum, it was observed that there will need to be a new settlement of some kind, and that, if Scotland eschews independence, a whole new set of questions about the nature of the union will be raised. Two points were raised in line with this; firstly, it will be unsustainable in the long-term to have a UK state in which the parliament in Scotland exists on the sufferance of the rest of the UK. Secondly, if a new settlement gives powers to Scotland which are seen as contributing to the long-term prosperity of Scotland, parts of the UK (for example the North-East) are likely to become very ill at ease with this settlement.

It was suggested that there is clearly some kind of relationship between the political decision to be the source of revenue raising and how people understand their identity. The political culture in Scotland is towards greater fiscal autonomy, and the question was raised: *in a culture where the trajectory is towards greater fiscal autonomy, does that not raise questions about the community of risk and who it includes? The question posed was: what kind of lessons can be learned from other types of fiscal federalism, and is there something distinctive and interesting in the Scottish situation and the move towards greater fiscal autonomy?*

Tax and Spending

In response, it was observed that an unusual feature of Scotland is that the Parliament spends nearly half of public expenditure in the country, but has virtually no tax-raising powers. It was further observed that there is nowhere in which a subnational unit raises all of its own taxes. The main reason for this is that without some degree of transfer and redistribution, it is impossible to take account of need.

A further response was offered which observed that there are some states in which a homogenous approach to the welfare state is taken, and there is a strong expectation that the state will do the same thing for everyone, regardless of location. There are other states in which attitudes to risk and to public services are more nuanced according to where people live, and in which welfare regimes vary significantly from one locality to another.

On the subject of Scottish exceptionalism, it was observed that there is a view amongst some that this exceptionalism can only be expressed through Scottish independence. The suggestion was made that this view is not as broadly held across Scotland as the present Government tends to believe, but that this view is certainly framing the present debate and needs to be taken seriously. It was observed that nobody believes that the referendum can be followed by the status quo and that regardless of the outcome it will need to be followed by a period of negotiation. The position of the UK Government with regards to pre-negotiation was criticised, on the basis that there needs to be a debate on what a new settlement between Scotland and the UK might look like in the event of a 'Yes' vote and in the event of a 'No' vote. It is very difficult to succeed in enlightening the constitutional debate without this information.

In response to this, a suggestion was made that the position of the UK Government is likely to be very influenced by what the opinion polls are showing. As long as opinion polls continue to indicate that the outcome of the Referendum will be the maintenance of the Union, it is unlikely the UK Government will invest time and resource in planning for an alternative outcome. It was suggested that if opinion polls did begin to show a likely 'Yes' vote in the Referendum, then the UK Government would seek to offer guidance on those things likely to become a political reality.

The position of the English was raised, and it was suggested that this has been somewhat neglected in the debate so far. The sustainability and coherence of some of the existing systems and processes for calculating the distribution of money in England was questioned, and the suggestion made that the manipulation of these processes by Local Authorities has been manifest. There has been an apparent desire to maintain this current system, and the question was therefore raised as to what the unforeseen consequences of changes to this system might be. The implication of discussion so far has been that it will be Scotland that has to change and adapt, but there might be significant implications, which are not yet being addressed, in relation to how things would operate in an England that is by far the greatest part of a remainder of the UK.

On the question of what the constitutional agreement will ultimately be, the point was made that dealing with fiscal issues sequentially is a risky approach, because any mistakes made on how the national debt is settled now could end up being very costly down the line. It was suggested that there is a need to think more broadly about how the questions around fiscal issues fit in with the rest of the debate.

Revisiting the question of pre-negotiation, it was suggested that a helpful approach might be to distinguish between different issues. There might be areas of the debate where we can expect a degree of candour, but this does not apply to all questions relating to Scotland's future. There are questions about things that are beyond the negotiating power of either side of the constitutional debate; for example, the question of an independent Scotland's relationship with the EU. While this can be influenced to some extent by the two sides of the debate, the question of whether the Scottish and UK Governments should try to find a joint position on this sort of issue is different from the question of whether they should seek a joint position on issues where they have different interests and negotiating stances to begin with. Understanding this distinction could help to interpret the levels of candour or pre-negotiation that might be encountered. In addition, there will also be questions about what an independence scenario will look like; for example, how the national debt will be shared, and about what the Unionist alternatives might be. The point was made that Unionist parties may not have a consensus on what the union looks like. It is important for the debate to separate these different questions and issues out.

Tax and Spending

The point was raised that there is a qualitative difference between the UK Government not pre-negotiating the possible terms of independence and the issue of whether there is clarity or consensus on what the available alternatives are in the event of a 'No' vote. A question was raised about who should be involved in developing proposals for such alternatives in the event of a 'No' vote. For example, if the three unionist parties in Scotland are negotiating consensus, will the SNP have a seat at that negotiating table?

In response to this question, the suggestion was made that this will probably depend on timing, and in particular on whether the discussion takes place before or after the Referendum. It was observed that the key time for these discussions is not 2014 but 2015, because the principal source for a mandate is likely to be the pre-election manifestos for the UK General Election in 2015. If there is a settlement that affects the whole of the UK, it can be considered by voters then.

The point was made that the Scottish question should not be dealt with in isolation, but that there is a need for UK-wide involvement. In the event of a 'No' vote in the Referendum, it was suggested that there should be recognition by UK political parties that the Union as it is has not been working and that a UK convention should be developed for how the Union will work on a UK-wide basis, i.e. not just focusing on one specific region.

Speaking of the SNP, a suggestion was made that if there is to be a post-Referendum scenario that is not Scottish independence, as the largest party in Scotland the SNP and their supporters will have to be part of this process. It was observed that the devolved Scottish Parliament is not functioning at its optimal level at the moment, in that it is not being held fully to account for policy outcomes. There will need to be a mechanism for measuring whether the Scottish Parliament is delivering positive policy outcomes.

Revisiting the earlier point on the need for a UK-wide convention on the future of the UK post-Referendum, it was suggested that part of the success of the UK to date is that it has never tried to 'essentialise' the union, instead the Union has meant something different in each region of the UK. Constitutionalism in the UK is about dealing with diversity in considering the ultimate purpose of the Union. The UK should be following a model of compromise, not trying to define the sovereignty or ultimate purpose of the UK. Referring to the devolution paradox discussed earlier, it was observed that policy making is not about asking what people want service by service, it is about finding out what people want from a compromise. This enables recognition of the deep diversity of the UK.

A question was raised as to whether the topic of tax and spending is likely to be one of the defining battlegrounds of the Referendum, or whether it is likely to be a peripheral issue. It was suggested that the complexity of the issues relating to tax and spending is quite high, and the UK and Scottish Governments have a tendency to produce complicated-looking graphs which support the political view they hold. The point was made that this is an area in which people are struggling to feel that there is an authoritative, independent view of the situation. Is this issue simply going to be too complex for the public to engage with, or is it seen as a defining battle ground? If the latter, what happens next?

It was suggested that in the event of a 'No' vote in the Referendum, the focus will be on fiscal devolution, and that the next logical step is to develop a convention on how fiscal devolution can be taken forward. A central question is likely to be: *What happens to England?* It was observed that debate will centre on the need for a genuinely needs-based formula to replace or modify the Barnett Formula. Another big question is likely to be the West Lothian question. It was reiterated that the status quo will not be the way forward.

At the end of the discussion, the Australian fiscal model was referred to. This is essentially an expenditure-based system, but one which does not dis-incentivise sub-national parliaments from thinking seriously about the tax structure. The point was made that the Scottish Parliament has never had to think about taxation and, therefore, never has. The Australian system is incentive-compatible, but does not rely on redistribution mechanisms to take the strain. The Canadian model, it was observed, is a much more revenue-based system, a requirement for this being that there is a lower expectation of national conformity than there is in the UK.

It was suggested that the Rate Support Grant system is broken, in that it is over-complicated and subject to 'gaming'. A re-thinking of formula funding for local government services and health is needed.

Regarding the constitutional convention, it was observed that this was felt to be a good idea in theory, but one which may be difficult in practice. It was suggested that were a political party to go into the next election promising a constitutional convention, this would give it a momentum that a Select Committee on its own cannot produce.

Referring to the deep diversity of the UK, it was observed that Scottish and English attitudes and approaches to 'big ticket' expenditure items are, and have been, quite similar. It was suggested that where there is deep diversity in the UK, it is in those historic areas referred to in earlier discussion, for example church and religion. On this point, the seminar was drawn to its conclusion.

Tax and Spending

PUBLIC DISCUSSION
ROYAL SOCIETY OF EDINBURGH, 29 JANUARY 2014

Because of the importance of the issues raised at this event, the RSE decided to hold a further discussion of issues relating to currency, banking and taxation in Scotland. The chair and speakers at this event were:

> **Ms Sarah Smith**, Newscaster, Channel 4 News (Chair)

> **Professor John Kay CBE FBA FRSE**, Economist

> **Dr Angus Armstrong**, Director of Macroeconomic research, National Institute of Economic and Social Research

> **Ms Jo Armstrong**, Independent Economist

> **Professor Gavin McCrone CB FRSE**, Former Chief Economic Adviser, Scottish Office

The points raised in relation to taxation and expenditure, are summarised here. This was an open, public event, and speakers were invited to present their thoughts ahead of a public discussion.

Ms Jo Armstrong proposed to discuss the likely consequences for public expenditure of Scotland becoming independent. She suggested that following the Referendum, whether Scotland becomes independent or adopts devo-max, expenditure and taxation will be issues that need to be addressed. Ms Armstrong proposed to discuss two or three key issues relating to expenditure and taxation.

She indicated that whatever the outcome of the Referendum, the Scottish Government faces a serious fiscal challenge in the shape of a fiscal deficit that it will have to close. Current projections indicate that Scotland will continue to have a deficit in the short term, so it will need either to erase its debt, or to raise taxes. Ms Armstrong acknowledged that an independent Scotland would have the option of simply spending less, for example by reducing spending on defence, but observed that to fill the gap, cuts to spending would have to be substantial. Scotland's current spending on defence is £3.3 billion, and the fiscal gap is £7.6 billion, meaning cuts to the defence budget alone would not fill the fiscal gap. To fill the gap, Scotland would need to look at cuts to spending and/or increased borrowing, and/or increased taxation.

Ms Armstrong observed that the UK is doing this, and is looking to balance the budget by 2017/18. She pointed out that if Scotland stays in the Union, it will have to take its share of the fiscal pain, observing that 50% of the UKs implied spending cuts are still to come into effect. If Scotland leaves the Union, without its Barnett allocation but with the revenues from North Sea Oil, it will need to outline an equally plausible fiscal plan so that it can continue to borrow, or seek to borrow, additional funds. Ms Armstrong observed that at the moment we have no indication of whether that plan would lead to the same level of cuts [as are being made in the UK], higher levels of cuts, or lower levels of cuts. She indicated that there is a need for greater clarity around what an independent Scotland's fiscal austerity plans will look like.

Equally important when considering Scotland's fiscal outlook is North Sea Oil, and the fact that Scotland's tax revenues are more dependent upon oil than are the rest of the UK's. Ms Armstrong indicated that initial projections, even those including a geographic share of North Sea Oil for Scotland, show that oil and gas revenues are not sufficient to close the funding gap. She observed that declining production coupled with increased operating costs have led to a downward projection in North Sea tax receipts. She suggested that if we saw higher oil prices, oil revenues would rise, but that the impact would not be a one-way bet, since higher oil prices reduce the profitability of non-oil companies. We therefore need to look at the whole picture of increased oil prices. Ms Armstrong pointed out that North Sea taxes account for 20% of Scotland's tax revenues, but only 2% of the UK's, meaning variability around figures relating to North Sea Oil revenues would have a greater impact on Scotland than on the rest of the UK. Ms Armstrong suggested that establishing an oil fund might be an option for an independent Scotland, observing that an oil fund would ensure that future generations are able to benefit from depleting resources. However, she pointed out that North Sea taxes (and more) are currently needed to fund Scotland's spending plans, so an oil fund would in fact exacerbate the fiscal challenge and make the fiscal gap larger.

In the event of a 'No' outcome in the Referendum, Ms Armstrong suggested that there would be a possibility of devo-max coming in through the side-lines. She observed that even if there is a 'No' vote, following the Referendum the current Scotland Act still comes into play, which extends Scotland's powers further. She acknowledged that there appears to be a desire in Scotland for some further extension of Scotland's powers, but made the point that Scotland has not yet tried and tested all the powers it will have. This means that the infrastructure is not in place for the extension of fiscal powers.

Tax and Spending

For example there is no revenue function, no Treasury, and no debt management office, and all will be needed in an independent Scotland, and even to some extent when the Scotland Act comes into full force. On this basis, Ms Armstrong suggested that there are fiscal risks for Scotland even without independence. The Scotland Act will create a Scottish rate of income tax, whereby HM Treasury will reduce income tax at the basic and higher rates [in Scotland] by 10%, and reduce the block-grant accordingly. The Scottish Government is empowered to levy a tax to fill that gap. Stamp duty land tax will also be replaced under the powers of the Scotland Act, with the land and buildings transaction tax. This is intended to be a more progressive tax. Finally, the new landfill tax will be roughly equivalent to the landfill tax which exists at the moment. The Scotland Act will also give Scotland additional borrowing powers, with Scotland able to borrow around 10% of its capital budget. By 2015/16, when these powers come in, that figure is projected to be around £230 million, to be used to fund infrastructure. Scotland will also have a short-term borrowing facility of around £200 million per year, which will allow it to deal with short-term revenue volatility that might occur as a result of the new tax-raising powers which are yet to be tested. Ms Armstrong pointed out that the powers extended under the Scotland Act are substantially different from what we currently have, with the *status quo* completely gone. Even beyond a 'No' vote then, the fiscal outlook will be different.

Ms Armstrong made the point that economic and fiscal policy that would lead to growth and productivity in Scotland are essential. She suggested that it is not yet clear how the Scottish Government will use its fiscal powers to make the necessary changes in fiscal productivity. There needs to be an understanding of how the Scottish Government will make this work. Within the Union, Scotland will continue to receive its block grant; however, there are those who want to see changes to the Barnett Formula. Ms Armstrong predicted that a 'No' vote in the Referendum will see a renegotiation of the settlement Scotland currently receives from Westminster. She observed that whatever the outcome of the Referendum, uncertainty on fiscal outcomes exists. She concluded by suggesting that these are questions to which we need answers in order to get some certainty as to whether the anticipated additional risks of Scotland becoming independent outweigh the anticipated benefits.

Professor Gavin McCrone suggested that although Scotland has a smaller deficit than the UK, both have deficits that are too large to be sustainable. Measures are needed to reduce these deficits. He added that estimations about Scotland's fiscal outlook rest on figures which are uncertain; for example, the assumption that an independent Scotland would get a 90% share of North Sea Oil revenues; the assumption that Scotland would take a population share of the national debt; and the assumption that if Scotland gets 90% of North Sea Oil revenues then GDP would increase, making Scotland's share of the debt a smaller proportion of its GDP. A further area of uncertainty is around the rate of interest that an independent Scotland would be expected to pay on its debt. Professor McCrone observed that Scotland would be a new borrower, with no established credibility, and that the UK has never defaulted on its debt, but that this record cannot be applied to a newly independent Scotland. It is likely, therefore, that Scotland will pay a higher interest rate on its debt than the rest of the UK. What is more, revenues from North Sea Oil are projected to decline. Coupled with Scotland's ageing population, this means that there is an expectation that revenue for an independent Scotland will be declining while public spending increases. At the moment, Scotland contributes tax revenue approximately proportionate to its population share to the UK exchequer, if taxation on North Sea Oil is excluded. However, it also has a public expenditure about 10% higher than that of the rest of the UK, so there is an imbalance. The importance of North Sea Oil revenues is therefore to try and bring them into balance. This is a problem, because if Scotland's public expenditure continued to be higher than that of the rest of the UK, then that would result in a deficit. On this basis, Professor McCrone cautioned against the assumption that under independence everyone in Scotland would be £500 better off, suggesting that people relying on this figure would do better to forget it.

Professor McCrone suggested that an independent Scotland would have to be fiscally conservative as a result of having no track record. This would require it to be very careful with its finances. He observed that due to quantitative easing in the UK, the Bank of England now owns one third of the UK debt, with the interest paid on this debt going back to the Treasury. He raised the question as to what might happen to that piece of the debt in the longer term, and queried whether, if the UK Government cancelled the debt, that would count as a default. He also queried whether, if an independent Scotland took a share of the UK debt, Scotland's bit of this debt would be reduced in the same way.

Tax and Spending

During the **Question and Answer session** which followed, a member of the audience asked the panel how Scotland should move forward in the event of a 'No' vote in the Referendum. Referring to the Barnett Formula, he asked how Scotland could ensure that it keeps its share of expenditure higher than the rest of the UK, on the basis of Scotland paying in high oil tax revenues, whilst also ensuring that the block grant is distributed to the regions on the basis of need rather than by head of population. Ms Armstrong responded that the Barnett Formula is a political fix which is not based on need, and observed that the Welsh Assembly have undertaken a piece of work showing that if looked at on a needs basis, Wales is being short-changed by the Barnett Formula. She pointed out that there are always opportunities to change the current Formula arrangement, and acknowledged that it is definitely up for change, but that the outcome of any changes would be as a result of negotiation. On the assumption that Scotland should get more than the other regions under this arrangement because is puts in more, she pointed out that this has only been the case since 1980, when North Sea taxes started.

A member of the audience asked Professor McCrone about a report he had written in 1974, which suggested that Scotland would be as rich as Switzerland if it used its oil revenues. The audience member suggested that this report had been 'suppressed' for over 30 years, and wanted to know why. He also commented upon the fact that in discussing tax, no mention had been made of the value of avoided and evaded tax. Referring to the paper, Professor McCrone responded that this had been written when he was a civil servant as a brief in the period before an election, and had indicated that North Sea Oil revenues in the 1980s would be larger than the outgoing Government had said. The report suggested that the Treasury of the outgoing Government had grossly underestimated the potential value of North Sea Oil for the forthcoming period. Professor McCrone pointed out that this report was a briefing paper written when he was a civil servant. Briefing papers by civil servants, especially those prepared in advance of a possible change of government, are never published. The paper had not been suppressed.

Ms Smith (the Chair) asked the panel to reflect on the quality of the debate about the Referendum and the information which has been made available so far, and asked whether there has been enough information made available. Ms Armstrong responded that there has been both too much and not enough information, observing that some of the information made available has been impenetrable and some of the information has been completely inaccessible. She pointed out that unless and until we are made aware of the realities of what an independent Scotland would look like, it is not possible to see how this maps against what we can and cannot afford to spend on and invest in. She suggested that the challenge is to look at the uncertainties presented by both positions, adding that transition costs in an independent Scotland could lead to capital flight. She asked the question, is it worth the pain [for Scotland to become independent]?

The discussion also dealt with issues relating to Currency, Banking and Financial Services, and the contributions made by the speakers in relation to this are summarised under the chapter heading of that name.

Defence and International Relations

Defence and International Relations

29 May 2013, at the Royal Society of Edinburgh

INTRODUCTION

This seminar was the third in the series. It examined questions on how the UK's role within NATO might be affected by constitutional change, and about the future of the UK's nuclear deterrence, given the SNP's anti-nuclear policies. The seminar also discussed how the UK's position on the international stage might be affected by constitutional change, and what the implications of separating the Scottish and UK armed forces might be. The latter half of the seminar addressed questions from the audience.

The subject of Defence & International Relations was addressed by a panel of four expert speakers:

> **Lieutenant Colonel Stuart Crawford,** Stuart Crawford Associates, former SNP defence advisor

> **Dr Phillips O'Brien,** Reader in Modern History and Convenor of the Global Security Network

> **Professor William Walker,** Professor of International Relations, University of St. Andrews

> **Rt Hon Lord Robertson of Port Ellen KT GCMG PC HonFRSE,** Former Secretary General of NATO and former Secretary of State for Defence

The discussion was chaired by **Lieutenant General Sir Alistair Irwin,** President of the Royal British Legion for Scotland.

The seminar was conducted as an open, public discussion seminar.

LIEUTENANT COLONEL STUART CRAWFORD,
STUART CRAWFORD ASSOCIATES, FORMER SNP DEFENCE ADVISOR

Lieutenant Colonel Stuart Crawford began by observing that the question around how an independent Scotland might organise its own armed forces has been central to recent debate on Scotland's future. He suggested that in recent years the focus of this question has shifted, so that it is no longer about whether or not Scotland could run its own armed services, but rather about whether it should. In making this point, he suggested that there is little doubt that Scotland could, if it wished to, manage an independent armed service.

In addressing the question of whether Scotland should seek an independent armed force, which would be a consequences of a 'Yes' vote in the Referendum, Lieutenant Colonel Crawford began by defining what the wider functions of a nation's armed forces are.

The three main tasks of any armed force, he suggested, are:

> ensuring the survival of the state against internal enemies (for example insurrection, non-democratic uprising and terrorism) and providing disaster relief;

> protecting the state against external aggression;

> promoting stability in regions where the state has strategic interests, for example through exchange training and diplomacy.

He also pointed out that a nation's armed forces may be deployed in voluntary ventures being undertaken by the UN or by NATO.

When considering what an independent Scottish defence force might look like, Lieutenant Colonel Crawford observed that a convenient suggestion is that Scotland would have armed forces around 10% the size of those the UK has at the moment; or that Scotland's armed forces would look the same as those of roughly equivalent countries, for example Denmark or Norway; or that Scotland would have a defence budget equivalently proportional to its GDP as the current average for EU countries.

While these suggestions make sense, or are at least acceptable, from the point of view of a straightforward size or GDP comparison, this sort of approach actually tackles the question from the wrong direction. A better way to approach the question, he suggested, is to look at the level of risk faced by an independent Scotland.

Defence and International Relations

This can be achieved by asking the following questions:

> What might Scotland have, which others might want to attack?

> What would Scotland need (in terms of military resource) to protect this?

> What would this cost?

There are no clear predictions about what an independent Scotland's foreign policy might be, but Lieutenant Colonel Crawford hypothesised that the focus of an independent Scotland's armed forces would be regional and not global, and that this focus would be primarily on defence; although an independent Scotland would have the option of contributing to allied engagements overseas, if it wished to.

On the question of what an independent Scotland would want to protect, he suggested that the main focus would be on territorial integrity, oil and gas revenues and fishing grounds. He observed that Scotland is not at high risk from conventional military attack, but that a more likely risk is from elements such as cyber warfare, terrorism and organised crime. Taking these interests into consideration, he suggested a model for what an independent Scotland might need in order to best protect its national security and assets from likely threats. This is as opposed to a model of what Scotland might want in terms of defence structure. Lieutenant Colonel Crawford suggested that Scotland would need something like 60 aircraft, 20 to 25 ships and two army brigades, one deployable and one for reinforcement and home duties, amounting to between 13,000 and 17,000 armed forces personnel across all three services. He suggested that an independent Scotland would be very unlikely to need the sort of hardware used by the UK military, for example aircraft carriers. On the question of how these forces might be raised and equipped, he suggested that much of this could be taken from Scotland's share of UK forces, and indicated that horse-trading might be required to facilitate this, including Scotland taking cash in lieu of assets, such as Trident, where appropriate.

Lieutenant Colonel Crawford estimated that the cost of the model proposed would be around £1.84 billion per annum, which is around 1.3% of Scotland's GDP. This compares favourably with the Scottish defence expenditure of £3.3 billion in 2010/11, and the SNP's recently declared defence budget of £2.5 billion per annum.

Summing up, Lieutenant Colonel Crawford suggested that there are three questions to ask when considering the potential for an independent Scottish armed force:

> Is it necessary?

> Is it feasible?

> Is it affordable?

On the basis of the model he had proposed, Lieutenant Colonel Crawford declared that we can answer 'Yes' to all three of these questions. The evidence, therefore, is that Scotland could have an independent armed force if it wanted to; the question which remains to be answered is whether this is an option that Scotland should pursue.

DR PHILLIPS O'BRIEN,
READER IN MODERN HISTORY, UNIVERSITY OF GLASGOW, AND CONVENOR OF THE GLOBAL SECURITY NETWORK

Following on from Lieutenant Colonel Crawford, Dr Phillips O'Brien referred to the nature of the debate around Scotland's constitutional future, and conducted a brief analysis of what the big issues to feature in this debate have so far been. He observed that the question of defence has been one of the largest issues to feature so far and that, under the heading of defence, the largest question has been around the Faslane nuclear base and what would happen to this base in the event of Scottish independence.

Dr O'Brien pointed out that Faslane is currently one of the largest employers in the west of Scotland, accounting for around 6,500 Scottish jobs, with current plans to see this rise to 8,000. The SNP has expressed a desire to maintain all of the jobs at this base; however, Dr O'Brien pointed out that the Campaign for Nuclear Disarmament (CND) has a loud voice in the independence debate and will want an independent Scotland to commit to removing all nuclear weapons and bases from Scotland. Dr O'Brien suggested that this may prove problematic for the SNP if Scotland does become independent. He pointed out that the issue of an independent Scotland's relationship with NATO is also a large one, especially now that the SNP has declared a change in policy and is now committed to Scotland becoming a member of NATO.

Defence and International Relations

Following the questions around Faslane and Scotland's relationship with NATO, Dr O'Brien suggested that the third biggest question under the defence heading has been around whether an independent Scotland would return to the original Scottish regiment model, with a permanent regimental identity. Questions that haven't figured as highly in the debate so far are questions around what would happen to Rosyth and other Scottish bases such as Inverness and Fort St George, or to the shipbuilding yards on the Clyde.

In relation to the big questions, Dr O'Brien suggested that most of these are not debatable, but refer to issues (e.g. NATO and Faslane) where there is not actually much to debate. On the issue of an independent Scotland's relationship with NATO, for example, Dr O'Brien suggested that Scotland has to be a member of NATO because the rest of the EU member states would make Scottish EU membership extremely difficult if Scotland was not a member of NATO. Walking away from NATO, he suggested, would damage Scotland's negotiating position on EU membership. On the question of Scottish regiments, he argued that this is not a model that Scotland can return to, and that to do so would make no sense. This is not, therefore, a realistic issue for debate. On the big question of what would happen to Faslane in an independent Scotland, Dr O'Brien stated that Faslane simply could not be expected to continue at its current size in an independent Scotland. By trying to consider and debate these issues, he suggested, the SNP is posing questions that are too politically difficult. On this basis, he proposed to address the question of what a politically feasible policy for the 'Yes' campaign would be, and what issues would lead to useful and worthwhile debate.

Dr O'Brien proposed starting with the question of money, and suggested that the defence budget of £2.5 billion proposed by the SNP is a mistaken figure, because it is either too much, or too little. Elucidating the point, he observed that this figure represents a much higher sum than Scotland actually needs for a feasible defence programme, but not nearly enough to maintain the status quo. He suggested that for a lower figure of around £1.75 billion, Scotland would get a very reasonable defence structure. He proposed Denmark as an excellent model for an independent Scotland. Denmark has two distinct facilities, one base for domestic patrols and another to train units for deployment with NATO operations.

This model would be very operable within an independent Scotland. Dr O'Brien suggested that an independent Scotland would have to place any domestic naval bases on the east coast, and observed that putting an entire Scottish navy at Faslane would be a dereliction of duty, because it would leave the east coast very exposed. A reserve base could be located at Faslane.

Dr O'Brien pointed out that the remaining 'big question' is around the size of an independent Scotland's air force. He suggested that this is a very debatable issue because the air force is a 'big ticket' item. Dr O'Brien suggested that Scotland would only need one air base, which could be located at Lossiemouth or Leuchars. He estimated that his proposed defence model would come in at around £1.75 billion, as opposed to the £2.5 billion proposed by the SNP. He suggested that the SNP, instead of arguing that Scotland would require a military that would cost £2.5 billion, should accept one that would cost £1.75 billion, but should place the difference between these two figures in a Transition Fund. Scotland would inevitably lose defence jobs if it became independent, so there would be a need to creatively address this issue. A Transition Fund could be used to manage the change. Dr O'Brien also suggested that in an independent Scotland, Glasgow would lose out to Edinburgh on the location of defence bases and the associated jobs.

This would also require creative management. The SNP should accept smaller defence facilities, but should use the money saved to manage the transition to fewer defence jobs in Scotland, especially on the west coast.

PROFESSOR WILLIAM WALKER,
PROFESSOR OF INTERNATIONAL RELATIONS, UNIVERSITY OF ST ANDREWS

Professor Walker focused on the question of Trident, which he observed to be central to the debate about Scotland's constitutional future. He undertook an analysis of the Trident replacement policy developed under the Labour Government, and the credibility of this policy in the current political and economic environment. Professor Walker suggested that the replacement policy is no longer as secure as it once was, and that this is not just because of the possibility of Scottish independence.

Defence and International Relations

The original replacement policy was for a fleet of four submarines carrying Trident missiles, of which one would constantly be at sea; the intention being the new system would be fully implemented during the 2020s. Professor Walker pointed out that this target is based upon an assumption that the UK can afford a like-for-like replacement of Trident. This assumption dates back to a pre-2007 climate in which it was not anticipated that there would be a shift from high public expenditure to austerity, or that the current Chancellor of the Exchequer would require that the costs for Trident's replacement be met entirely out of the UK Defence Budget. Neither was it anticipated that Trident would consume more than a quarter of the UK Procurement Budget, nor that the SNP would call a referendum on independence, nor that Trident's eviction from Scotland would be promised to the Scottish people as part of an independence package. In consideration of these unanticipated changes that have affected the political and economic landscape of the UK since the Trident replacement policy was first framed, Professor Walker asked why this policy has not been suitably revised. Answering this question, he suggested that any big spending on Trident's replacement will not need to take place until 2016, so any debate about this policy and its feasibility can be delayed until after the next UK general election. He observed that Trident is something of a 'sacred cow' of the Conservative Government, and added that the UK Government is observing a policy of not pre-negotiating, or contingency planning, on the question of Scotland's constitutional future. In spite of this, he asserted that the Trident replacement policy will need to be revised.

On the basis of the stated need for a revised Trident replacement policy, Professor Walker turned his attention to the available options. He raised the option of the UK adopting a different nuclear deterrence system, for example the use of cruise missiles, but observed that this option has been widely rejected. He also referred to the option of complete nuclear abandonment, according to which the UK would abandon its nuclear deterrent entirely, but suggested that there is not sufficient courage or conviction within Whitehall to contemplate this drastic step at the moment. Professor Walker observed that there is a third, less radical option, which involves the UK changing its nuclear posture and moving away from the idea of having a constant nuclear deterrent deployed at sea. In response to this third option, Professor Walker suggested that there is an argument that a part-time deterrent is no deterrent at all, and that if we do not have all four submarines, with a continuous deterrent at sea, there is no point in having a nuclear deterrent at all.

He added that reducing the number of submarines will not deliver substantial savings, and certainly not in the first five to ten years, and the opportunity cost would be substantial.

Professor Walker concluded that the decisions made on Trident and the UK's nuclear deterrence programme will depend upon the negotiations which take place between the Scottish and UK Governments, and that the situation will inevitably change after the referendum on Scotland's future. He suggested that in the event of Scottish independence, and assuming that Scotland pursued its policy of becoming a fully non-nuclear state, it would be difficult for the UK to have its main nuclear deterrent operating out of Scotland. It is not clear how tenable it would be for a nuclear weapons state to operate out of a non-nuclear weapons state, and this is likely to be a less than desirable arrangement. Professor Walker observed that there would need to be negotiation of a treaty, between an independent Scotland and the UK, on a range of contentious issues, including Faslane. He suggested that the stances taken on how to manage the UK's nuclear deterrence programme will depend on which political parties are in power when these issues come to the fore, and whether these parties have the power to make decisions on these issues. He closed with the observation that Scottish independence would inevitably increase the cost of Trident's replacement, and suggested that the Trident replacement policy is currently in a state of flux, but that the outcome is bound to be one of a diminished nuclear deterrent or no nuclear deterrent at all.

RT HON LORD ROBERTSON OF PORT ELLEN KT GCMG PC HONFRSE, FORMER SECRETARY GENERAL OF NATO AND FORMER SECRETARY OF STATE FOR DEFENCE

Lord Robertson opened with the observation that the referendum on Scotland's constitutional future represents a one-in-ten-generations decision and one which will be irreversible. He suggested that there are a lot of other countries watching the approach to the Scottish referendum, and that many are concerned that the potential break-up of the UK represents the potential break-up of a stabilising power in the international arena. He went on to suggest that the referendum and the lead up to it will be watched by enemies and potential enemies of Scotland and the UK.

Defence and International Relations

He observed that there are a lot of threats and challenges facing states today, including: terrorism; the proliferation of weapons; rogue states; cyber warfare; organised crime; climate change, which will be linked to conflicts over resources and to migration flows; pandemics; piracy; and fragile and failed states. He made the point that none of these threats has a national solution that can be dealt with by one government. Instead, collective solutions must be sought.

Lord Robertson suggested that other separatist movements will also be watching the debate around Scotland's constitutional future, for example in Catalonia, Flanders, the Basque country, Lombardy, Transylvania and Corsica, and that the states affected do not represent small or negligible factors in the world today. Lord Robertson speculated that a 'Yes' vote in the Scottish referendum could represent the first domino to fall in what he referred to as the 'Balkanisation' of the European continent.

Lord Robertson acknowledged that independence would give Scotland the opportunity to remain politically and militarily neutral in respect of global issues and conflicts, if it wished to. However, he added that he did not believe this stance would be in the spirit of the Scottish people. He observed that an independent Scotland could follow the model set by states such as Denmark and Norway, but noted that both Denmark and Norway are established nation states which have built up their defence forces over many years, observing that both accept the US and NATO nuclear umbrella without any equivocations, and both have deployed troops with NATO.

Lord Robertson made the point that if Scotland did become independent, it would need to create its own Ministry of Defence, army, navy, air-force, logistics and intelligence. He agreed with Dr O'Brien that an independent Scotland would have to be in NATO, and argued that there is no sense in an independent Scotland being outside NATO if it is to effectively defend itself. He pointed to the inconsistency between Scotland's proposed NATO membership and the Scottish Government's commitment to making Scotland a non-nuclear state, and suggested that the Scottish Government must either renege on its long-held commitments regarding nuclear weapons, or risk leaving a newly independent Scotland poorly defended and at risk. Lord Robertson concluded by stating his belief that Scotland should remain a part of the UK.

Questions and Answers

A comment was raised about Lord Robertson's reference to 'Balkanisation', and Lord Robertson was asked to clarify his meaning. It was suggested that the idea that people across the world are nervous or afraid of Scottish independence is a misrepresentation of the situation, and Lord Robertson was asked to offer evidence demonstrating this fear, in support of his comments. Lord Robertson responded by referring to the break-up of the former Yugoslavia, and the creation of new Balkan states that followed, as an example of the instability that may result from separatism and the break-up of nations. He observed that there are separatist movements in other parts of the world, and suggested that there is some apprehension in Europe that these movements are starting to get the upper hand. Lord Robertson pointed out that Belgium suffered a severe identity crisis at the onset of its independence, and that it took 1.5 years to establish a Government after the last national election. He observed that in Spain, there have been huge demonstrations demanding independence for Catalonia, and suggested that people across Europe will be watching Scotland because there is to be a referendum on Scottish independence. This gives the Scottish separatist movement a legitimacy not allowed to other separatist movements in Europe; a referendum on Catalonia's independence being prohibited under the Spanish constitution. He pointed to the example of the EU's inability to recognise Kosovo as a nation state as an example of the concern that other EU member states have over separatist and independence movements. The EU has not yet been able to take a position on the nation statehood of Kosovo because certain members of the EU, for example Spain, Italy and Slovakia, refuse to recognise Kosovo on the basis of their concerns over separatism.

Lord Robertson's earlier point that the decision made in the Scottish referendum will be a one-in-ten-generations decision was referred to, and the question raised as to whether speakers could think of any facts about Scottish defence which are true now, and which will still be true in 50 years. Lieutenant General Sir Alistair Irwin (the Chair) responded that it is very difficult to make these sorts of predictions, but indicated that those making decisions now do perhaps have a duty to be as "least wrong as possible" about the way things might look in the future.

The point was raised that the main threats facing Scotland today and in the future are from terrorism, organised crime and cyber-crime. The main weapon against these is intelligence, and yet it was observed that the issue of intelligence had not yet been addressed by the panel. The question was therefore posed as to how an independent Scotland might be expected to manage in respect of intelligence.

Defence and International Relations

Lieutenant Colonel Crawford responded that an independent Scotland would be unable to replicate the intelligence structure which is currently in place in the UK, for example GCHQ and all of the networks which feed into it. He did suggest, however, that there are aspects of UK intelligence in which Scotland plays an integral part. He suggested that an independent Scotland would have to rely on the UK for a lot of its information, for example regarding terrorist threats, but added that how much intelligence the UK might be willing to share was contentious. He referred to England's participation in the *Five Eyes* agreement[1] and suggested that the best an independent Scotland could hope for would be to be a part of this.

Lord Robertson added to this response, suggesting that intelligence is likely to represent a serious problem for an independent Scotland. He suggested that Scotland could not replicate the networks of relationships that currently exist as part of UK intelligence. He observed that these networks are based on long-established habit and trust, which have been built up over a very long time. The Scottish Government has indicated that it would create a Scottish version of MI5 and MI6 in the event of independence, but Lord Robertson asserted that this would be a Herculean task.

Picking up on Dr O'Brien's comments about an independent Scotland's membership of the EU, the question was posed as to how important it would be for an independent Scotland to be a member of the EU, and what would be required of the Scottish Government with regards to Trident if it wished for Scotland to become an EU member.

Dr O'Brien replied that states are hostile to Scottish independence because right now the UK meshes very well with existing defence structures, and breaking up the UK creates a question mark over how this might continue. States, as distinct from individuals, tend to be cautious and conservative. Dr O'Brien raised the question of why the United States would see itself as having a strategic interest in the UK or Europe if Scotland left NATO, and suggested that Scotland leaving NATO is not a realistic option. In negotiating entry into the EU, Scotland has quite a weak hand to begin with. If Scotland wishes easy entry to the EU therefore, it is not in a position to make demands around its cooperation with NATO.

Following these comments, Professor Walker suggested that it would be difficult for an independent Scotland, given the SNP policy on nuclear deterrence, to retain the principle of providing a base for NATO nuclear deterrents. However, he observed that if Scotland expelled Trident from its national waters, that decision would be frowned upon internationally, and would be inconsistent with Scotland seeking membership of NATO.

1 An intelligence operations alliance between the UK, USA, Canada, Australia and New Zealand

He added, however, that the UK should not be seen as coercing Scotland to host UK nuclear deterrents, as this form of coercion would also be frowned upon. Lord Robertson added that it is part of NATO's strategic concept to ensure the participation of allied states in collective nuclear defence planning, and suggested that it would be difficult for a non-nuclear state to seek to become a member of NATO. He observed that, following the break-up of the former Soviet Union, the Ukraine became a non-nuclear state, but the negotiations for this took 20 years, concluding in the decision that Russia would continue to use Sevastopol in the Ukraine as a nuclear base. He pointed out that the speedy removal of Trident, which Alex Salmond has promised as part of Scottish independence, must be understood in that context.

A point was raised that the title of the discussion seminar was 'Defence and International Relations', and the observation was made that International Relations has come up only sideways into the discussion. The whole panel were invited to answer the question; *would an independent Scotland have a) the capability to identify an international relations stance and b) the credibility to ensure that stance is respected by the international community?*

In response, Professor Walker suggested that Scotland is regarded with respect by the international community, as a place with many attributes, including a sound economy, good administration and a long democratic history. When compared to other small states, he suggested, it is seen as a place that could easily run itself. He observed that most countries don't want to see the UK broken up, but suggested that if this did occur, most would expect Scotland to be able to run itself with ease. He added that many foreign diplomats know Scotland well, and hold a deep respect for Scotland as a nation, and stated his expectation that an independent Scotland would be accepted by the international community.

Lieutenant General Sir Alistair Irwin (Chair) reminded Professor Walker that the question related to an independent Scotland's significance as an international player, as well as its acceptance by the international community, and asked him to comment on Scotland's potential significance. Professor Walker responded that Scotland would obviously be a small power, and the UK would be a much greater power. He observed that the aspect which concerns foreign governments about the potential breakup of the UK is not so much whether Scotland would cope as an independent state, but rather how stable the remainder of the UK would be and how it would relate to the EU. However, he acknowledged that Scotland could not expect to have a large influence internationally.

Defence and International Relations

Lieutenant Colonel Crawford added that in terms of defence, the model for an independent Scotland that he developed in his book, *A' the Blue Bonnets: Defending an Independent Scotland*, accepts that Scotland would not have global scope for its defence policy. He suggested that in the absence of a clear statement from the Scottish Government about what its foreign policy might be, we can do no more than hypothesise about an independent Scotland's potential international relations.

Lord Robertson asserted that an independent Scotland would certainly be able to stand on its own two feet with regard to defence and international relations, but suggested that the real question is why it would want to. He pointed out that Scotland is currently part of a union in which Scots play a disproportionate role in the way the UK as a whole is run, and suggested that Scotland has its own nation within the UK already, with more powers to be devolved to Scotland when the Scotland Act comes into force fully.

The question was posed as to what NATO's reaction to an independent Scotland seeking membership might be, if at the same time Scotland was committed to doing away with the Faslane base entirely, given that this base is part of NATO's strategy.

Dr O'Brien responded that an independent Scotland could not dictate to NATO, and would simply not be able to adopt such a contradictory position. He observed that Scotland could make the unilateral decision to become a non-nuclear state, but it could not dictate to the rest of the UK, which will have much more power and pull over NATO than an independent Scotland could hope to have. He added that an assumption can be made that Scotland and the UK would have a desire to reach a cooperative solution to the nuclear question, should Scotland become independent.

Professor Walker pointed out that any attempt by an independent Scotland to join NATO would have to come only after an agreement over the location of the UK's nuclear deterrent had been reached between Scotland and the rest of the UK. He suggested that the most logical position for the Scottish Government to take would be to allow the current deterrent to be based in Scotland, but to refuse to allow the replacements, once these are ready. The likely timeframe for this is between ten and twenty years, so this position would be regarded by the international community as quite reasonable. He added that NATO would find it difficult to turn down this position.

Responding to this, Lieutenant Colonel Crawford observed that the SNP have not so far placed a firm timetable on the removal of nuclear weapons from the Clyde. Lord Robertson observed that the problem the SNP will face is that they have made it very clear that they want to expel Trident if Scotland becomes independent, and have even proposed that this be included in the written constitution of an independent Scotland.

He added that NATO is not a monolith, but is made up of 28 member countries, so that every decision made by NATO must be taken by consensus. He suggested that if other countries within NATO have accepted the shared responsibility of nuclear deterrence, they might find it difficult to accept a state which has a policy of ultimately rejecting this responsibility.

A question was raised as to whether much thought has been given to the future international relations between Scotland and England in the event of Scottish independence. The question put to the panel was: *What would the transition from domestic neighbour to international partner be?*

Lord Robertson suggested that this would depend on the nature of the debate that takes place between now and the referendum. He observed that, so far, the debate about Scotland's constitutional future is largely taking place in Scotland, and has been given little perspective by the rest of the UK. Certain decisions, for example on the possibility of a currency union between an independent Scotland and the rest of the UK, are not just between Scotland and London. There are other nations within the UK (Wales and Northern Ireland) which might not be keen to share the pound with a Scotland which has claimed it will take 90% of North Sea oil, for example.

Professor Walker added that the question of the UK's membership of the EU is currently seen as a more important issue in England than the question of Scotland's future membership of the UK. He suggested that the dimension introduced by the possibility of the UK leaving the EU complicates greatly the politics around the possibility of Scottish independence.

The question was posed as to what the relationship between an independent Scottish armed force and a UK armed force might be, bearing in mind that there are obvious economies of scale to be achieved through cooperation.

Dr O'Brien responded by asking, *what does the rest of the UK become if Scotland leaves?* He suggested that people are not yet ready for this question, and made the point that if Scotland does become independent, the UK will probably have to de-nuclearise. He observed that if the UK does scale down its nuclear role on the international stage, it could probably cooperate well with an independent Scotland. If the UK wishes to remain a major world power, however, it will mesh well with NATO and the other NATO member states.

Defence and International Relations

Lieutenant General Sir Alistair Irwin made the point that Scots are embedded within the entirety of the UK armed forces, and suggested that to try and separate the UK armed forces out into a Scottish-only and a UK-only segment would be organisational pandemonium. He added that mutually-agreed cooperation would probably be achieved between two such forces eventually, but that this would not be possible until all of the complex organisational aspects of separating out the armed forces had been addressed. He observed that this would be a long time coming.

Lieutenant Colonel Crawford suggested that the relationship between separate UK and Scottish armed forces would be based upon mutual cooperation. He pointed out that there is currently no army officer training school in Scotland, for example, and that Scottish soldiers would therefore continue to go to Sandhurst to train. He stated that he could not foresee a situation in which relationships between distinct Scottish and UK forces are less than cordial.

Lord Robertson observed that the UK armed forces are highly integrated, and that they are respected and acknowledged across the world. He suggested that unpicking these forces would render the armed forces of both Scotland and the UK sub-scale and sub-optimal. On the basis that two such forces would be sharing and cooperating, he posed the question of why we should consider separating them in the first place.

A question was raised about the opportunities that would be available to an independent Scotland with regard to the decisions it makes about international engagements. An independent Scotland, for example, would be able to make its own decisions about whether or not to go to war.

Lieutenant Colonel Crawford agreed that an independent Scotland would have the option to participate in foreign military engagements. He observed that much has been made, in the debate so far, of the idea that those in the armed forces would have reduced opportunities in an independent Scotland. However, he suggested that a reduction in the size of the military based in Scotland would not necessarily mean a reduction in the number of commitments Scotland might have as a nation. This means that there might actually be an increase in opportunities for those employed in the armed services in Scotland.

The Chair then asked the rest of the panel for their thoughts on what opportunities and advantages might be accrued through having an independent defence force.

Professor Walker observed that an independent Scotland would have the opportunity to make its own choices about its levels of activity and engagement. He suggested that the UK had made some enormous mistakes in the past, and quoted the Iraq war as a pertinent example. He added that an independent Scotland would be free to make its own decisions, and potentially its own mistakes, observing that there is a degree of responsibility and accountability which inevitably goes with the power to make these choices.

Professor Walker added that there is a role for small states to play in diplomacy and conflict resolution, but suggested that while there are certainly opportunities, there may also be risks, and that being a small state can be very lonely and uncomfortable.

Dr O'Brien made the point that people from smaller countries tend to be happier, and suggested that there is a 'cosmic notion' that smaller nations are more optimistic. He observed that the real advantages for an independent Scotland would probably be found outside the arenas of security and international relations.

Lord Robertson acknowledged that an independent Scotland would have the option of remaining neutral, or of picking and choosing which operations to become involved with. He pointed out that the SNP has suggested Scotland would take part only in UN-mandated operations, and observed that the war with Afghanistan was just such an operation.

A final point was made that there is a democratic component to this debate which had not, so far, been mentioned. It was observed that if Scotland does vote for independence, it will be voting 'Yes' to doing things differently on an international scale, and that if mistakes are made, these will be made on Scotland's own terms.

CONCLUDING REMARKS

The seminar was brought to a close after a very engaging discussion, during which the audience posed both interesting and challenging questions. A range of topics under the heading of Defence and International Relations were addressed, and a range of stances on the challenges and opportunities for an independent Scotland were explored by the panel. The overwhelming point which emerged from the discussion was that questions about Scotland's constitutional future are not thought to rest on whether an independent Scotland could manage its own defence and international relations, but rather on the question of whether this is a preferable alternative to maintaining the Union.

The Real
Economy

The Real Economy

20 June 2013, at the Royal Society of Edinburgh

INTRODUCTION

This seminar was the fourth in the series. The 'real economy' refers to aspects of the economy besides banking, currency and financial and monetary policy. The seminar examined Scotland's global reputation and attractiveness as a trade and business destination, Scotland's energy market and Scotland's labour market and how these might be affected by constitutional change. This seminar aimed to bring new perspectives into the debate on Scotland's constitutional future.

The subject of The Real Economy was addressed by a panel of four speakers:

> **Mr Brandon Malone**, Chairman, Scottish Arbitration Centre;

> **Mr Stephen Boyd**, Assistant Secretary, Policy and Campaigns Department, Scottish Trades Union Congress;

> **Professor Gordon Hughes**, Professor of Economics, University of Edinburgh; and

> **Professor Jeremy Peat OBE FRSE**, Director of the David Hume Institute.

The discussion was chaired by **Mr Douglas Fraser**, Business and Economic Editor, BBC Scotland.

The seminar was conducted as an open, public discussion seminar.

Mr Brandon Malone,
Chairman, Scottish Arbitration Centre

Mr Malone suggested that, with reference to the Real Economy, the decision to vote 'Yes' or to vote 'No' in the Scottish Independence Referendum would not be made on the basis of accounting issues. He therefore proposed to examine the business case for independence. Mr Malone began by observing that much of the debate about Scotland's future has centred on the notion of risk; for example, the potential risk of Scottish independence to aspects such as Scotland's global competitiveness, to Scottish pensions, to Scotland's membership of the EU, etc. In business, however, risk tends to be associated with reward, and taking calculated risks is an integral part of business decision making. He acknowledged that there are risks associated with Scottish independence, but suggested that the question to ask is not whether there are risks, but whether the potential reward outweighs these risks.

Mr Malone briefly referred to the fact that Scottish independence would enable the Scottish Government to have more fiscal levers available to it, but he did not wish to focus on the issue of taxation and spending. He proposed to look at the wider picture, and to focus on Scotland's branding, PR and promotion.

Addressing the issue of branding first, Mr Malone suggested that UK branding is slightly confused, with the nations of the UK operating under several different brands; for example Great Britain, the UK and the national brands of each nation (England, Wales, Northern Ireland and Scotland). He suggested that the international perception of Scotland as a nation with its own distinct and unique identity suffers as a result of this, with Scotland being subsumed by the UK brand. Mr Brandon referred to his work as a solicitor and suggested that when trying to promote Scotland as a destination for international arbitration, he is often called upon to explain to people that Scotland has its own distinct legal system. He suggested that internationally there is a lack of understanding about what Scotland is, but indicated that since the Scottish Referendum has been announced, there has been greater global awareness of Scotland as a unique and distinct entity. He argued that it is only through the attainment of independent statehood that the problems around Scotland's branding will be resolved.

The Real Economy

On the subject of Scotland's global PR, Mr Malone suggested that Scotland's global reputation is suffering as a result of the UK intention to hold a referendum on EU membership. Mr Malone suggested that the Scottish Government is more pro-European than the UK Government, and pointed out that the UK Independence Party (UKIP) has so far made no progress in Scotland. He made the point that international perceptions of Scotland are coloured by UK foreign policy.

Turning finally to the question of how Scotland is promoted abroad, Mr Malone observed that, at the UK level, this promotion is undertaken by the Foreign and Commonwealth Office (FCO). He referred to a document entitled *Plan for Growth*[1] produced by the UK Government, purporting to promote UK legal services internationally, but observed that the original document referred to the 'supremacy of English contract law', which is different from Scottish contract law.

He argued that this demonstrates a tendency to conflate UK law with English law, and in particular with the London legal scene. The document was subsequently revised, but Mr Malone suggested that it is still heavily focused on London and the English legal system, and promotes English lawyers over Scottish lawyers.

Summing up, Mr Malone concluded that brand confusion, negative PR and confusion in promoting Scotland could all be eliminated by Scottish independence. He added that Independence presents an opportunity for Scotland to manage its own PR internationally, to showcase Scottish business without caveat, and to create a world capital in Edinburgh.

1 https://www.gov.uk/government/uploads/system/uploads/attachment_data/file/184602/2011budget_growth.pdf.

MR STEPHEN BOYD,
ASSISTANT SECRETARY, POLICY AND CAMPAIGNS DEPARTMENT, SCOTTISH TRADES UNION CONGRESS

Mr Boyd addressed the issue of the labour market, and suggested that this is an area which has so far not been discussed as part of the debate on Scotland's constitutional future. Mr Boyd observed that the economy is affected by how the labour market functions. He added that the labour market is also highly relevant to some of the issues that have been at the forefront of the constitutional debate; for example, options for a currency union, which is heavily influenced by labour force mobility, as well as policy around taxation.

Mr Boyd suggested that tackling inequality has been a key theme of the constitutional debate. He pointed out that inequality at the Scottish level cannot be tackled unless and until inequalities in the labour market are tackled. Mr Boyd observed that in spite of its relevance, the only aspect of the labour market which has been addressed by either side of the constitutional debate is pensions, but that even this area has not been addressed in a very enlightened way.

Mr Boyd observed that the labour market is a complex entity. Recent statistics on the Scottish labour market have been reasonably positive relative to the rest of the UK, and the Scottish labour market is highly integrated with the rest of the UK. The Scottish labour market is lightly regulated, and has labour market institutions which are UK-wide and/or UK-affiliated. He added that trade union density in Scotland is higher than for the UK as a whole. In relation to the performance of the Scottish labour market, Mr Boyd observed that it has performed well since devolution, elative to the UK and by international standards. Scotland has maintained relatively high employment levels, but does suffer from long-standing regional unemployment, as well as high levels of low-paid work and high levels of under-employment. Mr Boyd suggested that some of these, and other, negative labour market trends were apparent before the recession began in 2008, and asked what might happen with regard to these trends as Scotland and the UK move towards recovery. He suggested that these negative labour market trends will have to be addressed, especially if the aspirations of the 'Yes' campaign in Scotland for the Scottish economy are to be achieved.

Mr Boyd turned to the question of what Scottish independence might entail with regard to the labour market. He suggested that it is difficult to discern a rationale for devolving labour markets under enhanced devolution, but observed that independence is an entirely different matter. He suggested that a newly independent Scottish Government might want to do as little as possible to upset the levels of integration between Scottish and UK labour markets. On the other hand, it may wish to shift towards a model more aligned with that of small European nations, for example the Nordic nations to which Scotland often compares itself.

Mr Boyd addressed the question of what this might look like. He observed that, contrary to popular belief, Nordic labour markets are not heavily regulated; only slightly more so than the UK. Instead these labour markets are characterised by high trade union density and wide collective bargaining coverage.

The Real Economy

Nordic nations invest massively in European labour market programmes, as compared with the UK, which invests very little as a proportion of GDP. Unemployment insurance in the Nordic states is amongst the most generous in the world, and significantly more generous than that in the UK. Given this very different environment, Mr Boyd posed the question: *How might an independent Scotland begin to move towards this model?*

Responding to this question, he observed that the Scottish Government has recently published its economic case for independence, which introduced into the debate some issues around the labour market. Mr Boyd observed that, within this document, there are demonstrations of a shift towards a system of centralised bargaining mechanisms like those of the Nordic states. This proposal included introducing mechanisms to formalise the relationship between Government, employer organisations and employee associations.

Mr Boyd indicated surprise at how little response this proposal has generated, given that it could have a profound impact on the Scottish economy and the labour market. He suggested that the challenges involved in bringing about a shift towards centralised bargaining mechanisms are significant. He pointed out that bargaining structures are part of the cultural and historic fabric of societies, and are therefore not easily changed by Government action. While the social and cultural conditions exist in Nordic states to allow social partnerships to flourish, the same is not true of Scotland, which has no recent history of successful bargaining mechanisms. He added that social partnerships in Scotland are weak and that the employer side of these partnerships is fragmented and unrepresentative. Mr Boyd referred to a recent report by Michael Heseltine which stresses that the way employer organisations in the UK are set up is detrimental to the policy development process, and recommends establishing a mechanism closer to the European Chamber model. Mr Boyd also observed that the way Government in Scotland is set up is not conducive to social partnerships. He argued that there is a capacity issue; the institutional infrastructure does not exist to support a move towards more formal styles of social partnerships.

Discussing next steps, Mr Boyd suggested that there is not likely to be much consensus for reform of the current structure, observing that the UK flexible labour market has very widespread political support and suggesting that any initiative for heavier monitoring of social partnerships is likely to face strong opposition.

Concluding his discussion of labour market issues, Mr Boyd observed that significant change is required to address some of the problems of the Scottish labour market, and suggested that it is incumbent upon both sides of the constitutional debate to present their arguments for how they would address these issues and bring about the required change. He added that the way people are treated in work on a daily basis has to be a part of the debate about Scotland's constitutional future.

PROFESSOR GORDON HUGHES,
PROFESSOR OF ECONOMICS, UNIVERSITY OF EDINBURGH

Professor Hughes proposed to focus on the energy sector, as a key aspect of the Real Economy. He pointed out that the energy sector in Scotland is large and will, in a variety of ways, be central to any prospect for an independent Scotland.

Professor Hughes observed that, according to Scottish Government figures, the gross value added (GVA) by the energy sector in Scotland is around 15% of Scottish GDP, with this figure varying from year to year depending on the oil price. However, he suggested that if all of the industries that are dependent on the energy sector are added in to this, the figure is above 20%. He also pointed out that employment in energy accounts for less than 2% of Scotland's employment, revealing that the energy sector is very capital intensive.

He observed that the energy sector in Scotland is projected to attract between 60% and 80% of all business investment over the next ten years. The energy sector is therefore hugely important in terms of investment activities, and in terms of the energy sector's contribution through taxation and rents (meaning the various forms of income which accrue through the extraction of oil, or the exploitation of renewable energy).

For those numbers to continue, Professor Hughes observed, there has to be a large continuing flow of investment, and this investment has to come in a variety of forms. Scotland therefore faces a need to maintain a continuous flow of investment back into the sector. This is a major lesson which many countries with large energy sectors have ignored, he observed. Professor Hughes provided the example of Norway to illustrate this point. The crucial feature of Norway is that it has a state-owned oil company; Stat Oil, and has ploughed back a very large share of the earnings back into Stat Oil.

The Real Economy

A contrary case is PeMex in Mexico. The lesson to be taken from this example is that an economy with a large energy sector cannot consume the investment required to keep this sector going. Energy nations must therefore make a choice between using the benefits of the energy sector for enjoyment in the future, or consuming the revenue earned by this sector today and foregoing what those benefits might be worth in the future. The more that is consumed now, the lower the incomes that can be generated by the sector in the future will be. The major challenge, Professor Hughes observed, is in getting the balance between these two options right.

Professor Hughes raised a second issue about the energy sector in an imagined independent Scotland, in which Scotland would have a small, energy-dependent and relatively open economy. Economies of this kind, he observed, tend to suffer enormously from volatility of prices. All energy prices have a tendency to extreme swings, which can be cyclical, or dependent upon external factors. The more reliant an economy is upon the energy sector, the more likely it is to find itself squeezed if energy prices work adversely, and the greater the bonus will be in terms of revenue if they work positively. Spending this revenue has a consequence however, which is widely referred to as 'Dutch Disease'. This is endemic in all energy-dependent countries. The manifestation of this phenomenon is that in times of economic growth, the prices of non-traded goods (goods made and consumed at home) are driven up by demand, meaning that the costs for other traded sectors (e.g., manufacturing) are higher than they would otherwise be. These sectors ultimately find themselves squeezed, the consequence being that in all energy-dependent countries, traded goods outside the energy sector get squeezed out and eventually die. In Scotland, this is likely to have a huge impact, because manufacturing industries account for a far larger proportion of employment in Scotland than the energy sector does. Professor Hughes provided the analogy of the car industry in Australia, which doesn't exist, because mineral booms have driven up prices such that Australian car manufacturers cannot compete with the prices of imported cars.

Thinking about the possible solutions to this problem, Professor Hughes suggested that finding a solution will pose a considerable challenge to an independent Scottish Government. One option would be to create a 'sovereign wealth fund' as Norway has, funded by revenue from the energy sector.

Norway's sovereign wealth fund was started a long time ago, and Professor Hughes pointed out that Norway's real wealth is not its sovereign wealth fund, but Stat Oil. Scotland would not be starting from this pattern; the state does not own the resources or the infrastructure of North Sea Oil, and even if the Scottish Government began receiving the rents from North Sea Oil, Professor Hughes argued, it has already committed to spending this money to finance public spending. The choice that would be faced by an independent Scotland is therefore between setting up and paying into a wealth fund, or continuing to pay for what is needed today out of the revenue of the energy sector; this is a choice which all energy-reliant economies must make.

Professor Hughes also observed that, with regard to the need for energy-reliant economies to maintain investment, if this investment is not being financed by the revenue from the sector itself, there would be a need for large inward flows of capital from outside. This means becoming extremely highly integrated with capital markets around the world. The consequence of this level of integration is that independent management of policy, for example monetary and fiscal policy, would be heavily constrained. Professor Hughes observed that the idea that Scotland's energy sector would provide Scotland with the freedom to be independent is correct in one sense, but that this freedom would come at a very high cost to independence in another sense.

Professor Hughes observed that there has been an assumption that Scotland's separation from the UK would not disrupt UK energy markets. He suggested that this is a naïve assumption, and is not borne out by the experience of other separations, or by other independent countries. By way of example, Professor Hughes suggested that if England could no longer rely on gas from the North Sea, it is naïve to assume that it would continue to import North Sea Oil. In this scenario England might just as easily import its energy from elsewhere, or produce energy itself using alternative sources; for example, shale gas. Professor Hughes suggested that the separation of Scotland from the rest of the UK would radically change the calculation in England about the way its energy policy is managed. England and Wales, he pointed out, have a lot of options available and need not necessarily rely on 'foreign' sources of gas or electricity. He pointed out that Scotland is a large exporter of energy to English and Welsh markets, and that the energy Scotland produces other than through gas is expensive, so losing these markets would hit revenues that can be earned from renewables, etc.

The Real Economy

Professor Hughes concluded that Scotland's energy is a great benefit, but one that needs to be managed in ways different from what we are used to. He suggested that this is a challenge which neither side of the debate about Scotland's constitutional future appears to understand or acknowledge.

PROFESSOR JEREMY PEAT OBE FRSE,
DIRECTOR OF THE DAVID HUME INSTITUTE

Professor Jeremy Peat spoke about competition policy and regulation in the context of Scotland's constitutional future. He opened with the observation that excessive regulation and the non-empathetic implementation of competition policy is a nuisance to business and is expensive to the economy. A well-functioning market, however, is necessary to stimulate efficiency, so regulation is required. He suggested that there is a need to strike a balance, and this requires skilled staff to implement these policies.

Speaking about competition policy, Professor Peat observed that, at the UK level, we are already observing major structural change, with the Office of Fair Trading and the Competition Commission being brought together to form the Competition and Markets Authority (CMA). He observed that the CMA has committed to having a presence in Scotland, which the Competition Commission has not, and suggested that, given the increased levels of devolution across the UK, it will be crucial to take account of the policy differences between different regions. He pointed out that there are differences in policy in different regions of the UK, and that these differences matter. It is crucial for all regulatory bodies to recognise these differences. Professor Peat observed that there are difficulties that arise from working with so many separate policies, because many policies transcend the boundary between Scotland and the rest of the UK, and would transcend those boundaries at least for the first ten years after the Scottish Referendum, in the event of a 'Yes' vote. He suggested that it would be neither efficient nor effective to undertake separate studies for the UK and Scotland. There are many instances when regulatory bodies are looking at distinct sectors, and the policies governing these largely apply across national and regional boundaries. In these cases, there is a need for close cooperation and working by regulatory bodies across these boundaries.

On the subject of regulation, Professor Peat suggested that Scotland can operate an independent regulatory regime very successfully, and provided the example of the Water Industry Commission for Scotland as demonstrative of this. A distinct Scottish water regulatory body was merited, he pointed out, because Scotland has a distinct water industry. Whether a distinct Scottish regulator is needed for other sectors is not certain. If there is to be a single energy market operating across Scotland and the UK after a 'Yes' vote in the Referendum, are separate regulatory bodies for Scotland and the rest of the UK warranted or desirable? Professor Peat suggested that a single regulator would work, provided it took account of distinct regional policies. On the other hand, he observed, the existence of completely distinct energy markets in Scotland and the rest of the UK would warrant distinct regulatory bodies. There is a need to select an approach which makes sense for the individual circumstance.

Professor Peat concluded by suggesting that the Scottish Government's proposition is perfectly tenable: that – following a 'Yes' vote in the Referendum' – regulatory functions would be brought together under one body, which in the UK are carried out by diverse bodies. He suggested that the UK is showing evidence of going down this route already, by bringing the OFT and the Competition Commission together, and pointed out that this system can work, indicating New Zealand and the Netherlands as examples. He added, however, that there are always caveats as to how this works. There would be a need for a highly skilled and expensive staff to implement this system, comprising lawyers, accountants and economists, with genuine business experience. He added that it would be critical for any new regulatory body to be seen as wholly independent of Government. Regulatory policy would need to be established by the Government, but the implementation of these policies would need to be entirely separate. He also observed that such a body would need to have links with the UK and with the EU, because a lot of policies would transcend the national level, and links with the EU would be critical.

Professor Peat finished with several observations. First, under Scottish independence or increased devolution there would be an increasing need to look at the Scottish dimension when implementing regulatory policy. There would be a need to work in close harmony with the UK and under the constraints of EU policy. Greater efficiency might be achieved through aggregation, but the costs of this should not be underestimated, and finally, no market is perfect, some intervention is always needed, but this would need to be well argued and carefully implemented.

The Real Economy

Questions and Answers

Mr Douglas Fraser (Chair) opened the question and answer session with the suggestion that, throughout the discussion so far, a clear theme has been that the Real Economy is an open economy. He asked the panel whether, with or without Scottish independence, the debate around Scotland's constitutional future is in fact a way of hiding from questions about a globalised economy. Mr Malone responded to this question by pointing out that globalisation is about participation at all levels, and suggested that a question exists around how Scotland wishes to participate in this process; i.e., as a region or as an independent state. Mr Boyd added that the international debate has not really been engaged with yet. He suggested that the question of how globalisation can be reconciled with nation states and democracy is a great issue of our time, but one that has been ignored by the independence debate so far. Professor Hughes observed that, around the world, arguments are being had about subsidiarity – i.e. what is the right level at which decisions should be made. This argument has been based around assumptions that Scotland has the power to make some of these decisions. He posed the question, what are the things we want to keep Scottish and what are the things we want to pool into a larger entity, and will independence allow us to do these things? Professor Peat suggested that the debate around Scotland's constitutional future is hiding away from questions around globalisation, and observed that a number of the issues that relate to the Real Economy are already open to polices within Scotland. Most labour market policies are devolved, as are many of the policies for intervention in industry. There are also aspects of the energy market which are devolved, although there are other aspects which cannot be devolved, even in independence. Professor Peat suggested that, with regard to the real issues which merit our attention under the heading of the Real Economy, the debate is very similar regardless of whether it refers to the existing constitutional settlement, the scope for further devolution or a move to independence. It was suggested that in talking about independence, it is much more on the macro side that we need to look at the big issues. On the micro side, the issues themselves matter more than the constitutional context.

A question was raised around the phenomenon of Dutch Disease, and the suggestion was made that the phenomenon sounds more like UK Disease; it was observed that resources from the North Sea and elsewhere in the UK have been squandered through being left in the hands of the private sector.

The failure of the UK to create a Sovereign Fund was observed and the question was posed as to whether an independent Scotland might have the opportunity to correct this. The point was also made that the UK is not currently meeting its target for renewable energies and that England would therefore still be reliant on Scotland for the provision of renewably sourced energy, even if it decided to procure its non-renewable energy from elsewhere.

Responding to the question around Dutch Disease, Professor Hughes pointed out that the effects of this disease would be much worse in an independent Scotland than they have been in the rest of the UK. He pointed out that there has been a tradition in the UK of spending the rents generated by North Sea Oil, and that Scotland does not need ownership of these resources to save the rents generated, but that Scotland has grown used to spending these resources. Shifting towards a policy of saving these funds now, he observed, would be difficult. Turning to the point about the UK's renewables commitments, Professor Hughes warned against overestimating Scotland's negotiating power in this area. He suggested that it is conceivable that the UK would not honour its commitments, or that it would go down a stronger nuclear route. Professor Peat observed that up until now Scotland has managed to get the whole of the UK to pay for its renewables, but pointed out that this is costly and that there are no signs of this energy becoming quickly competitive. He questioned whether England would continue with its renewables commitment in the event of Scottish independence, and suggested that England might prefer French nuclear energy over Scottish wind energy. Professor Hughes added that the UK could, in theory, meet all of its renewables targets by importing biomass.

A question was raised about the affordability for Scotland of inheriting the decommissioning liability of the North Sea Oil industry, given the potential challenges of decommissioning. Professor Hughes responded to this by pointing out that decommissioning is a future liability and does not represent a fundamentally difficult problem for an independent Scotland.

A suggestion was raised by a member of the audience that Scotland seems to have ceased to have a real economy. It was pointed out that during the 19th Century, Britain was a manufacturer to the world, but this is no longer the case. The question was put to the speakers as to whether they see a difference between Scotland being independent or remaining part of the UK, with regard to its ability to regenerate a viable Scottish economy, as had existed in the 'great days of engineering'.

The Real Economy

Mr Boyd responded to this question by observing that Government certainly can influence the economy, but that to do so Government has to be at the heart of an innovative system. He pointed to NASA as an example and suggested that the work and progress of NASA has Government very much at its heart. He suggested that Scotland is capable of rebuilding its manufacturing sector, and that it probably does not need to be independent to do this. He pointed out that restructuring of the financial sector would be crucial to re-energising manufacturing in the UK, and acknowledged that there are arguments that this restructuring might be easier for an independent Scotland, but pointed out that there is nothing to suggest that independence is necessary for this, or that independence will inevitably lead to this.

The Chair, Douglas Fraser, put the question to Mr Malone as to whether an independent Scotland could husband resources more successfully than the UK. He prompted Mr Malone to respond to the suggestion by Professor Hughes that funds raised through North Sea Oil are not available for Scotland to spend because these funds have already been allocated elsewhere. He suggested that Mr Malone had implied in his presentation that there is some economic dynamism which is waiting to be unleashed by an independent Scotland, and asked Mr Malone to elaborate on what or where that is. Mr Malone responded to the first part of this question by suggesting that the establishment of an Oil Stability Fund is one proposal for enabling Scotland to absorb economic shock. In response to the second part of the question, Mr Malone clarified that he did not wish to make the claim that there are certain types of industry not coming to Scotland because of the current constitutional situation. He suggested that since Scotland got its own Parliament there has been increased dynamism within the country, and he anticipates this growing with independence.

Mr Malone suggested that Edinburgh could become a world capital comparable to London if Scotland became an independent country, and pointed out that Government attracts companies which want to influence Government. He referred to the example of international arbitration, and observed that Scotland doesn't have much of this at present, with the majority tending to go through London. He suggested that Scotland does not currently have an international legal personality, and that opportunity for international arbitration is lost as a result. Professor Peat responded to this by suggesting that he could not see any separate policies that could arise through independence which aren't already there.

He observed that Scotland is very good at creating intellectual capital but very bad at utilising this, and indicated that he could not see what independence would change about this fact. He posited one possibility as being that independence might bring about a change in psyche which would lead to some sort of change taking place in this area, but pointed out that this would be person-led rather than policy-led if it did occur.

A request was made from the audience for an explanation of what is meant by the *real economy*. This question was addressed by speakers in combination with their answers to subsequent questions.

A point was raised about the 'intent' of the Westminster Government and whether this is something that the Scottish people wish to be guided by. The suggestion was made that there have been 35 years of growing inequality in the UK, and the assumption derived from this is that the intent of the Westminster Government is in fact to generate income for the wealthy elite. It was suggested that the alternative to this is an independent Scottish Government with the intent, subject to its own competence, to enrich the broader population of Scotland. Mr Boyd responded to this question with the observation that the Scottish Government's independence campaign has started to focus a little on inequality, but suggested that this has been done in quite an inefficient way. He pointed out that there has been no serious consideration of why inequality has grown, or what can be done under various constitutional scenarios to address this. He suggested that, in addressing these questions, attention needs to be turned towards the present structure of norms and institutions, and argued that a whole new debate exists around this issue.

Mr Fraser addressed the question of inequality to Professor Hughes, and suggested that, to some extent, global forces drive inequality. He posited that inequality is not just a choice that is actively made by Governments, but that the choice relates to what you do about global forces. Professor Hughes chose to tie his answer to this point together with his response to the earlier question *what is the real economy*. He suggested that the real economy is sometimes thought to be about goods, but interpreted it as actually being about the way things are in the world, which is where issues of globalisation arise. He argued that the freedom of choice of all economies in the world is far less than we would like to believe. Capital and skills are highly, and increasingly, mobile. An independent Scotland would be subject to this, and could not expect that it had a right to retain people and capital.

The Real Economy

Instead, Scotland must create an environment which is attractive to both. Professor Peat suggested that the real economy refers to what is actually happening in production and distribution. He agreed that intent matters, and suggested that Scotland should have in mind a clear idea of what it wants to achieve. He suggested that this would require consideration of what trade-off Scotland would be willing to accept; would it be willing to accept slower growth in order to achieve greater equality, for example? He added that it is conceivable that an independent Scotland might have different objectives to the rest of the UK.

A question was raised around defence. It was pointed out that there has been no discussion about whether the UK can afford Trident, or its replacement, and the suggestion made that the removal of Trident and non-participation in a nuclear strategy would save something in the region of £2.2 billion[2]. The question was put to the panel: *if there was a 'Yes' in the forthcoming Referendum, how would they advise that the Scottish Government use those savings to rebalance the economy and restore confidence in it?* Mr Boyd suggested that the Scottish Government would need to address the failure of the financial sector to support Scottish business and innovation. He added that funds should be directed towards boosting the productive side of the Scottish economy.

Professor Peat responded that the amount that could be saved through non-participation in the UK's nuclear deterrence is negligible. He added that the worry for the Scottish economy is not about the availability and supply of funds, but about the demand for them. He observed that businesses are not currently trying to grow, and suggested that businesses need confidence in the environment in order to grow. Mr Malone added that reducing levels of inequality should boost the economy. He suggested that the problem is not just around inequality but also around poverty, and expressed the hope that the priority of the Scottish Government would be to address these areas rather than Trident.

The question was raised as to whether an independent Scotland would be better or less able to deal with challenges such as global debt, an ageing population and terrorism, and how Scotland might respond to these. Professor Hughes made the point that for small countries, shocks such as these are of great importance. He suggested that there is a need for flexibility, and that this needs to be built into national institutions. He observed that the capacity for flexibility becomes increasingly important for small countries.

2 Figure quoted by audience member but not referenced.

Mr Malone suggested, with reference to some of the shocks that the UK has already been through, that an independent Scotland should not be prepared to allow these sorts of shocks to occur again. He suggested that the existence of an Oil Stability Fund might assist in providing a buffer against any future shocks and observed that this could be an advantage over nations that don't have resources. Professor Peat pointed out that there are a number of small economies that have worked against shocks, but suggested that these economies have very tight monetary and fiscal policies. If Scotland wishes to go down this route it will need to be more flexible, but also more tight, which could make the creation of an oil fund even more difficult than others have suggested. Mr Boyd added that trying to predict Scotland's ability to absorb shocks in the future is hard, especially given that we do not know what the macroeconomic climate will be. He observed that Scotland is generally held to have a worse demography than the rest of the UK with regard to its ageing population, but that this is largely due to the higher levels of immigration to the rest of the UK [higher levels of immigration means a larger working age population, which redresses the demographic challenge of an ageing population]. He suggested that it might be possible for an independent Scotland to attract higher levels of immigration than the rest of the UK, if Scotland had a different immigration regime.

The point was made by an audience member that the financial services sector is typically described as the backbone of the Scottish economy, and the question was posed: *what suggestions would the panel like to offer as to how this sector could be restructured to contribute effectively to the growth of the economy, in the event of an independent Scotland?* Professor Peat suggested that the financial centres in Glasgow and Edinburgh are something to be proud of, and suggested that that financial sector in Scotland should continue as it is, provided that a degree of certainty could be provided about the regime that would operate. He suggested that it is uncertainty around this that will cause those sectors that are still flourishing to flourish less. Mr Boyd agreed that a degree of flexibility would be needed, but expressed doubt as to whether an independent Scotland would have the power to adopt a very different fiscal policy than that adopted by the rest of the UK at present.

The significance of Scotland becoming independent to the functioning of the real economy was raised, and the question was posed: *does putting a border across a market make a difference?* Professor Hughes suggested that this does make a difference, and observed that other countries which have separated and now have a border between them do much less trade with each other than they do with other countries. He pointed out that borders do matter in terms of integration.

The Real Economy

Mr Malone suggested that his greater concern was around the potential border between Scotland and the EU. He added that he felt confident there would continue to be high levels of integration between the UK and Scotland in the event of Scotland becoming independent. He suggested that he was willing to defer to the expertise of the economists on the panel, but expressed doubt that the rest of the UK would stop buying Scottish products if Scotland separated from the UK. He expressed a belief that quality and price have more of an influence than borders.

Mr Fraser directed the question about borders to Professor Peat, and suggested that London, as a world capital, will influence Scotland, with or without a border between Scotland and the rest of the UK. He asked the question: how will London influence Scotland? Professor Peat responded that London has a huge impact, observing that it does attract business and industry. He suggested that competing with that is very difficult, and that Scotland and Edinburgh could not compete with the type of centre that London is. He suggested that Scotland would need to establish a different kind of centre, based on the reputation of the financial centres of Edinburgh and Glasgow.

At this point discussion was brought to a close, and the speakers and audience members were thanked for their contributions.

Currency, Banking and Financial Services

Currency, Banking and Financial Services

24 July 2013, at the British Academy

INTRODUCTION

This seminar was the fifth in the series. It took place at the British Academy in London, and assembled invited economists, academics and other experts to discuss the options for currency, banking and financial services following the Referendum.

The seminar was conducted under the Chatham House Rule, which encourages frank exchanges by not attributing comments to named participants. Each speaker presentation was followed by a Question and Answer session, and the seminar concluded with an open, roundtable discussion.

Chair: **Tim Besley FBA**

Speakers:

> **Professor John Kay CBE FBA FRSE**, Economist

> **Jan Fidrmuc**, Brunel University

> **Frances Ruane**, The Economic and Social Research Institute

> **Dr Gary Gillespie**, Chief Economic Adviser, Scottish Government

This chapter also covers discussion held at a related public discussion seminar in the series on Currency, Banking and Taxation (the tenth in the series), which was held at the Royal Society of Edinburgh on 29 January 2014. The discussion held at this event is summarised at the end of this chapter, with speaker contributions attributed to named speakers.

INTRODUCTION

In the event of Scotland becoming independent, it will have to confront decisions around what currency to adopt and how to regulate banking and financial services. Monetary policy issues have an overlap with fiscal issues, to the extent that there is interdependence between monetary and fiscal policy. Moreover, the background context of a significant budget deficit in the UK and the aftermath of the financial crisis make the issues considerably more complicated than they would have been in 2008. Thus it is important to learn from the experience of other nations which have made related decisions as well as looking at the specific issues facing Scotland. This seminar examined the experiences of other countries which have undergone a break-up similar to that proposed for Scotland and the UK. It then examined the options available to Scotland in the event of independence, and gathered views and feedback on these options.

EXPERIENCE FROM OTHER COUNTRIES

The seminar opened with a discussion of the experience from other countries which have broken up a monetary union. The examples discussed were Czechoslovakia and Ireland.

Czechoslovakia

Czechoslovakia is one of few monetary unions to have broken up without a war. It is therefore a good comparator for the Scotland–UK debate. There has been some discussion as to whether Austria–Hungary represents a good comparator. However the break up of this monetary union occurred after a war, and is therefore not analogous. Czechoslovakia underwent a peaceful breakup of its monetary union, which was managed with diplomacy and negotiation. In this respect it represents a much better analogy for Scotland and the UK. It was observed in discussion that when Czechoslovakia ceased to exist, a monetary union was initially maintained; however, this was dissolved after only six weeks. Ultimately, the two currencies (the Czech koruna and the Slovak koruna) were formally separated and two national currencies introduced. It was suggested that there are three main lessons that can be learnt from the Czechoslovakia example.

Currency, Banking & Financial Services

First, credibility is of paramount importance. In the Czechoslovakia case, it was observed, there was no clear commitment from the two countries (the Czech Republic and Slovakia) to maintain monetary credibility. The monetary union was announced as a temporary arrangement to be re-evaluated after six months, and the institutional set-up of these two countries was flawed; there was no central bank; instead, the two countries set up their own central banks and appointed committees to agree monetary policy. The committees were intended to decide upon monetary policy for the union. Each country possessed the same number of votes, but there was no provision in place to deal with disagreements. Credibility was clearly lacking from these attempts at a monetary union.

The second lesson is that in this example, betting against the common currency was very easy and cheap. The Slovak currency was seen as weaker, so people began transferring money into the Czech Republic. During the monetary union, transferring money was easy, and could be done without much cost. It was suggested that in the Scotland and the UK case, the transfer of currency from Scotland into the UK, or vice-versa, would be even easier because of online banking. The gain of transferring money in the Czechoslovakia example was around 20%, which was gained through the depreciation of Slovak currency.

The third lesson to be taken from the Czechoslovakia example is that when the monetary union was severed, the cost was not huge. Trade between the two nations was already declining due to the opening of Czechoslovakia to trade with the West, and at the time of the break-up, this decline accelerated and lasted for around two years. It was suggested that this extended the recession that both countries were experiencing at the time by one or two years.

At the break-up of the monetary union, introducing separate currencies was very easy. It simply involved attaching stamps to the face of bank notes to indicate which currency they represented. This meant that there was not the need to print new bank notes. The point was made that, potentially, it will be even easier for Scotland to have its own currency in the event of separation from the UK, because Scottish banks already issue bank notes.

Ireland

In 1922, Ireland became the Irish Free State. At this time, all Irish banks were headquartered in Ireland, and all issued their own notes. Sterling circulated freely within Ireland and, at the time of its separation from the UK, currency was not considered a problem, because 98% of Ireland's trade was done with the UK. A big issue, however, was concern with interest rates and inflation, and with minimising uncertainty. Shortly after separation from the UK, Ireland introduced the Coinage Act. This was the very first act of change, and replaced the UK Sovereign who appeared on coins, with the cláirseach, the Irish harp. At this point, it was decided not to break the link with sterling, in order to maintain the credibility of the currency. In 1926, a Currency Commission was set up, influenced by the Federal Reserve. This Commission decided to maintain the link with sterling and to take the currency board route (i.e, to maintain a fixed exchange rate with the UK currency). This was formally introduced in 1928, and notes issued in Ireland after this were issued jointly by banks and the Currency Commission. In 1942, the Central Bank Act was passed, which provided for standard central bank powers; however, these were not worked out in any serious way until the late 1960s/early 1970s. During this time, residents of Ireland could be handed a UK or an Irish note in a shop and it made no difference; the value of the two was the same.

In the late 1960s, decimal currency was introduced, and this again prompted consideration about whether Ireland should break its link with sterling. It was decided to maintain the link. However, in 1971, a new Central Bank Act was passed, which effectively gave the Central Bank the power to agree to sever the link, a power which had not existed formerly. Ireland never formally broke the currency link with the UK; rather it became engaged in discussions about whether to join the European Monetary System (EMS), as did the UK. Relatively late on the UK decided not to join. At this stage, Ireland's trade with the UK was down to 50% as opposed to 98%, and it was felt that there should be some diversification from British markets. Ireland therefore joined the EMS in 1978.

Having considered the Irish example, it was suggested that lessons for Scotland – should it separate from the rest of the UK – could be drawn from this. In the Irish example, movement was very gradual, with the Central Bank taking on more powers only very slowly and gradually. It was suggested that it may not be possible for such gradual moves to be made today, in the event of Scottish independence, because of the general speed with which things now happen.

Currency, Banking & Financial Services

In Ireland, there was a big question around whether Ireland as a small nation had the skills to manage its own currency. It was pointed out that Ireland never had a voice at the sterling table and had no real influence over what was happening with monetary policy in the UK. There was recognition that Ireland was a small, open economy, and that it might therefore be sub-optimal as a currency area on its own. As such, the decision for Ireland was whether it should stick within the sterling currency area or join the EMS. The link with the UK was ultimately severed very quickly. It was suggested that there is an issue with the timing of these things and thinking things through thoroughly. This worked well in Ireland during the early stages, but less so later on.

When the issue of the Euro came up, Ireland was in a position of choosing between two sub-optimal positions. From an Irish point of view, being in the same monetary union as the UK made sense; being with the UK alone made less sense; as did being in a union without the UK. It was suggested that Brussels was always very generous if you were going to follow its policies, and this became apparent when Ireland joined the EMS. There was a feeling that Ireland, as a small, open economy, was always going to be linked with either the UK or Europe, and the euro delivered on low pricing and low interest rates, so became the favoured option for businesses and consumers.

Questions and Answers

It was suggested that in the Ireland example, communication with London regarding Ireland's monetary future was lacking. The question was therefore posed as to whether there had been much debate with London, or whether decisions about Ireland's currency were made entirely unilaterally. There is a question, with regard to Scotland's constitutional future, around the need for debate between Edinburgh and London on the future of Scotland's currency. In response, it was observed that in the Irish example, decisions made, to leave the sterling union and adopt the euro, were very much Irish decisions. There was a courtesy relationship between Ireland and the UK. It was also observed that once the suggestion had been made that Ireland might break the link with sterling, the markets did not wait for this decision to be formalised.

A question was raised as to whether there was any evidence, in the Irish example, of constraints on fiscal policy occurring as a result of the link with sterling. It was observed that Ireland inherited no debt when becoming an independent state[1], and that this is unlikely to be the case for Scotland should it become independent. In answer it was suggested that UK policy at that time fitted reasonably well with where Ireland was, and that by and large it worked to Ireland's advantage to be within the sterling regime. With regard to fiscal policy, it was observed that Ireland tended to look to the UK for changes to fiscal policy, and tended to follow the UK on this. The question of fiscal independence was not tested; there was no Irish involvement in the setting of UK monetary policy.

A question was raised about credibility, and whether any lessons can be learnt from Ireland in terms of establishing a credit rating; in particular, whether there is anything from the Ireland example that would be done differently now. In response, it was suggested that at the time there was a lot of concern in Ireland that the country was not ready for the break with the UK, and that decisions had been made very quickly. A question was raised about investment and what happened in the two examples, of Czechoslovakia and Ireland, with regard to investment before and after the break up of the respective currency unions. With regard to Czechoslovakia, the response was given that there was not a major difference. The Czech Republic was seen as a more attractive destination for investment, so funds were not readily moving east before the break-up of the currency union. However, there was some expectation at this point that if Slovakia was to become independent they would be better able to manage the flow of investment. This did not happen immediately after the break-up of the currency union however; only when there was a clear prospect of Slovakia entering the European Union and the Government began implementing 'sound' economic policies, did Slovakia come to be seen as a favourable destination for manufacturing etc. With regard to Ireland, it was pointed out that a lot of British companies in Ireland began gradually moving out in the run-up to Ireland's break with sterling. Ireland had a Foreign Direct Investment Strategy for bringing in foreign (mostly American) multi-nationals, and Ireland's link into the European currency union at that time attenuated some of the flows of investment.

---

1 This observation was made at the roundtable discussion, but it was commented afterwards that the Anglo-Irish Treaty of 1921 stated; "The Irish Free State shall assume liability for the service of the Public Debt of the United Kingdom as existing as the date hereof and towards the payment of War Pensions as existing at that date in such proportion as may be fair and equitable, having regard to any just claim on the part of Ireland by way of set-off or counter claim, the amount of such sums being determined in default of agreement by the arbitration of one or more independent persons being citizens of the British Empire."

Currency, Banking & Financial Services

The point was raised that with regard to the break-up of Czechoslovakia, at the time this seemed like a huge event, but now this event does not seem so huge. The Czechs are happy not to be in the Euro and the Slovaks are happy to be in the Euro. It was asked whether this observation can be generalised. The response was that it probably can be; the separation of Czechoslovakia into two distinct states allowed two peoples to have Governments closer to their preferences.

THE OPTIONS (FOR SCOTLAND)

In discussing the currency options facing Scotland in the event of independence, the following questions were posed: what do we mean by money and what is the purpose of it? In considering examples of currency options, it was observed that Ecuador has no currency of its own, but uses the US dollar. The Ecuador option, it was suggested, is one of the possible options for Scotland. In all, it was suggested that there are three basic possibilities for Scotland: it could join the Euro; continue to use sterling; or have its own currency.

Joining the Euro

On the possibility of Scotland joining the Euro, it was suggested that this option does not provide a sensible long-term basis for economic policy. It was observed that joining the Euro if the rest of the UK is outside is not an optimal currency-area solution for Scotland. Further, it is unlikely that such a solution would be accepted by Europe, since an independent Scotland is unlikely to be able to meet the criteria for joining the Euro, which will be more tightly enforced in the future than has previously been the case. Should it become a member of the EU, however, Scotland would be required to accept the Euro as the currency of the European Union; it was suggested that this could be got round with a loose promise by Scotland to adopt the Euro in the distant future. In reference to this option, it was noted that as soon as the possibility of Scotland joining the Euro is created, the markets are likely to respond to that possibility.

Monetary union with sterling

It was suggested that monetary union is not a straightforward option, and is made less so by the problems the Eurozone has recently experienced. It is now a conventional political and market position that it is difficult, if not impossible, to achieve a stable currency union unless this is accompanied by banking or fiscal union, or at least a step towards these. It was suggested that this is in fact an exaggerated position, and the example of the US was referred to, as a nation which has currency union without, in any real sense, a fiscal union. It was pointed out that there are 51 treasuries in the US; so that California, for example, has its own budget and its own debt. This offers a counter-example to the idea that currency union must be supported by fiscal and banking union. However, it was suggested that the very fact that those in political and market circles believe that fiscal and banking union matters, even if this is not necessarily the case, will make the negotiation of an acceptable monetary union between Scotland and the UK difficult. The point was made that in any such negotiation, account would have to be taken of the fact that an asymmetry exists, with Scotland accounting for around only 8.5% of the monetary union, so that the rest of the UK would expect oversight of Scotland's economic policies. It was suggested that the negotiation of monetary union would, on that basis, prove very difficult, with Scotland unlikely to be able to negotiate acceptable terms.

Unilateral use of sterling

The alternative to maintaining a currency union with the rest of the UK would be for Scotland to follow the Ecuador model, and to use sterling unilaterally. Ecuador is the largest country not to have its own currency, but there are lots of other interesting examples of this around the world. Montenegro, for example, uses the Euro without the agreement of the European Central Bank. The question was therefore raised as to whether Scotland could do the same. It was suggested that it probably could, although it is unlikely that it could print its own notes. The unilateral option would therefore mean that an independent Scotland could not print its own notes: Scottish banks would simply be part of the rest of the UK's financial system, and Scotland could not have a separate monetary policy. This limits the availability of fiscal policy, but perhaps less so than a monetary union would.

Currency, Banking & Financial Services

Independent Scottish currency

It was suggested that having an independent currency is a serious option for an independent Scotland. On the subject of the negotiation of a monetary union with the UK, it was suggested that this would only be possible to conduct on the basis that the independent currency was the default option, which would be pursued if acceptable terms of the monetary union failed. The independent currency could in turn either be pegged to sterling or allowed to float unilaterally. It was observed that relevant comparisons can be offered by Denmark, which has its currency pegged to the Euro, and Hong Kong, which has its currency pegged to the dollar. It was pointed out that both of these currencies would appreciate against the Euro or dollar respectively if they were free to float. Sweden offers an example of a nation which has a currency that floats loosely against the Euro.

Concluding the discussion on the currency options available to an independent Scotland, two final remarks were made. The first was that there has been a tendency to assume the results of this process would not be chaotic. It was suggested that this cannot be safely assumed. The only reason there has not been more speculation on this issue already is that not many people in financial circles believe that the Referendum will go in favour of independence, so the possibilities are given less attention. The second point was around what was referred to as an insufficiently discussed question; the relative negotiating positions of the parties to the debate – Scotland, the UK and the EU – and what happens if agreement is not reached. In relation to the current discussion, it was pointed out that it is not possible not to reach agreement; if Scotland becomes independent there will have to be some agreement. It was observed, however, that there is no agreement on the urgency of the negotiations. The EU and the UK have no interest in achieving a rapid outcome, but the position of the Scottish Government is very different. The Scottish Government needs answers to questions which the other parties to the negotiations do not. The real difficulty for Scotland, it was concluded, will be in achieving acceptable results to these negotiations on some quite difficult issues.

Views on the Options

Responding to the discussion of an independent Scotland's currency options, it was suggested that a move could be made quite quickly away from talking about the Euro or sterling options, on the basis that these are not seen as credible or realistic at this point in time. Focus was therefore directed towards the issue of a formal sterling union. The earlier point about the US providing a relevant example of how the difficulties of fiscal and banking union might be surmounted was referred to, and the point made that the US has a very strong political union, which substitutes for a fiscal and banking union. There is no anticipation that there will be a change of currency in the states of the US. This is not true in the Euro area, and is much less likely to be true in an independent Scotland, given the political divergence that will be generated in the process of Scotland potentially becoming independent. It is therefore still necessary to decide how feasible it is to get around the challenges of fiscal and banking union if there were to be a formal monetary union between Scotland and the rest of the UK.

Discussing what these challenges are, it was observed that common agreement suggests that wherever there is a monetary union, there is greater pressure on fiscal policy. Within a currency union, there is a need for greater fiscal stabilisation, so the question was posed as to how this stabilisation might be achieved when monetary policy cannot operate and the automatic fiscal transfers that currently exist between Scotland and the rest of the UK are lost. It was suggested that this poses a fundamental coordination problem, because while, in theory, an independent Scotland could just replicate any fiscal transfers required itself, the reality is that neither the benefits nor the costs of fiscal policy are born solely by the implementing agent. Rather, the impacts of fiscal stimulus tend to leak across currency unions. The assumption with regard to the Eurozone was that if any one country got into difficulty, it could increase its own fiscal deficit to stabilise the economy, without the need for a transfer across national boundaries. This only works for small economic shocks, however. When there are large shocks, as seen in Spain and Ireland, this has been shown not to work.

Examining the potential solutions to these challenges, it was pointed out that simply designing a better set of deficit and debt rules for Scotland and the rest of the UK is not a realistic solution. There is something more fundamentally challenging occurring in the Scotland case, not least the asymmetry of the relationship between Scotland and the rest of the UK, referred to and characterised earlier.

Currency, Banking & Financial Services

This asymmetry leads to a much greater asymmetry of fiscal risk between the two nations, which will make any set of rules even more challenging than the current blueprint of the Eurozone. Further difficulties exist in the size of Scotland's banking sector, which raises major problems. There is also the question of whether the Bank of England could provide lender-of-last-resort facilities to an independent Scotland. It was pointed out that the Bank of England is accountable to UK Parliament under UK law, so it is not straightforward to see how the Bank of England could be allowed to commit these facilities without some sort of supporting political process. It was observed that there are also solvency concerns for Scotland's very large banking sector, in the event of crises. There would therefore need to be an arrangement between the Scottish and UK Governments to account for the large risk that the rest of the UK would be bearing if Scotland's financial sector remained as large as it is at present.

Moving on from the discussion of the challenges and risks of a monetary union, the views of the Scottish Government were brought to the fore. It was observed that there will be three issues facing the Scottish Government in relation to its currency options. These are: which currency option to choose; what will be required to deliver that currency option; and what the merits of the chosen currency option are.

On the first issue – the choice of currency option – it was observed that the Scottish Government has said formally that it would recommend retaining sterling as part of a formal monetary union, seeing this as the best option, in particular with regard to trade and flows of labour and capital. It is also thought to represent the best option for any period of transition in which Scotland moved from being part of the UK to being independent, in particular in relation to the division of assets and debt. Finally, it is thought to represent the best option with regard to governance, sustainability and stability, on the basis that a formal monetary union would come with other agreements, for example monetary and fiscal policy and financial stability.

On the second issue – what is required to deliver that option – it was suggested that there is a need to negotiate with the UK, and that in the proposed time-line for independence there is an explicit period built in for negotiation. It was suggested that the Scottish Government proposal is to have an eighteen-month negotiation period with the UK and the EU immediately following a 'Yes' vote in the Referendum, although the point was raised that this is complicated by the fact of UK elections prior to the conclusion of the proposed negotiation period, and by other factors.

It was pointed out, however, that the negotiation period has been built in to the timetable for a move towards independence, in the event of a 'Yes' vote. The Scottish Government believe that the model of retaining sterling within a monetary union would benefit the UK. It was observed that there is an argument about UK institutions and who they are currently responsible to. Again, the Scottish Government position is that the Bank of England is a UK institution which serves the whole of the UK and would be part of any negotiations, irrespective of which currency options an independent Scotland decided to take.

On the final issue – the merits and risks of the proposed currency option – the questions were posed as to whether the UK Government would agree that this model was sustainable, and what this model would deliver to the Scottish people. On the question of sustainability, it was pointed out that any economy can be subject to an external or an asymmetric shock, and that in taking forward the proposed arrangement, the Scottish Government would accept monetary policy created at the sterling zone level and agreements on fiscal aggregates. On this basis, the UK Government would gain a lot of control over fiscal issues in Scotland, although the monetary side would look broadly the same. It was suggested that for the UK Government, retaining control over fiscal policy is regarded as key. With regard to what this model would deliver for the Scottish people, it was suggested this process of a formal monetary union would facilitate them getting the Government they wanted. The point was made that small, open economies do not tend to have much scope for creating their own monetary policy, but tend to take this from elsewhere (for example the Eurozone). Neither do they set their own financial regulation; this is done at the international level.

Returning to an analysis of the available currency options, the suggestion was made that none of the currency options for an independent Scotland dominate across all selection criteria. For example, the best way to minimise transaction costs in cross-border trade is by using sterling, whether independent or not, but having one's own currency gives most flexibility in setting monetary policy. The decision on which currency option to choose therefore comes down to comparing the consequences of the different criteria. It is clear from historical cases of currency unions with separate governments and different economies, that unions can be unstable and vulnerable to capital flight. It was suggested that the welfare costs (i.e. the consequences to the economy as a whole) of this outcome far outweigh the welfare costs of changes to exchange costs. Therefore, any currency arrangement has to be robust in defending the economy against capital flight.

Currency, Banking & Financial Services

It was observed that much of the debate so far has thought about currency as a medium of exchange, and the consensus view has therefore been that Scotland should continue to use sterling. It was suggested that a more appropriate approach is to see currency as a store of value, with focus being on Scotland having a hard currency. A 'hard' currency was explained as one in which investors are willing to accept long-term debt contracts in that currency, at a reasonable price. This emphasises the importance of government solvency, market expectations and the capital market infrastructure of a country. A pre-requisite of being considered a 'hard' currency is that the solvency of the sovereign is beyond doubt.

If Scotland uses sterling, the value of the debt it issues will be limited to the expected sum of future primary fiscal surpluses in Scotland. This is simply the fiscal constraint that all governments face. If the expected surpluses are not enough, this translates into expectations of default. The question was therefore posed as to how this solvency condition can be assessed.

It was posited that one way to get at this issue is to estimate the interest rate spreads of Eurozone countries against Germany between 2000 and 2012, as explained by certain macroeconomic factors. The parameters could then be used to estimate the spread that a hypothetical independent Scotland's debt would have over Germany. Given the closeness of German and UK bond yields, this could be a reasonable proxy for the cost of Scotland's debt versus the rest of the UK. Initial estimates suggest that this spread could be very significant.

It was suggested that there would be several implications of sharing the same currency. First, independence would imply two very different countries to those that exist within the UK today; Scotland would be an oil exporting country and the rest of the UK would be an oil importing country. This means they would be more likely to have asymmetric shocks in future. It was suggested that under any reasonable governance structure of the Monetary Policy Committee (MPC), there is almost no means of adjustment to country-specific shocks within a sterling monetary union. In addition, real economic imbalances are mirrored by financial imbalance, but the lack of capacity for a flexible fiscal response in an independent Scotland might mean that there would be no obvious corrective mechanism.

Finally, the point was made that with the high cost of capital and the economic consequences of this, there is a question as to whether there would be strong political will to maintain the currency union, particularly if people in the UK are seen to be able to borrow at much cheaper rates than people in Scotland. It was questioned whether an independent Scotland, even using sterling within a currency union, would have a hard currency regime.

In agreement with an earlier point in the discussion, it was suggested that a fiscal union is not always necessary for a monetary union. However, there needs to be some capacity for conducting risk sharing. It was pointed out that although currency regimes are likely to be negotiated by the UK and Scottish Governments, the final arbiters will be private investors, and what they decide to do with their own money. If there are two exchange rates, this will be reflected in the foreign exchange markets; if there is a single currency it may happen through credit risk and the ability to raise bond financing. It was observed that under the current payment system, foreign counter-party banks based in London have access to the Bank of England liquidity system. This would presumably be the same for London-based counter-party banks of an independent Scotland. However, it is far from clear that the Bank of England would provide liquidity services to what would effectively be an offshore sterling area with its own regulation. Any shortage of sterling liquidity north of the border might be intermediated by a London-based subsidiary, but the Bank of England would be likely to require additional collateral to provide liquidity. The point was made that a pre-arrangement may not even be desirable for an independent Scotland. In the event of a crisis, the UK would hold most of the cards on how to impose losses on Scottish institutions. The point was made that with regard to decisions on currency, governments need to ask themselves which choices will be robust in all eventualities.

The unwillingness, in the debate so far, to talk about the debt that would be transferred from the UK to an independent Scotland, was seen as a big problem. This discussion needs to be in the open and well ahead of the Referendum so that voters know what sort of country and future they are voting for. In conclusion it was suggested that a shared currency between Scotland and the UK would be unstable and capital flight likely to occur. The suggestion was made that with regard to risk management, there has not been adequate understanding of the potential financial risks the day after the Referendum on Scotland's future.

Currency, Banking & Financial Services

QUESTIONS & ANSWERS

An observation was made that the financial sector in Scotland is very large, and that this invited speculation as to whether, as part of negotiations between the UK and Scotland in the event of a 'Yes' vote in the Referendum, London authorities would wish to allow that to continue. It was suggested that the precedent for this might be taken from when HSBC wanted to buy the Midland Bank, at which point they were forced to move their Head Office to London, on the basis that the British authorities did not want a foreign bank with such a large domestic network in the UK. It was suggested that there is a likelihood that the Royal Bank of Scotland (RBS) would be told that if they wish to keep the rest of their operations in the UK they will also have to be headquartered in the rest of the UK, rather than in an independent Scotland. It was therefore suggested that the size of Scotland's financial sector would be resolved in the negotiations following a 'Yes' vote in the Referendum, and the point was made that it might be unlikely that Scotland would be left with a banking sector thirteen times its GDP by the time these negotiations are concluded. In response to this point, it was observed that the question of where a bank is to be headquartered ultimately lies with its shareholders. The shareholders of RBS are, at present, predominantly the British Government, and if the British Government wanted it to be relocated, then that is likely to be what would happen. The prediction was therefore made that, almost immediately after a vote for an independent Scotland, the share-holders of RBS would vote for this bank to relocate its headquarters.

A second point for discussion was raised, namely that there is an assumption being made that during the negotiations following the Referendum, a rational outcome would prevail. It was suggested that this is not necessarily the case. The observation was made that it could even be the case that there were elements of the negotiations which were hostile. It was suggested that there will be elements in the EU which do not wish to see an independent Scotland secede too smoothly, for example Spain. The point was made that not everyone desires a prosperous, independent Scotland as part of the EU as their first objective. Scotland therefore needs to have a fall-back position in the event of a worst-case scenario.

Returning to the point about the potential relocation of RBS, a suggestion was made that the UK Government might not have to do much in order to encourage RBS to relocate. It was also suggested, however, that the assumption that an independent Scotland's financial sector would need to be smaller is not true. The suggestion was made that there are two currency options in which maintaining a large Scottish financial sector could be viable. If Scotland joined the Euro, it is feasible that it could choose to set itself up as a financial sector specialist within the Eurozone. It would also be viable if Scotland were to have its own currency. It was noted that Hong Kong was offered as a good template for this, as a successful small, open economy with a very large financial sector. However, it was also pointed out that Hong Kong has very large foreign exchange reserves and an enormous capacity for government support if needed. Neither would be the case for an independent Scotland. While it would be possible for Scotland to maintain its large financial sector, it would need the monetary and fiscal policy to support this.

Discussion around the size of Scotland's financial sector continued with reference to the estimate that the balance sheet of Scotland's financial sector represents 13 times the size of Scotland's GDP[2]. In reference to this figure, the question was posed as to whether it would be in anybody's interests to have this degree of mismatch post-independence. It was suggested that the figure relates to investment banking activity in London, and the question was raised as to whether investment banking activity in London would continue to be allocated to Scotland. The point was made that EU law requires banking headquarters to be in the country of their main activity. It was suggested that in the event of independence, there might be an unwinding of financial registration with regard to where people are located and what they do. The suggestion was made that the current situation, with regard to the size of Scotland's financial sector, has arisen due to the nature of the UK market.

The point was made that the size of the banking system depends upon the fiscal back-stop, which is why Hong Kong and Singapore and many other small countries can afford to have large banking sectors. With regard to the negotiations, it was pointed out that if the UK leaves the EU before any negotiations with an independent Scotland are concluded, Scotland's whole negotiation with the EU over its own membership will change.

---

2   This estimate was quoted during discussion, and echoes the figure expressed in the UK Government paper 'Scotland Analysis: financial services and banking', which describes the Scottish banking sector as currently accounting for 1254% of Scotland's GDP; close to 13 times its GDP.
https://www.gov.uk/government/uploads/system/uploads/attachment_data/file/206166/banking_assets_vs_gdp_explanation.pdf

Currency, Banking & Financial Services

It was suggested that the Referendum on Scotland's future is contingent upon the present context, and if this context changes there should be another Referendum. In response to this, it was observed that the greater the possibility of the UK leaving the EU becomes, the easier it will be for Scotland to negotiate membership of the EU on comfortable terms.

Commenting on this discussion, it was suggested that from the EU perspective, the Referendum on Scotland's future is a constitutionally lawful one, and is therefore materially different to the situation with regards to Spain and Catalonia, or to other parts of Europe.

MONETARY POLICY AND FINANCIAL REGULATION

On the subject of monetary policy and financial regulation, the question was raised as to what would happen to the UK debt in the event of Scotland becoming independent, and what constraints the debt would provide to the development of fiscal policy. Referring to experiences of other countries, it was observed that earlier discussion had suggested that in the case of Ireland, there had been no debt[3]. With reference to Quebec, it was observed that the debt played a very crucial role in the debate before the most recent referendum. It was further suggested that the fiscal constraints on an independent Scottish Government would be considerably tighter than they are under the Scotland Act 2012. The risk would be even greater if negotiations for a monetary union were to fail and Scotland's debt repudiated. This is because the danger of the market pushing up interest rates under these circumstances would be considerable. It was suggested that, on this basis, the risk of the flight of Scottish assets into the rest of the UK would be high, and that to counter this, the Scottish Government would have to run a very tight ship with regard to fiscal policy. Independence therefore implies the need for a tight fiscal policy. It also implies that the interest rate the Scottish Government would have to pay on their share of the debt would be higher than the interest paid by the rest of the UK. The question was posed: how would that affect the rest of the Scottish financial system and Scottish borrowing costs? In answer to this question it was suggested that if RBS and Halifax Bank of Scotland (HBOS) had to relocate to the UK, their borrowing costs would not be affected very much.

---

3 Again, this comment was made during the course of discussion and clarified afterwards, see footnote 1.

It was suggested that Scotland's pension funds and asset management would not be affected much, although it was conceded that there might be a possibility that Scottish borrowers became subject to a credit risk, particularly if Scotland had an independent currency. In this instance, interest rates for Scottish borrowers would be much higher. If Scotland took sterling, it was suggested, there would likely be a marginal increase in interest rates, but not enough to make a huge difference.

It was observed that there has been little focus on how the division of the debt would be carried out, and that this question appears to have been far less controversial for the UK than it was for Canada, when Quebec was seeking independence. It was observed that on the subject of UK debt, there is a general acceptance that something like 8.5% of the debt would be acquired by Scotland. Assuming there can be a division of debt, the question was raised as to how the transition to this debt division would be achieved. It was suggested that there are several potential ways of doing this. One possibility is to go into the transition 'cold turkey'; i.e. for Scotland to raise a huge amount of funding at the outset and take over their whole portion of the debt in one go. This strategy was considered to be very risky. Another possibility would be for Scotland to pay its share of all principal repayments and interest rates as it went and to clear the debt gradually that way. A further alternative would be to have a halfway house, whereby Scotland raised as much as it could at the outset to repay the small issues, and kept the large issues to repay as it went.

Concluding this part of the discussion, it was suggested that whatever currency option it takes, Scotland's debt will, at least initially until credibility has been established, attract a higher interest rate. In order to keep the higher interest rate within bounds, Scotland will need to have much tighter fiscal policy and, on the assumption that RBS and HBOS will relocate to the rest of the UK, this will account for a marginal negative for the rest of the Scottish financial system.

Currency, Banking & Financial Services

General Discussion and Summing Up

Fiscal policy, oil revenue, division of debt

A further point about fiscal policy was raised, and this theme was linked with the position of Scotland as an oil exporting country. The point was made that when an economy is dependent upon a volatile sector, such as oil, this creates an additional need for robust fiscal policy. It was observed that this presents a very difficult challenge for a government that is used to running a relaxed fiscal policy, and it was suggested that this difficulty has not yet been sufficiently addressed in discussion or debate around Scotland's future. Commenting on the division of debt in the earlier Czech and Slovak example, it was observed that in this case debt was divided in a 2:1 ratio, with the Czechs taking two-thirds of the debt and the Slovaks taking one-third. This was roughly proportionate to the ratio of the population, not necessarily of GDP. On the fiscal position, it was suggested that, if we look at Scotland as a 'mini UK', Scotland is roughly the same as the UK. Referring to Government Expenditure and Revenue Scotland (GERS) data, it was observed that if oil revenues are excluded, onshore Scottish tax revenues account for around 8.1% of total UK revenues. The GDP share for Scotland, again excluding oil, is around 8.3%. On revenue per capita, then, it was suggested that Scotland generates much same amount as the UK. On the expenditure side, however, expenditure per capita in Scotland is about 15% to 20% higher than for the rest of the UK, although including oil revenues offsets this. The challenge for any Government will be containing the expenditure side. One position that has been put forward is that an independent Scotland would spend less on reserved issues than it currently does, but that only gives limited scope. The challenge then is managing the flow of revenues. It was suggested that the Scottish Government would view North Sea Oil as a positive, because it represents an asset base with a revenue stream, but it does represent a challenge for the Scottish Government. The suggestion was that this is a manageable challenge. The real challenge will be to control Scottish public expenditure.

Answering this point, it was observed that the Scottish Government is currently talking about using some of the Oil and Gas revenue to create a fund, in order to avoid spending all of this revenue straight away. This was deemed a good approach; however, it was pointed out that the Scottish Government cannot both save those revenues to create a fund and use them to plug the gap between onshore revenue and excess public expenditure, especially if it must also tighten its fiscal policy. There has to be a means of further taxation revenue, and/or cuts in expenditure compared to the present position, in order to deal with the risks presented by the volatility of the oil revenues.

On the subject of Scotland's share of the existing UK debt, it was pointed out that the lack of discussion or even respective positions on this issue was of serious concern. This is particularly the case for the UK, as in the event of a 'Yes' vote, the negotiating position on a share of existing public debt could be significantly weakened. Assuming that the division of debt follows a similar basis of the Czech–Slovakia precedent, then an independent Scotland would inherit around 8.5% of the existing UK public sector debt. This is around £85 billion. However, there was some discussion about how this could be done in practice. If the UK accepted an IOU from an independent Scotland this would be likely to damage its credit standing. It was pointed out that it would be very difficult for an independent Scotland to raise this much finance in the short term. On the topic of negotiations about debt, the question was posed as to whether the Scottish Government would be likely to be open to negotiations about asset sales possibly including the Trident bases. It was also asked whether it is likely that the Government would face pressure from the Scottish people to accept only what they took to be a fair share of the debt, without exchanging this for anything else.

Continuing the discussion on fiscal policy, it was observed that Office for Budget Responsibility (OBR) figures show a UK deficit of around 5% in 2016, the assumption being that Scotland would have a deficit of roughly the same size. This deficit would have to be immediately financed post-Referendum, in the event of a 'Yes' vote. It was suggested that even if Scotland did not take the 'cold turkey' option of trying to tackle the deficit immediately, there would still be quite a lot of the deficit that had to be financed quite quickly after a 'Yes' vote. It was suggested that this is something which is quite often forgotten.

Currency, Banking & Financial Services

A point was made that estimates on Scotland's borrowing costs have tended to be based on fairly conservative estimates. It was also observed that, given the magnitude of the debt, each percentage point in credit spread is approximately a percentage point of GDP annually, which represents a lot of money and a big fiscal constraint.

A suggestion was made that UK companies are likely to want to pressure Governments on the costs of decommissioning North Sea Oil, and the question was posed as to whether the Scottish Government has started thinking about that yet. In response it was observed that the Scottish Government has published an Oil and Gas strategy which sets out their framework for dealing with decommissioning.

A point was raised about human capital, and the suggestion put forward that following the Referendum, in the event of a 'Yes' vote, there would likely be a flow of human capital going south.

In response to the points raised under this theme, it was acknowledged that questions about how the debt should be handled would be a key part of any negotiations which took place in the event of a 'Yes' vote. It was observed that small open economies do tend to run tighter fiscal policies, and are subject to greater flows of capital and labour. With regard to how hard or soft the negotiations undertaken by the Scottish Government would be, the suggestion was made that this would depend upon what their mandate was; for example what the percentage of a 'Yes' vote actually was.

Banking and the financial sector

The suggestion was made that the discussion on where banks such as HBOS and RBS might be headquartered has been predicated on a belief that the creditors of the organisation concerned have a call on the taxpayers of the country where the headquarters are located. It was observed that the Scottish Government cannot sensibly accept that proposition. The point was made that there is a need to frame this issue in a wider context than discussions of Scottish independence. A further point was made that, whatever the location of the headquarters, RBS and the Lloyds Banking Group are run out of London, not Edinburgh, and that ought to underpin the discussion. It was suggested that the activities of these banks would not change very much, regardless of the location of their headquarters. Provided the possibility of creating uncertainty about the state of Scottish assets can be avoided, it was suggested that the position of the Scottish financial services sector as an industry is not impacted much by the possibility of independence.

It was suggested that the main issue is around what possibility there is for an independent Scotland to engage in regulatory arbitrage and to attract activities to Scotland that are not currently being attracted.

Responding to these points, the suggestion was made that if Scotland took on large financial liabilities and got into trouble, the question is whom it would draw on in the event of needing a bail-out? Would Scotland prefer, under those circumstances, to draw on Brussels or Washington, rather than London? The observation was made that if the UK were to accept a formal currency union with an independent Scotland, it would be London which provided lender-of-last-resort functions, whereas if it joined the Euro it would be Brussels. If Scotland had its own currency it would probably be Washington which provided these functions.

The discussion was directed towards what options an independent Scotland would have had in 2008, at the point when RBS and HBOS failed. It was suggested that at this stage there would have been three options for Scotland. The first option would have been the 'Irish option', of Scotland underpinning everything itself. This would have left Scotland permanently in the hands of the IMF and the European Union. The second option would have been to put together a support package for the banks, involving primarily the UK and US Governments, to which Scotland would have made a modest contribution. The third option would have been to deny that the banking failure was a problem for Scottish taxpayers to solve. It was suggested that the only sensible option would have been option two, with clear implications for the UK taxpayers, moving to option three if this did not succeed in the first few days. It was acknowledged that option three would have been a disastrous option for the rest of the world; on the basis that the next country which got into trouble after one country had followed option three would find itself with nobody willing to help out.

A point was raised about the reaction of the markets in the response to the different options available to an independent Scotland. Some suggested that agreement could probably be reached between Scotland and the UK regarding a currency union, if that was regarded as the ideal outcome. The observation was made however, that the challenge is not so much in agreeing a deal 'in principle' as making the deal stick, particularly if there is any perception that the deal is only temporary. The question was therefore posed as to how Scotland might agree and adopt one currency option to begin with, without closing down all other options for the rest of time. The point was made that it might be sensible for Scotland to agree a currency union for the first ten years or so, with the proviso that this might change.

Currency, Banking & Financial Services

General points

The point was made that Scottish voters voting in the forthcoming Referendum will be doing so in a situation of huge uncertainty, in which they do not have clear knowledge of the costs and benefits of the various potential outcomes. One such uncertainty was provided as an example; this being whether, in the event of Scottish independence, Scottish MPs would be returned in the UK General Election of 2015. If the answer to this is no, this would affect the balance of parties in Westminster and increase the likelihood of their being a UK referendum on Europe.

In response to this point, it was observed that there are two layers of uncertainty in relation to the possibilities for an independent Scotland: economic uncertainty and political uncertainty. The question was asked as to whether voters would benefit from the articulation of a clear economic plan in the lead-up to the Referendum, or whether such a plan is infeasible because of all the political uncertainty. The answer provided was that it is not entirely infeasible to develop a clear economic plan, and that there are certain things we do know about the economic position of an independent Scotland; for example, that it would need to run tighter fiscal policy. It was suggested that there is evidence of a move towards fiscal realism in Scotland, irrespective of the outcome of the Referendum.

On the subject of uncertainty, the Czechoslovakia example was returned to. It was pointed out that in this example, the possibility of a break-up was not a clear option in the election which precipitated it. There was no referendum on the break-up, but rather an election in which it became clear that the two governments had very little common ground. It was questioned whether, in the event of a 'No' vote in the Referendum, the Scottish people would accept the status quo, or whether they would seek greater autonomy in other ways.

It was suggested that the Scottish Government would see the options faced by Scotland as an independent nation as the same, or very similar, to those it would face as part of the UK. It was observed that small, open economies tend to run smaller deficits and less debt, and tend to build up stocks to deal with shocks. It was suggested that there is a lot of work to be done around whether an independent Scotland could build such a reserve, but that this would be the ideal.

At the conclusion of the seminar, the importance of facilitating independent debate on Scotland's constitutional future was emphasised, and the aim of the series, to 'enlighten the constitutional debate', was reiterated.

PUBLIC DISCUSSION
ROYAL SOCIETY OF EDINBURGH, 29 JANUARY 2014

Because of the importance of the issues raised , the RSE decided to hold a further discussion of issues relating to currency, banking and taxation in Scotland. The chair and speakers at this event were:

> Ms Sarah Smith, Newscaster, Channel 4 News (Chair)

> Professor John Kay CBE, FBA, FRSE, Economist

> Dr Angus Armstrong, Director of Macroeconomic Research, National Institute of Economic and Social Research

> Ms Jo Armstrong, Independent Economist

> Professor Gavin McCrone CB FRSE, Former Chief Economic Adviser, Scottish Office

The points raised at this event, in relation to currency, banking and financial services, are summarised here. This was an open, public event, and speakers were invited to present their thoughts ahead of a public discussion.

Professor John Kay contrasted the historic example of Ireland's leisurely pace of change from a currency union to an independent currency, with the more recent example of the Czech Republic's separation from Slovakia, and the speed with which it was forced to adopt a separate currency. In light of the recent example of the Czech Republic, Professor Kay suggested that a decision on the currency an independent Scotland would choose would be the most urgent decision to be made in the lead up to the Referendum on Scotland's future. He referred to the main currency options faced by a Scotland seeking independence (joining the Euro; using sterling either as part of a monetary union, or unilaterally; and having a Scottish currency) and suggested that in a negotiation with the rest of the UK, he would expect that Scotland would fail in getting all of its preferences met, and would therefore need a plan B to turn to. This plan B would probably be Scotland having its own currency, pegged to the British pound.

Currency, Banking & Financial Services

Dr Angus Armstrong referred to the Scottish Government's White Paper on Independence, in which it has stated that independence is about 'the power to build a country which reflects our priorities as a society and our values as a people'[4]. Given this understanding of what independence means, Dr Armstrong proposed to look at the question of what kind of currency arrangement an independent Scotland would need in order to match the aspirations of the White Paper. What kind of currency arrangement would allow these priorities to be expressed? The Scottish Government has made it clear that it wants a full-blown monetary union, and has suggested that this is in the best interests of all sides. Dr Armstrong indicated that while a currency union means sharing the same currency, a monetary union means sharing a currency, a payment system, a central bank, and usually bank regulations.

Dr Armstrong therefore asked, *what is in a monetary union for each side?* He observed that each side would benefit from the minimum disruption allowed by a monetary union. People in Scotland could continue to receive their pensions and pay their mortgages in pounds, the Scottish Government could issue debt in a currency recognised and trusted around the world, and there would be no additional costs to trading between Scotland and the rest of the UK. However, Dr Armstrong pointed out that all of this could also be achieved in a currency union. The difference, he observed, is that a formal monetary union comes with an implicit insurance policy that just in case one side of the union gets into financial trouble, the other side may help it out. In the case of Scotland and the UK, the Bank of England would provide this insurance policy, but UK taxpayers would be the main underwriters. So, what would the rest of the UK get in return? Dr Armstrong suggested that a formal monetary union would allow the UK to avoid trade costs when trading with Scotland, and to avoid losing oil and gas exports. However, because the rest of the UK is ten times larger than Scotland, it would not get the insurance policy that Scotland would be getting. This means an independent Scotland might take more risk, because it has an insurance policy should this risk taking backfire. As discussed at the earlier roundtable on currency and banking, it is probably that the UK would therefore want to apply fiscal constraints to prevent an independent Scotland from taking such risks. Dr Armstrong observed that the more debt Scotland inherits, the higher this risk, and the tougher the fiscal constraints on an independent Scotland would need to be.

4 Scotland's Future – Your guide to an independent Scotland, November 2013

Given the difficulties of maintaining a formal monetary union, Dr Armstrong asked whether such a union would fulfil the priorities for independence set out by the Scottish Government in the White Paper. He reiterated that with the rest of the UK representing 90% of this monetary union, and with the only prospect of a bailout existing in favour of Scotland, the UK would want to apply strong fiscal constraints to an independent Scotland. He also observed that the UK could choose to end this monetary union at any time, which could prove quite inconvenient for Scotland. The White Paper on Independence sets out the view that in an independent Scotland, it would be open to the people of Scotland to make different fiscal arrangements in the future. In reality however, if an independent Scotland seeks a formal monetary union with the rest of the UK, this is unlikely to be the case.

On this basis, Dr Armstrong suggested that rather than a formal monetary union, the best option for an independent Scotland might in fact be a new Scottish currency. He observed that the Scottish Government's Fiscal Commission has suggested that the creation of a new Scottish currency provides an independent Scotland with the greatest opportunity for autonomy. He added that it would be in the interests of the rest of the UK to help Scotland to do this without creating uncertainty or instability. However, he also pointed out that in order to achieve this, an independent Scotland would need its own central bank, its own exchequer, a tax office, a currency conversion law, a debt management office, an independent fiscal commission, and its own mint. This is a lot to achieve in a year and a half, so the Scottish Government would need to start preparations for this early, ahead of the Referendum. Once Scotland has its own currency, this could be pegged to sterling and Scotland could choose its own policies, those that meet the priorities of Scotland and not the rest of the UK.

Professor Gavin McCrone agreed with the general consensus that there are really only two viable options for an independent Scotland; a formal monetary union with the rest of the UK, and a separate Scottish currency. He pointed out that establishing a monetary union depends upon what terms can be agreed and whether Scotland can ensure sufficient independence with regard to its fiscal policy in the event of a monetary union. The prospect of a monetary union raises questions, for example, would Scotland have a separate central bank? This is a requirement of EU member states, so is presumably something that an independent Scotland would need to set up.

Currency, Banking & Financial Services

A further issue is around debt. Professor McCrone pointed out that an independent Scottish Government would issue its own Government debt, which the UK would not be guaranteeing, meaning the interest rates would be higher. He floated the question of whether the rest of the UK would become a lender of last resort for an independent Scotland, and pointed out that Brian Quinn, who has written a paper for the David Hume Institute, and who is a former Deputy Governor of the Bank of England, sees a great difficulty with this. Finally, he pointed out that if a monetary union is to work, not only would the level of fiscal deficit have to be agreed but discriminatory taxes would have to be avoided. This would make it difficult for an independent Scotland to keep corporation tax 3% lower than the rest of the UK, because this would not be acceptable within such a union.

Having a Scottish currency would give Scotland greater flexibility, Professor McCrone suggested, because Scotland would have the option of changing the exchange rate in the long-term. However, he suggested that there are problems with this. Scotland has a large financial sector with the bulk of its clients based in England. As discussed at the roundtable, there is therefore a danger that some institutions would simply move their headquarters into the rest of the UK when Scotland became independent, for example life insurance companies. That would apply also to fund managers. Professor McCrone also made the point that the structuring of the banks raises a further question. He suggested that Iceland and Ireland both provide examples of the dangers faced by a small country that has a bank too big for it to cope with. He therefore voiced an expectation that at least the two main Scottish banks, in the event of independence, would be headquartered in England.

Professor McCrone suggested that a further problem with Scotland having its own currency is that this will affect existing pensions and mortgages, meaning that people could end up having a mortgage in sterling and the asset in a Scottish currency. This is a risky situation to be in. There will inevitably be a degree of exchange in repaying the loan, for example if the Scottish currency fell against the pound. Speaking about pensions, he suggested that some of the same problems arise. He observed that at the moment, most of the pension companies in the private sector are suffering from a substantial deficit, but the EU requires pensions that cross national boundaries to be fully funded. This would cause real trouble for a lot of these pension providers, and some of them would have to be wound up if the requirement were interpreted strictly. Professor McCrone suggested that this could probably be negotiated with a suitable transition period, but added that it represents another sticking point that creates potential difficulties.

In summary, Professor McCrone suggested that Scotland would face a lot of problems in becoming independent. Scotland is a wealthy nation with the resources to be successful, but whether it is or not would greatly depend on the Governments in power at the time.

Ms Smith (the Chair) opened the **Question and Answer** session by asking the panel whether they thought it likely that in the event of Scottish independence, the Bank of England would give lender of last resort facilities.

Professor Kay expressed his uncertainty about what the concept of 'lender of last resort' is taken to mean under these circumstances. He observed that this is not a concept that has ever arisen previously, pointing out that a lender of last resort used to mean that the central bank would step in and lend money at a penal interest rate to solvent banks which were suffering from a liquidity crisis. In 2008, lender of last resort appeared to be turned into a description for somebody who lends money at a concessionary rate to insolvent banks. Professor Kay indicated that he does not understand why anybody would wish to do that. He suggested that in an independent Scotland, the Scottish Government policy should be that if there are insolvent banks in Scotland, then the Scottish Government will seize the ring-fenced assets of the bank which relate to its deposit taking activities in Scotland, pay off depositors who are resident in Scotland, and not worry about the global creditors of international banks, which are not the Scottish Government's or the Scottish tax-payers' problem.

He indicated that an independent Scotland should seek to avoid the mistakes of the Irish Government, which thought it was guaranteeing the deposits of Irish depositors, but ended up guaranteeing everything that had ever been lent to an Irish bank. He observed that this liability almost bankrupted Ireland, and had this been done in the Scottish case it would certainly have bankrupted Scotland, because the liability of HBOS and RBS at the time that these banks failed were around 13 times Scottish GDP. If the Scottish Government had guaranteed these liabilities, Scotland would be bust. The implication of the Scottish Government taking the policy suggested is that there would not be any globally operating banks headquartered in Scotland, for as long as they can find other countries to underpin their liabilities.

Responding to this suggestion, Ms Smith asked whether such an approach would be practical for an independent Scotland. Dr Armstrong responded that the lender of last resort is something which takes place under the sterling monetary framework. The Bank of England's counterparties include American banks and German banks, and Dr Armstrong suggested there was no reason to believe this would not include Scottish banks.

Currency, Banking & Financial Services

However, these are subsidiaries which are regulated in the UK, meaning a lender of last resort should and could extend to Scottish banks too, but only if they are subsidiaries which are regulated in the UK. He added that this is intended to be against good collateral. He suggested that the question was really around the provision of exceptional liquidity assistance, not really lender of last resort facilities. Responding to the suggestion by Professor Kay, that Scotland simply adopts a different type of banking system which excludes international banks, Dr Armstrong added some caveats to that. He first indicated that the sterling monetary framework includes not only banks, but financial institutions, pointing out that a very large insurance company was also bailed out during the financial crisis. He therefore expressed doubt about the idea that this would always apply only to banks. Secondly, he pointed out that an independent Scotland might have more opportunity to regulate the banks than it has done as part of the UK, but added that there is an apparent political resistance to tougher regulation of the banks, which he stated he did not really understand. He observed that in theory, Scotland could implement the type of policy described by Professor Kay, but questioned whether it actually would do it, and whether Scotland would be willing to have no big banks operating within its territory.

Professor Kay suggested that a policy of supporting the banks is observed because of the political power of the financial services industry. However, Dr Armstrong responded that regardless of the political power of the financial sector, Scotland is a democracy and must, on that basis, have some way of containing the behaviours of the financial sector.

A member of the audience suggested that the UK Government has not been very successful in its monitoring of the Scottish banks. He asked whether independence for Scotland might allow the Scottish Government to change this and to create a banking system like that which used to exist – i.e. one which is very conservative and safe. Taking up this question, Ms Smith asked the panel whether the risks taken by Scottish banks did occur because Scotland was part of the UK. Professor Kay responded that this was not the case, and observed that regulators have not been successful [in regulating banks and financial institutions] anywhere, and are unlikely to be successful in the future. Ms Smith addressed the same point to Professor McCrone, asking if there is any reason to believe that the financial sector would be more safely regulated in an independent Scotland. Professor McCrone responded that it would not be possible to have huge banks without these risks, and reiterated his belief that large banks would be headquartered in the rest of the UK, in the event of Scotland becoming independent.

These banks, he suggested, would operate through subsidiaries in Scotland, which would be regulated in Scotland and whose liabilities would be very much less. Professor McCrone suggested that much of the issue of bank regulation goes back to the Conservative Government's 'big bang', which freed things up and enabled bank takeovers to occur much more easily. He suggested that attempts to take over the Royal Bank of Scotland had been made before, but had been resisted, and observed that after the 'big bang' resisting these attempts was no longer possible. Discussing the possibility that Scotland's big banks would headquarter in England in the event of Scotland becoming independent, the Chair asked how dangerous it would be for Scotland to lose that part of its financial services sector.

Ms Jo Armstrong pointed out that the information available on the revenue side is very poor, so it is difficult to tell how much corporation tax Scotland currently received from institutions headquartered here and whether an independent Scotland would lose a lot of corporation tax if large financial institutions were to headquarter elsewhere. The implication is that this would be the case, but the data available makes it difficult to know. She suggested that part of the reason that massive losses by the banks can still result in bankers bonuses is that there is still a belief that the banks will make lots of money in the future. The reality, she pointed out, is that we just don't know what the banking sector will look like in the future. She observed that if banks are only allowed to grow to the deposit size available within the country, this limits the size of the banks that Scotland can have, and probably also limits the number of banks it can have. She suggested that the question to ask is what sort of banking sector we need to support business, not what sort of banking sector do we need to try to make huge profits.

A member of the audience asked the panel to clarify whether Scottish GDP includes the earnings of Scottish banks made anywhere, or just the revenues which have been raised in Scotland. The question was posed as to whether the Scottish Government could offer to transfer bank headquarters out of Scotland to reduce its GDP when entering into negotiations with the UK Treasury. Professor McCrone clarified that Scottish GDP includes the earnings of all people working in banks in Scotland. On this basis, he suggested, it would be easy for a Scottish bank to move its profits elsewhere. However, he observed that what is in Scottish GDP figures for the profits of companies is only an estimate, and that if Scotland became independent a lot of companies might begin declaring their profits in England. On the other hand, if Scotland could get away with charging a lower corporation tax than the rest of the UK, there might suddenly be a lot of businesses who would wish to declare their profits in Scotland.

Currency, Banking & Financial Services

Professor Kay added that the inclusion of North Sea Oil in Scottish GDP greatly exaggerates how rich Scotland is, because much of the revenue from North Sea Oil is earned by international oil companies and never comes near Scotland. Another example of this is Scotch whisky, a lot of the profits of which are apparently earned in the Netherlands.

The panel was asked to comment on the perceived future of Scottish bank notes. It was observed that in the White Paper it is suggested that Scottish banks will continue to issue their own bank notes, but the point was made that this statement might be one of wishful thinking. It was suggested that it would seem strange for the Bank of England to be expected to supervise the circulation of bank notes in a separate country. It was therefore asked whether, with the prospect of independence, the future of Scottish bank notes is under threat. In the event of a monetary union with the rest of the UK, would it be Bank of England notes which circulate in an independent Scotland? Dr Armstrong responded that Scottish bank notes are backed by notes in the Bank of England, so any new Scottish notes would also have to be backed. He suggested that this becomes something like a currency board[5], with the possible paradox being that if the Scottish Government became concerned they could just replace these notes with English pounds. Professor Kay observed that due to a loophole, Scottish notes don't have to be backed seven days per week, so Scottish banks could, in theory, profit by the arrangement. He pointed out that this is plainly an anomaly which causes irritation, but which it has so far been considered unwise to disturb. He suggested that this arrangement would be up for grabs in any negotiations following independence.

A question was raised as to whether the debate on Scottish currency would raise questions about the UK budget and financial stability, because it is the UK which is running a deficit and undergoing quantitative easing. Professor McCrone responded that in the UK as a whole, things are gradually getting better. He pointed out that the UK has faced a major financial crisis, and that this wasn't because of excessive UK Government borrowing, but over-lending by banks to the private sector. He suggested that this will take a long time to unwind. Ms Smith asked Dr Armstrong to comment upon whether the debate being held in Scotland changes the way in which the economy as a whole is viewed from London. Dr Armstrong responded that the debate has not yet had real resonance in London, in spite of the fact that the rest of the UK's debt to GDP ratio would rise by 10% almost immediately upon Scotland becoming independent.

5 A monetary authority which is required to maintain a fixed exchange rate with a foreign currency

A member of the audience picked up the point that so far, the Scottish Government has failed to propose a 'plan B', in the event that a satisfactory monetary union cannot be achieved. She asked the panel, if they were in the Scottish Government's shoes, would they state a 'plan B'? Professor McCrone suggested that if the Scottish Government were to propose a 'plan B', everyone would immediately speculate upon this. He observed that the only 'plan B' the Scottish Government could feasibly have would be for a separate Scottish currency. He indicated that there could be some advantages to this, but that there are also horrendous problems in relation to things like mortgages and pensions. Dr Armstrong added that in his view, investors and private citizens are smarter than people think they are, and like to know that there is a 'plan B' in place if the current proposals are not adding up and cannot be made to work. To avoid stating a 'plan B' is slightly disingenuous, and once people realise that things don't add up, avoiding stating a back-up plan could actually create some of the problems that are trying to be avoided. If people are concerned about 'plan A', he suggested that there is a case for having a public 'plan B'. Professor Kay suggested that if he was making this decision on behalf of the SNP, he would keep the 'plan B' in the safe so as to persuade undecided voters that nothing would change in the event of independence. He suggested that he would then announce the 'plan B' the day after a vote for independence, observing that an independent Scotland can only negotiate effectively with the rest of the UK if it has a 'plan B' to refer to with regard to its currency options. Ms Armstrong added that the option of an independent Scotland adopting its own, independent currency, is probably being kept 'in the closet' by the Scottish Government at the moment because it is viewed as too scary for voters. However, she agreed with Dr Armstrong that voters will need to know that the Scottish Government has somewhere to go if a satisfactory currency union cannot be negotiated with the rest of the UK.

A member of the audience asked the panel whether, in the event of a 'Yes' vote in the Referendum, there would be a flight of capital out of Scotland. Dr Armstrong responded that this depends on where banks are and how they are regulated, and suggested that capital flight happens if it is believed that there is going to be a compromise [i.e. on the currency option]; for example, if it appears that an independent Scotland would seek a monetary union with the UK to begin with, but would look to adopt its own currency in the long-term. He observed that if an independent Scotland's currency arrangement was viewed to be temporary, this could be a disaster, because the markets would pre-empt the change and thereby force it to come about quicker than planned. He also indicated that interest rate risk that would have to be paid would then become higher, because this is not only an interests rate risk but also a currency risk.

Currency, Banking & Financial Services

Ms Smith asked Dr Armstrong whether it would be possible for capital flight to occur before the Referendum. He responded that there could be a situation of citizens moving capital and holding their money in UK banks, but he indicated that the risk of capital flight really happens afterwards. He pointed out that the real difficulty would occur when an independent Scotland started to issue its own debt. Professor Kay argued that he saw the dangers [of capital flight] as being much greater than indicated by Dr Armstrong. He suggested that if people believe there is going to be a 'Yes' vote in September, the problems of capital flight would be much wider. It is the opinion polls, which currently show a majority in favour of retaining the union, that are keeping the situation stable at the moment. Professor Kay observed that the risk is that every sophisticated individual and business will try to position itself to profit. The risk of Scottish independence to business is extreme instability and uncertainty affecting Scottish investment. If a 'Yes' vote looks possible, there would need to be clear contingency planning on the part of of these businesses and individuals.

Ms Smith asked the rest of the panel whether they felt this to be a pessimistic position. Dr Armstrong responded by asking how one would speculate against an independent Scotland. He suggested that one way would be to move money from RBS in Edinburgh to RBS in Newcastle. However, he pointed out that if RBS became a bank headquartered in London, it would not be in the interests of the rest of the UK to refuse to recycle money back up to Scotland. Dr Armstrong stated that he was sympathetic to capital flight, but expressed surprise at the view that this was a potential risk for an independent Scotland, acknowledging that the risk of this is certainly one way, i.e. from Scotland to the rest of the UK. In response, Professor Kay made the point that Scotland's currency options will affect the way mortgages and pensions are paid in Scotland, and that this is something everyone should be thinking about. He referred to the problem experienced by the Eurozone, of people taking out assets in what they thought were the stronger currency regions in the Eurozone, and matching these with liabilities in another part of the Eurozone. He observed that this sort of behaviour is typically a one-way bet. Dr Armstrong acknowledged this, but suggested that in the instance of mortgages, it is usual to bring in a currency conversion law.

He made the point that international currency conversions are quite complex, but indicated that this has been done before. He suggested that in the event of an independent Scottish currency, there would be a conversion process to ensure that everyone's mortgages were not automatically in a different currency. He observed that the process and the institutions required for this are very cumbersome, and questioned the idea that this could be done in 18 months. Professor McCrone raised the point that if it became clear that the UK would leave the EU, this would be damaging to Scotland. There is therefore a merit to Scotland staying in the EU. He suggested that this has the potential to complicate issues further. Professor Kay commented that Scotland's membership of the EU brings the question of the Euro as a currency option back onto the agenda.

The discussion also dealt with issues relating to Taxation and Spending, and the contributions made by the speakers in relation to this are summarised under the chapter heading of that name.

Culture and Broadcasting

Culture and Broadcasting
24 August 2013, at the Scottish Parliament

INTRODUCTION

This seminar on culture and broadcasting was the sixth in the series. The speakers were invited to discuss the impact of constitutional change on the culture of Scotland, asking how Scotland's artistic, literary and cultural contribution would be affected by the outcome of the Referendum. The speakers were also asked to discuss the impact that there might be on the media in Scotland, whether broadcasting, the traditional print media or new outlets that have emerged in recent years through the rapid growth of digital communications.

The subject of culture and broadcasting was addressed by a panel of four speakers:

> **James Boyle,** Chairman of the National Library of Scotland and former Head of Radio Scotland and Controller of BBC Radio Four;

> **David Elstein,** Chair of Open Democracy;

> **Ruth Wishart,** Journalist and Commentator; and

> **Rt Hon Brian Wilson,** former MP, former Minister for Energy and the Founding Editor and Publisher of the *West Highland Free Press*.

The discussion was chaired by **Magnus Linklater CBE FRSE,** former Editor of *The Scotsman* and also the Scottish edition of *The Times*.

The seminar was conducted as an open, public discussion seminar.

James Boyle,
Chairman of the National Library of Scotland and former Head of Radio Scotland and Controller of BBC Radio Four

Mr Boyle addressed a series of issues, including people's engagement with culture in general, social stratification and literacy, as well as the arguments for and against creating a new TV network in Scotland, and the need to invest in new talent and higher-quality content creation.

He said that successive governments have been "good to the arts," particularly when it comes to the performing arts, our national companies and the national collections. The last Labour Government, for example, pumped an extra £20 million into the arts, and the overall performance of government is "what one would wish." He then discussed some headline statistics relating to culture. About 500,000 tickets were sold for performances by our national companies two years ago, dropping to 430,000 last year. But if you drill into this data, looking at people not tickets, only 2–3% of the whole population engages with the "higher end" of the arts – older, better educated and wealthier people.

The broader definition of "cultural engagement," including going to the cinema, shows that the percentage of people actively involved is almost 90%. Excluding visits to the cinema, this figure drops to about 66%. But this may be a misleading indicator, because there is a huge gap between the higher arts and other activities, such as watching television and going to libraries. This gap is something that "obsesses" Boyle, who added that these figures don't begin to tell us what people's "life experience" is.

He also suggested that independence would not necessarily make a big difference to spending on the arts, since successive governments in Scotland since devolution have "both done well by culture." Mr Boyle also stressed the need to engage with pre-school children and early primary school-age children, educating people through the arts to "build confidence, performance and presentational skills, to build skills and capacity," rather than simply focusing on the "admittedly very costly" funding of the "rarefied and other-worldly" high arts. The question is, however, where to find the resources to "prime" people to enjoy a broader cultural life, as well as to become well-educated citizens.

Culture and Broadcasting

Mr Boyle then turned to the issues of social class and literacy, saying that the Government has been "brave" to admit that 20% of Scotland's population are functionally illiterate; which means, for example, being unable to follow simple medical instructions. Mr Boyle described this as "a colossal drag on the economy, as well as a personal tragedy" for all those affected, and suggested that although the devolved Government is addressing the problem, more could be done. When it comes to culture, we should also think more broadly about social stratification, because illiteracy is a blight on our society. We should focus on teaching people basic reading skills, so they can "go to the library, not just go along to hear the Scottish Chamber Orchestra." We have the power now to do something about it, but not the resources. But we have identified the problem, and people will need to support this, he added.

Turning to broadcasting, Mr Boyle focused on the issue of whether or not to spend Scotland's £75 million broadcasting budget on creating a new TV network, or investing in talent and content creation. The Broadcasting Commission has not recommended devolving broadcasting, but Mr Boyle said he is still "at right angles" to its conclusions, particularly the idea of broadcasting "more about Scotland for Scotland," exploiting the potential of new digital channels. He is also sceptical about broadcasting being "accountable" to government, and said that since the 1990s, he has become increasingly worried about the trend towards "aggravated rebuttal" by successive governments – their over-vigorous defence at the first sign of any attack, including attempts to "censor" jokes at government expense.

Mr Boyle agrees that the priority in broadcasting should be to produce more high-quality programmes – taking risks and linking it to higher education. But do we want a new TV network about Scotland for Scotland – for ourselves by ourselves? "That is not nearly ambitious enough," Mr Boyle continued. We should be sending our message out to the world, taking advantage of our "technological brilliance" and innovation. The £75 million budget is also not enough to create a quality channel (broadcasting four hours per day) and compares unfavourably with the £122 million budget of BBC Radio Four. It would be better to "throw the money at talent," said Boyle, enabling the creative community to come up with new content, including new digital content – not just for transmission in Scotland but all around the world. Broadcasting is like every other industry in Scotland. We are a small to medium-sized country and we need to put more money into research and development. "Be more ambitious. Throw the money at talent and let them go for it," he said.

DAVID ELSTEIN, CHAIR OF OPEN DEMOCRACY

Mr Elstein focused on broadcasting, suggesting it was time to create a new TV channel for Scotland, run by Scotland for Scotland and funded by Scotland. He also suggested that in the period leading up to the Referendum, the devolved Scottish Government should negotiate a new deal with the BBC, using the threat of a fully independent new channel and the loss of £300 million in licence fees as leverage.

He opened by saying that he has no special knowledge of Scotland and is only an occasional visitor. He also has no links with any political party and has nothing to offer in the debate about Scottish independence. But he does know something about broadcasting, after 40 years in the industry.

There are two key issues with regard to broadcasting, he said. First, there is the question of spectrum. And second, the structure of finance. To understand this, it is essential to understand the early history of broadcasting and the role of the BBC, which "must be at the heart of the debate,"as a public corporation, run from London, just the same as central government. Broadcasting "follows the money," he added, and the BBC grew up in an era when the British Empire was still a major influence on how people thought.

About £3.6 billion comes to the BBC in licence fees, plus about another £1.65 billion in commercial revenues (overseas sales, etc.), and it's all controlled from London, apart from BBC Alba. "Even when the Chairman lives in Edinburgh," he added, "board meetings still take place in London."

The BBC has invested about £100 million in "an impressive series of fortresses" in the regions – e.g. Glasgow's Pacific Quay, Cardiff, Birmingham and Manchester – and promised to devolve about 60% of production to these new facilities, as well as editorial decision making. But this is more "an expression of power," he said, than devolving real power to the regions.

Mr Elstein then argued that greater independence for BBC news would lead to greater plurality and greater democracy. And he then declared that a channel run by Scotland for Scotland and funded by Scotland was "overwhelmingly overdue," as an expression of the Scots nation. The concept of a Scottish digital network needs to be broadened, he added, to deal with the talent base in Scotland.

Culture and Broadcasting

The Scottish Government currently spends about £12 million a year on BBC Alba, without having any direct broadcasting powers or control of spectrum, but this should come from licence fees, he argued, rather than being an extra. The issue of spectrum is less of an issue today than it used to be, now that we are in the digital age, but nonetheless Scotland should pre-empt any future discussion to negotiate spectrum, ahead of next year's Referendum, so that spectrum becomes a non-issue. Online channels are not the answer and Scottish Television would struggle to deliver a new Scottish channel because it is still dominated by ITV. Scotland should "confront the BBC" and demand a new Scottish channel by winning concessions from Westminster now. In Wales, some people went on hunger strike to demand a new Welsh-language channel. Mr Elstein said, however, that Scotland and First Minister Alex Salmond didn't need to go that far to "attack the BBC's soft underbelly."

The BBC is coming under increasing pressure, and three years ago it made significant concessions on the BBC World Service and local TV, spending an extra £400 million in order to prevent the loss of £600 million in revenue. Charter renewal is also a threat to the BBC's future, so the time is ripe for Scotland to "reach a concordat" with the BBC over the next 12 months, using the potential loss of £300 million in licence fees to leverage the discussion and take broadcasting off the agenda before the vote is held on independence. This would win real editorial independence rather than simply new digital channels.

"The BBC's mindset is resistant to real change," he continued, "never mind constitutional upheaval." But the BBC is also vulnerable. There is already pressure on BBC news, so more independence for BBC Scotland could be achieved by a "determined campaign." The prospect of a fully independent broadcaster in Scotland – and the subsequent loss of revenues from Scotland – could be used as a lever to deliver more spectrum and increase the budget for BBC Scotland. Scotland already controls education and law, so why not broadcasting? A successful negotiation may mean "leaving unharvested some of the fruits of independence, should it be voted through," he concluded, "but I'm a great believer in the bird in hand."

Ruth Wishart,
Journalist and Commentator

Ms Wishart emphasised the flowering of talent in Scotland in recent years and said that independence would be "a golden opportunity" for the creative community in Scotland to do even better in future, as part of a wider international community – the kind of opportunity that everyone living in Scotland should have.

She began by recounting how thirty years ago, a literary critic in Scotland vowed to review every single new publication in Scotland, and pointed out that this would now be virtually impossible because of the number of new works released every year, and "the explosion of confident voices." She then heaped praise on Scotland's diverse literary talent – highlighting various novelists, poets and playwrights such as Liz Lochhead, the late Iain Banks, Ian Rankin, Janice Galloway and David Greig.

Ms Wishart said that as we enter the last year of the vital debate and contemplate our constitutional future, the most thoughtful contribution has come from our writers and the rest of the creative community in Scotland, rather than from the conventional print media, who are "still dominated by the tribal warhorses" and seem "more intent on wounding political enemies" than on constructive debate about the future of our country. She compared this to the lead-up to the 1979 Referendum debate, when the creative voices, especially musicians, were ahead of everyone else, according to political commentator Iain Macwhirter. In those days, there was also a new confidence in Scotland – for example, the successful singing duo The Proclaimers proudly sang with Scottish accents. And once again, she said, the country is alive with debate, even though it can sometimes be inhibited by "the stifling garment of party loyalty."

Ms Wishart then addressed the controversy over novelist Alasdair Gray's "now infamous" remarks about "settlers and colonists" dominating the arts institutions in Scotland, saying many critics missed the point by dismissing it as "nationalism in the raw." She said that even though nationalists may believe that the solutions to our problems lie within our own borders, we are also enriched, nourished and inspired by importing people and influences from abroad. For example, Celtic Connections started off as a relatively modest affair and is now "a glorious festival of interconnected traditions" from all around the world.

"Internationalism will always have at its core the belief that Scotland's identity and traditions can only benefit from an infusion of the exciting and the exotic," she added. "The building block of that internationalism is a self-confidence born of the pride and knowledge of your own cultural traditions."

Culture and Broadcasting

She then defended non-Scots taking charge of our national arts institutions, saying she has "no difficulty"with incomers as long as they have the credentials, the right motivation and the right attitude. For example, when Vicky Featherstone was appointed the first Director of the "shiny new" National Theatre of Scotland, she encountered a lot of scepticism, but her vision of a "theatre without walls" has been a big success. She also commissioned some of our best young writers and, when she left, she emphasised the importance of respecting and understanding the culture in which you come to work.

Not everyone appointed to senior positions in Creative Scotland has understood that imperative, but the artistic community has been quick to point out any failings, and the new Director, Janet Archer, has declared the needs and aspirations of artists in Scotland should shape Scotland's cultural future. At the same time, importing and exporting talent is a "two-way street," and cross-fertilisation is good for all of us.

The Broadcasting Commission is broadly right about the need for the creation of a dedicated digital channel for Scotland, she said, but the whole debate about broadcasting has changed a lot since digitalisation. A new digital channel could deliver what's needed. It is "not a big ask," she said. We have come a long way since the earlier debate about a separate national news bulletin (the so-called "Scottish Six"). After devolution, BBC visitors to Scotland used to think they were coming to the "dark side of the moon," and needed to be told about the powers of the parliament, but nowadays, BBC Radio is careful to point out that some issues affect only England and Wales.

What difference would a 'Yes' or a 'No' vote make? "To be honest, the current vibrancy would continue," she said. "But I am convinced we have a golden opportunity to build new values. I think we can do better." Ms Wishart then compared two recent statements from the respective culture secretaries in the UK and Scotland which illustrate the "cultural divide" between the countries. In Westminster, Maria Miller said "the arts should pay their own way," while in Holyrood, Fiona Hyslop said that the most important function of the arts should be to "enable and inspire." Ms Wishart said the creative community on both sides of the border would sign up to Fiona Hyslop's view rather than Maria Miller's, and she also believes that Scotland has different political values.

Ms Wishart said that "creativity should be at the heart of education," to produce collaborative, enquiring and curious minds," rather than placing the emphasis on how to decline Latin verbs and write in immaculate copperplate script. Finally, Ms Wishart held up Venezuela's Simon Bolivar Orchestra as a great example of what can be achieved in the arts, with its influence extending to Stirling and, more recently, to Glasgow, where young people have been following a similar formula (El Sistema), and achieving the same remarkable results. "That is the kind of visionary thinking I want to see applied throughout our cultural policy," Ms Wishart concluded. "Talent is not a postcode lottery but too often opportunity is."

Brian Wilson,
former MP, former Minister for Energy and the Founding Editor and Publisher of the *West Highland Free Press*

Mr Wilson believes that the constitutional debate is getting in the way of the debate about culture and broadcasting. There is always room for improvement, but independence is not the critical factor and we already have the means to make things better. "We should change our priorities, not the constitution," he said.

In the debate about culture and broadcasting, the burden of proof is on those who want to separate. We all know what we have and all of us are proud of it, but supporters of independence say they want to change it. What has the constitution got to do with it? For example, the Edinburgh Festival has flourished for well over 60 years, attracting people from all around the world, "without inhibition from the constitution or the political status of Scotland." So what is to change? Our national institutions and galleries have also flourished during that period, not necessarily because of the Union but while we are part of it and not inhibited by it. Many people quote the names of all the painters, writers and composers who have plied their talent in Scotland under the status quo, but these artists have succeeded regardless of the constitutional set-up. There is no *a priori* evidence that a different constitution would produce a great flowering of talent, but there is a lot of evidence that talent has flourished over the last 300 years, and there are many other examples. The new Victoria & Albert Museum planned for Dundee is another example of how the arts can continue to flourish "without inhibition," just like the Celtic Connections Festival, before and after devolution. Mr Wilson also said he believes El Sistema is a good example of young people being given the opportunity to develop their talent, and that this is in line with his own Socialist principles rather than anything to do with nationalism. The difference is that he wants to extend those opportunities to children everywhere, not just in Scotland.

Culture and Broadcasting

Those who support independence should be able to prove that the current constitution has inhibited the arts and that somehow "what's on offer is going to make things better," taking into account the cross-border and cross-cultural benefits which Scotland now enjoys and also exports to the rest of the UK and beyond. If independence can't be proved to offer an advantage, then culture and broadcasting should be treated as a separate subject and discussed on their own merits, not as part of the constitutional debate. If there is anything wrong with our culture, then whose fault is it?

All powers relating to the arts are already devolved. When artists don't like how the arts are being run here, they don't complain about London or Westminster or the Union, but they do complain about Creative Scotland, he added, and that is Scotland's own responsibility, appointed and funded by the Government. "So why don't we just do things differently here instead of worrying about the constitution as a kind of alibi for everything that's wrong?" he asked.

Mr Wilson then echoed Mr Boyle's words, saying that Scotland's literacy rates are "appalling." But to solve this and other problems, we should change our priorities, not the constitution. We create opportunities through economic and social policies, including early education, "not by pretending that everything changes when we change the constitution," he added.

"It would be an act of wanton vandalism to break up the BBC," he continued. The BBC is a good example of a national institution that has benefited from scale, and it has been and still is disproportionately influenced by Scots. If we vote for independence, we will lose that. It is all very well to say we should leverage the debate, as David Elstein suggests, but if we vote 'Yes', we are no longer part of the Union or part of the BBC.

We should invest the £75 million in excellence and creating new content, not in talking to each other about each other. Take away 10% of the BBC's revenues, and there would be a big drop in standards. In Scotland, we would still be tuning in, as "a nation of eavesdroppers," but we would not be part of it. It wouldn't be our state broadcaster any more but working to another state's agenda. So what would we get in exchange? RTE in Ireland is the equivalent of Scottish Television, but its output is mainly cheap programmes and imports, funded by advertising. Our small share of the BBC adds up to bigger benefits.

"I would love to have a rational debate about these issues, but the debate about broadcasting is obfuscated by everything being fed into the constitutional debate. We should focus on creating content, and stop seeing everything through the prism of the national question and the constitution," he concluded. "After thirty years of talking about nothing but the constitution, we have to get back to real politics and talk about real economic policies to make Scotland a better place."

DISCUSSION

Chairman Magnus Linklater then led a discussion, asking each of the speakers in turn to expand on particular points. First, he asked David Elstein if broadcasting has an obligation to culture or entertainment, and how that fits in with the BBC's guidelines. Mr Elstein said the argument has raged for 90 years. When spectrum was scarce (because the Ministry of Defence had over-riding requirements), there was a trade-off between culture and entertainment. The BBC got spectrum in return for delivering the benefits of public broadcasting, while also entertaining its audience, as part of Lord Reith's dictum for the BBC to "inform, educate and entertain." Does this mean documentaries, the arts, children's programmes or religion? There is also a very high cost associated with regionalism, and over the last 15 years, ITV has virtually abandoned its commitment to public broadcasting because its share of the spectrum has diminished with the launch of so many new channels and alternative media. ITV now spends only £100 million of its total budget on non-commercial programmes, while Channel 4, which is publicly owned, spends the vast majority of its budget on entertainment. "Privileged broadcasters are required to give something back," said Mr Elstein, who then suggested that Sky Arts was doing an "impressive" job compared to the BBC. "My concern here is not whether broadcasting owes a duty to culture but that broadcasting is part of culture." Mr Elstein then expressed "mild Sassenach wonderment" at everyone's caution and "nervousness" with regard to a separate channel for Scotland, as if the choice is giving up the BBC or being forced to continue as part of an unequal relationship. Also a small country, Denmark is doing a very good job with its broadcasting output, with very little money, but why would it want to be part of the BBC heirarchy, and become a junior partner?

Magnus Linklater then turned to James Boyle, suggesting that the output of BBC Scotland was "pretty poor," and that a new channel may be an opportunity to unleash new talent.

Culture and Broadcasting

A budget of £40–50 million would not go very far, said Mr Boyle, and when it comes to news and current affairs, the suggestion of an "opt-out" system for BBC Scotland would be hard to schedule because of the "yawn factor" and the need for mixed programming, including entertaining content as well as more serious programmes. We also have an obligation to diversity and the needs of different audiences. Fragmentation is a problem. For example, young people tend to engage more with music channels, and that is a pity. "We have all the resources and talent," said Mr Boyle. "Broadcasting is part of the economy as well as part of culture, and it needs to be properly funded." We should get all the money we can and "leave behind the old-fashioned models." We should focus on creating new content, including new apps, whether we opt for independence or not. "Take the risks instead of same old thing, same old thing," he concluded.

Ruth Wishart was then asked what is being denied to the creative community by the current system, and what would be the cultural "add-on" of Scottish independence. "What are we being deprived of by the current broadcasting system?" Mr Linklater asked. "Quite a lot," Ms Wishart responded. There is not very much Scottish material being broadcast today. We could do better. And whether we vote for independence or not, we will still be able to view content on the BBC and continue to have access to hundreds of digital channels. She also held up the documentary programme *Eorpa*, which is produced by BBC Alba, as an example of what can be achieved, "with the money and the political will."

Magnus Linklater then suggested to Brian Wilson that Radio Scotland has "a very low standard of cultural output" which he described as "very feeble." Mr Wilson said he would not defend Radio Scotland but wanted to discuss it in a broadcasting context, not as part of the independence debate. There should be far more serious programmes, more serious discussions and documentaries, but policy decisions are the problem, not the constitution. He also said he did not want to lose the "very substantial" Scottish input to BBC Radio Four, which he described as "excellent." It is not an economic or financial argument but a domestic issue, said Wilson. Ms Wishart questioned Mr Wilson on the Scottish contribution to BBC Radio 4, and Mr Wilson cited several examples. Mr Linklater then begged to differ from Ms Wishart and added his personal view that Scottish input to Radio 4 was indeed "very good." What Mr Linklater questioned was the fact that regardless of the Scottish contribution, all decisions on BBC Radio Four were made in London, not in Scotland or in any other region.

Mr Boyle then suggested that the decision to fund Radio Scotland now belongs in Scotland and should be an entirely Scottish responsibility, adding "we can restore Radio Scotland to strength with higher-quality content," including mixed programming. Does every programme made in Scotland have to be "identifiably Scottish?" Many radio programmes produced in Scotland are simply brilliant, said Mr Boyle, and they are produced without "the skirl of the pipes." Their strength comes from our unique selling points – thinking and science.

QUESTIONS & ANSWERS

Magnus Linklater then invited the audience to pose three questions.

Question 1: Does the Scots language have a place in Scottish culture, and does the neglect of the Scots language in education have an adverse effect on literacy because people feel their own language is not valued? **Question 2** concerned the consumption of cultural output and spending priorities, observing that the Gaelic-language channel BBC Alba has much higher viewing figures and a higher penetration than the Welsh-language channel in Wales, despite the fact that BBC Alba has a much lower budget – about £15 million compared to S4C's more than £100 million. The same questioner also asked if culture which reaches the audience via the medium of radio or television has a "lesser value" than the collective experience of going to the theatre or musical festivals, etc. **Question 3** was about the performance of BBC Scotland and a recent BBC Trust survey which suggested that half the population of Scotland is dissatisfied with BBC Scotland's overall output, asking if the made-in-Scotland programme *Mrs Brown's Boys* satisfies the quota for Scottish cultural output.

Turning to Brian Wilson, Magnus Linklater asked if broadcasters have a responsibility to keep the Scots language alive. Mr Wilson wondered if the Scots language was in fact neglected, and commented that he used many Scots words and spoke English with a Scottish flavour, like many other people in Scotland, rather than "Scots," adding that in Northern Ireland, "Ulster Scots" was an invented language, used politically to balance native Gaelic. Wilson is more concerned about the neglect of localism and regionalism, believing that more children should be educated in the history of how their own environment around them was created – e.g. how the Outer Isles was influenced by the land struggle, or the industrial heritage of the central belt. Ruth Wishart commented that Scottish history is just as important as regional history and should not be an afterthought in education, complaining she knew more about the Corn Laws than the Covenanters, because Scottish history was not taught at all in school in her day.

Culture and Broadcasting

She also said we only have ourselves to blame for neglecting the Scots language, unlike the effort we have made to keep Gaelic alive. She then praised attempts to create more educational materials in Scots and use more Scots content in children's books – e.g. Itchy Coo books who, according to their website, publish "braw books for bairns o aw ages."

Is television of less value than the high arts? David Elstein said that many programmes, even from the BBC, were "not worth bothering about," but also said that broadcasting was the best way we know to distribute culture – for example, the BBC had built its reputation by changing England into a musical nation by broadcasting concerts, etc. He also praised the distinctive character of the Scots, and "the rhythms and musicality" of the Scots language, urging Scots to make more of their "fantastic" cultural assets, including their language and their great "ability to be themselves."

"It's great to hear a lot of really strong Scots accents in a drama produced here," he added, "even if it isn't a very good drama." With £300 million to spend, a Scottish network could create a lot of "proudly Scottish" content for Scottish consumption, properly packaged and presented, at the same time as making a greater impression abroad. When he was running Sky, he would have loved to have a Scottish channel to draw from. A distinctly Scottish channel would be a great way to "nourish, enrich and transmit the culture."

Mr Elstein also cited the example of *The Fall*, a BBC drama produced by a Welshman in Northern Ireland, directed by a Belgian and written by an Englishman – a good example of what Lord Reith meant when he said that "nation shall speak unto nation." Then Mr Elstein added: "Scotland is a nation. Let it speak."

Magnus Linklater then said that the "angry" audience reaction to a number of points reflected the wider belief that BBC Scotland is not living up to its potential, and that there is a problem with funding as well as with quality of output. Brian Wilson then defended the production in Glasgow of *Mrs Brown's Boys*, pointing out that it was a good example of a UK network programme made in Glasgow, watched by millions of people, which created jobs in Scotland without using up any of BBC Scotland's regional budget, as intended by creating the Pacific Quay facility. He did not attempt to defend the quality of the specific programme, but questioned whether BBC Scotland should only make programmes which are "icons" of Scotland: "I want to see all sorts of programmes made in Scotland. We should concentrate on excellence and speak out to the world."

Just because some people in Scotland don't like a programme like *Mrs Brown's Boys*, he asked, is it "beneath our dignity" to make it here? It simply meets the BBC's objective to make more networked programmes in regional centres.

Ruth Wishart said that everyone welcomes the creation of new jobs at the "shiny new" headquarters, but also wants BBC Scotland to do a lot more than "put a brass plate on imported programmes." Much as she enjoys the programmes made there, she would prefer the new facility to be used to make more Scottish programmes and encourage more indigenous drama, rather than being tacked on to the end of existing programmes. "There is not enough happening," Mr Linklater added, and Mr Wilson agreed there was not enough good Scottish drama produced here.

James Boyle then said there is a lot that we could criticise about both STV and BBC Scotland, and that the idea that *Mrs Brown's Boys* is "the triumph of the year" is absurd. He then compared assembling programmes here to the car assembly plant at Linwood, which closed in 1981 and is now widely regarded as a national failure. More creative input is needed.

Mr Boyle then commented that BBC Scotland has failed to introduce the rest of Scotland to the Edinburgh Festival, describing this as "a disgrace." Could we use new digital channels, and the extra money, to promote our own culture and do new things which were not possible until now, Magnus Linklater asked. "What in the system is holding that back?" Mr Boyle replied that the broadcasting network in Scotland is "an old fashioned and sclerotic system," and said that it is hard to talk about return on investment when you only reach one, two or three per cent of the whole population. "If you want something to change, you have to do more than just bolster the existing system," he said. BBC Alba may appear to be successful, but the audience figures are being distorted by the popularity of 'live' football.

Magnus Linklater then invited three more questions. **Question 4** concerned David Elstein, praising him for having "more vision than some of the Scots," when it came to broadcasting, and asking him if he would like to come here to run a new national network. The questioner also expressed concern about the "dreadful" propaganda in the media as a whole. **Question 5** was: "What actually is culture?" Can we expand our idea of culture beyond elitism – e.g. including folk culture? **Question 6** focused on the "regrettable" loss of regional channels, including Grampian TV, and asked how we could foster greater regionalism – including a channel for Orkney, where the questioner lives.

Culture and Broadcasting

David Elstein declined the invitation to move up to Scotland, and said that Scotland had produced a lot of "superb broadcasting talent," including Stuart Hood and Alistair Milne – as well as the inventor of television, John Logie Baird. He said that there are many opportunities for talent in Scotland. He also said he wouldn't want to appear to be an "English carpet-bagger" by accepting a job as Controller, but that he is willing to help the Scottish Government negotiate a better deal with the BBC to "deliver real value to the people of Scotland." Brian Wilson commented that all the best talent in Scotland has tended to move on to UK national positions, to perform on "a bigger stage." Is it not a good thing that the most talented people run the national networks, thus spreading their talent nationwide instead of limiting themselves to to the regions? "Would they have stayed to run BBC Scotland?" he asked. Mr Elstein said there is plenty of traffic in both directions and that this is the way it should be. Talented Scots will always have something to give back to Scotland, he added.

Ruth Wishart then suggested that the issue is that London and the southeast of England are "over-heated," and that talent has no choice except to move there. "That is why we must create more opportunities here," she said. It would be good if more talent opted to stay here and build here, she added. "People go away because they want to broaden their experience," said Brian Wilson, and that is a good thing. Scots continue to play a major role at the BBC. Many of them also come back. Surely, he continued, it is better to add to the overall quality of programming for the benefit of broadcasting and a much larger audience, rather than stay in a Scottish broadcasting service forever, especially one which is no longer part of the BBC as we know it today.

David Elstein repeated that Scotland has "the opportunity to leverage a better deal for Scots broadcasting which is not possible under the present structure," suggesting that "the BBC responds to pressure." The BBC has spent £65 million "disposing of unnecessary managers," he added, with a third of them being rehired. It has also lost £100 million on a failed IT project, so £75 million for BBC Scotland is actually a trivial amount by comparison. What the BBC currently offers is not good value for money. "There is an opportunity. You should not let it pass," he concluded.

James Boyle suggested that the break-up of the BBC has always been David Elstein's main point in such debates, adding: "Be careful what you wish for." Mr Boyle believes that it is more important to focus on finance and on improving the quality of programmes made in Scotland.

We all want to make BBC Scotland better, but not at the price of breaking the whole thing up. "It is all about determination, ambition and vision," he added, rather than simply money. Magnus Linklater than asked Ruth Wishart why STV and BBC Scotland have retreated from the regions, and she said she is all in favour of restoring localism in Scottish broadcasting.

Magnus Linklater summed up by saying that the speakers had raised many critical points, not only about broadcasting and culture but also wider issues, as we embark upon the last year of the debate about independence for Scotland.

"I would argue that culture must be right at the heart of it," he said. Everyone agrees there is huge room for improvement, even though there may be disagreement on how to achieve this.

Borders, Immigration and Citizenship

Borders, Immigration and Citizenship

25 September 2013, at the Royal Society of Edinburgh

Introduction

This seminar on borders, immigration and citizenship was the seventh in the series. The speakers were invited to discuss how constitutional change might affect the citizenship rights and status of those living within and outside an independent Scotland, including the relationship of residence to nationality, questions of dual nationality, and freedom of movement within the British Isles and the wider European Union, as well as the relationship between citizenship and national identity in a new Scotland.

Chair: **Professor John Curtice FRSE**, Professor of Politics, University of Strathclyde

Speakers:

> **Professor Bernard Ryan,** Professor of Migration Law, University of Leicester;

> **Professor Jo Shaw,** Salvesen Chair of European Institutions,
> Dean of Research and Deputy Head, College of Humanities and Social Sciences,
> University of Edinburgh;

> **Professor Christina Boswell,** Professor of Politics, University of Edinburgh;

> **Ms Sarah Craig,** Lecturer in Public Law, University of Glasgow, and
> Co-Convenor, GRAMnet (Glasgow Refugee Asylum and Migration Network).

The debate was conducted as an open, public discussion seminar.

PROFESSOR JOHN CURTICE FRSE,
PROFESSOR OF POLITICS, UNIVERSITY OF STRATHCLYDE

Professor Curtice set the scene for the debate by saying that borders, immigration and citizenship involved "some of the most important questions" facing Scotland in the event that the Referendum resulted in independence. The first obvious question was how to police our borders and who would be allowed to come here, under what conditions. Did we want to change the open borders we have at the moment? Then there are the questions all new states have to address: Who can be a citizen? Will new citizens have to be born in the country, have lived here for a certain length of time, be resident when the new state is formed or qualify by having parents or grandparents born here? Another major issue was who would be able to vote – citizens or residents? How would the new state deal with asylum seekers and naturalisation?

For the purposes of the debate, Professor Curtice also suggested that the issues should be discussed irrespective of personal views concerning the pros and cons of independence itself. It was important to stand back and examine what the answers to these questions should be in the event of independence, rather than declare what should or should not happen vis-à-vis independence – not a "partisan" debate but a more reasoned analysis.

Professor Curtice also said that one issue that had perhaps been underplayed in the debate until now was the fact that this was not the first time the UK or the EU had been faced with such issues. One precedent to consider, but not necessarily to follow, was the creation of the Irish Free State in 1922. He also said that the UK and Ireland, and a future independent Scotland, would all expect to be part of the EU in the future, and that this was not a new phenomenon for the EU, which had already dealt with the creation of new states in the Balkans and Eastern Europe, after the break-up of the Soviet Union.

Finally, Professor Curtice touched upon the issue of national identity. Just as people had asked who is a Serb and who is a Bosnian, so one of the fundamental questions for Scotland is: "Who are we?"

Borders, Immigration and Citizenship

Professor Bernard Ryan,
Professor of Migration Law, University of Leicester

Professor Ryan outlined the fundamental issues an independent Scotland would face when it came to shaping nationality laws and immigration policies, including how it would define its relationship with the UK and other countries, as well as details such as automatic citizenship and dual citizenship. In many cases, he used Ireland as a reference point.

He started by saying that borders and immigration are issues that matter. As someone who comes from "south of two borders," an Irishman living in England, he is "fairly neutral" when it comes to independence and is more concerned with looking at the implications for nationality law and immigration control in the event of independence, focusing on the early decisions that a new government would have to make immediately after independence. Referring to Professor Curtice's remarks about the precedent of Ireland, he also pointed out that it took Ireland thirteen years to draw up its own nationality laws, after the creation of the Irish Free State in 1922. The situation, however, is different today, because the UK now accepts the principle of Scotland becoming independent and will sit down to negotiate the terms of independence, unlike the more adversarial situation in 1922.

A newly independent Scotland would clearly have a "relatively liberal" attitude to immigration and nationality laws, and establish residence as the primary criterion for citizenship. Advocates of independence also have an open view regarding the possibility of many people opting out of Scottish citizenship, and are open to the possibility of dual citizenship. His conclusion here was based on statements made by the Scottish National Party (SNP).

Professor Ryan identified three major issues that Scotland would have to address immediately after independence.

1 The fundamental issue is to determine the nature of Scottish citizenship. Is it a completely new status, or will it succeed the previous status (i.e. UK citizenship)? There are "real risks" of being over-inclusive or under-inclusive if reference is not made to the current regime. How would a future Government deal with residents who had non-UK citizenship at the time of independence (e.g. Irish citizens) and also non-residents whose parents or even grandparents were born here who may wish to apply for Scottish citizenship?

2 Working out the details of nationality laws would require some very difficult decisions. For example, would Scottish citizenship be conferred automatically, or would it be a matter of choice? Some people would have citizenship "thrust upon them," or else there would be very few new citizens, but how far should we go? The criteria would be hard to resolve, including how to deal with people born here but no longer resident and people who were residents at the time of independence but were not born here. Who would have the right to choose, in the initial stage of independence and subsequently? Rather than starting "with a blank sheet of paper," current UK citizenship would be a useful starting point for these complex issues. On a more personal note, Professor Ryan also said that he feels "Irish" and has no desire to become a UK citizen, even though he has lived here for a long time. He also said it would be "strange" and "arbitrary" for residence to lead to automatic citizenship, although it would make sense for residents to be offered the option.

3 He then moved on to a more general point to discuss how the future government of an independent Scotland would define citizenship law without making arrangements with the UK – for example, how to deal with people who would lose their UK citizenship and whether or not they should lose their UK citizenship automatically or be offered the choice. "It's very difficult to see how Scottish nationality laws could be decided without UK agreement to decide the best way forward," he said.

Professor Ryan then said he had observed "a certain amount of loose rhetoric" about immigration control. Some people have argued there would have to be border posts set up between Scotland and England, while others have argued there would not need to be any controls; but he said that both these propositions were very unlikely. Referring to the Irish example, his "best guess" is that Scotland would not be expected to join the Schengen zone, even though it may be legally obliged to do so as a condition of becoming a new member of the EU. He also said there would be an open border between Scotland and the UK, much the same as the open border between Northern Ireland and Ireland, mainly because it would otherwise be very costly, for social, economic and administrative reasons. The most likely outcome is that Scotland would become part of the Common Travel Area (currently the UK, Ireland, Isle of Man and Channel Islands). Scotland would be open to a range of different outcomes, he suggested. For example, the UK currently does not impose restrictions on travel from Ireland to the UK, but this is not reciprocal because Ireland is not fully open – it allows free movement from Northern Ireland by land but not to arrivals by sea or by air. There is another precedent, however, because there is some cooperation at present between Ireland and the UK when it comes to visas and the treatment of individuals considered to be "undesirable." There would be pressure to establish long-term immigration policies, but "deep coordination" may not be needed.

Borders, Immigration and Citizenship

Professor Ryan concluded by saying that he was "intrigued" by the prospect of three countries, including an independent Scotland, being part of the Common Travel Area, but also wondered if the "somewhat informal" nature of this would survive in its current form. When the current Scottish Government draws up its White Paper to cover these issues, Professor Ryan hoped that all the points he had addressed would be resolved, despite the fact that tactical "politics" – both by those who are pro-independence and those who oppose it – may have an impact on initial policy decisions.

PROFESSOR JO SHAW,
SALVESEN CHAIR OF EUROPEAN INSTITUTIONS, DEAN OF RESEARCH AND DEPUTY HEAD, COLLEGE OF HUMANITIES AND SOCIAL SCIENCES, UNIVERSITY OF EDINBURGH

The major issues for Professor Shaw are citizenship versus nationality or national identity, the politicisation of citizenship, the constraints on future policies posed by EU laws, the difference between the initial and long-term decisions on citizenship, and the risks involved in permitting dual citizenship, as well as the lack of historical precedents. Professor Shaw welcomed the opportunity to be part of the panel because she believes this subject needs much wider discussion. She began by saying she is particularly interested in the EU context of citizenship and the issues raised by people of one state living in another EU member state, as well as the more recent issues raised by citizens living in new states – for example, what it means to be a citizen of one of the countries created after the break-up of the former Yugoslavia, and what value this adds. This may not be a model for an independent Scotland, but it raises interesting issues – for example, the politicisation of citizenship. She also said that citizenship is very different from ideas of nationality.

In general, said Professor Shaw, drawing on her own study of central and south-eastern Europe, nationality is understood in terms of national identity and is often the driving force behind state nationalism and the creation of states in the first place. This is a phenomenon which first emerged at the end of the nineteenth century and after World War One, and happened again after the break-up of the Soviet Union, Czechoslovakia and Yugoslavia. Our experience of the break-up of these federations has taught us there are "some things to avoid" when new states are created, such as making people stateless, failing to protect transitional families and avoiding the excessive "ethnicisation" of the citizenship regime. "Citizenship is very much about democracy and respecting the requirements of individual justice," she said, and citizenship and nationality fit together in different ways.

The situation in Scotland is also unique, she continued, with the prospect of one new state being created within an existing state by democratic will, with the consent of the "rump state," within the framework of the EU. The creation of the individual ex-Soviet states are also not very useful models to follow. The creation of the Czech Republic and Slovakia, for example, did have some federal guidelines to follow, but we could not "hark back" to the existence of a previous state. We therefore have to find another set of principles to determine who might be the Scots.

According to Professor Shaw, there is also a difference between the determination of policies in the initial stages of independence and what would happen thereafter, and she pointed out how this could be an intensely political subject in the current debate. In new states, "citizenship law tends to be one of the most politicised issues," she said, and this is also likely to be the case in Scotland.

Professor Shaw then discussed the criteria for citizenship such as birth and residence, including length of residence and residence at time of independence, time away from the country and consanguinity – acquiring citizenship on the grounds that parents or even grandparents were born here, despite not being resident. The First Minister, Alex Salmond, has referred to the Irish model of consanguinity as one of the criteria for citizenship; a somewhat "ambiguous" model, in Professor Shaw's view, which makes it easy to acquire citizenship "externally" up to two generations back. And it is the issue of acquiring citizenship externally that is one of the most political elements of setting up a new state, she added. Would being a UK citizen prior to independence also be an underlying condition? Would Scottish citizenship be acquired automatically or be offered as an option? How generous would that offer be? And what about voting rights?

The Scottish Government has taken a broadly inclusive stand on issues such as citizenship and wants to be seen as a good global citizen, and may also wish to distinguish itself in the future by being different from its neighbours; but there will be constraints. A new state may be able to do what it likes, but assuming that Scotland does become a member of the EU, then its policies must take account of EU legislation and not do anything that interferes with the principles of EU law. There is also evidence that having different policies on citizenship (e.g. being allowed dual citizenship until the age of 23, then being asked to choose between the two) may be challenged by EU laws, so it would be useful to consider international practices and transnational research when drawing up the appropriate new legislation; particularly when it comes to residence, both initially and in the long term.

Borders, Immigration and Citizenship

Professor Shaw then commented that so far, much of the debate about independence has been framed in terms of "soft secession" issues that will not change very much no matter what happens, "not breaking many of the unions that hold the state together," such as currency and monarchy, but that it was important to realise that what was being proposed would lead to "constitutional rupture," and may not be so easy in terms of new laws. "Could we deal with citizenship in soft-secession mode?" she asked. For example, how would the new state deal with dual citizenship – one of the keys to a smooth transition? This would have to be handled on a mutual basis, but the current UK Home Secretary, Theresa May, has suggested that the residual UK may not be so open to this, notwithstanding the UK's historical record on the principle of dual citizenship. Toleration of dual citizenship is key, but this would work only if there were reciprocity and agreement between Edinburgh and Westminster.

Once you have dual citizenship, she continued, "the risks are legion" when it comes to the framing of new legislation, and decisions made in Scotland "could be hollowed out by its much larger neighbour." Some citizens may choose not to exercise their rights to Scottish citizenship. There may not be good reasons to do so, and voting rights could be an issue. Would proactive registration make a difference? Should a future Scottish government offer "cheaper passports" as an incentive to taking up citizenship? "The relationship with the existing 'gold plating' of EU electoral rights (in the referendum and in the Scottish Parliament elections) raises some difficult questions when it comes to the initial 'offer' of citizenship and the extent of non-citizen voting that might be applied in a post-independence Scotland," she added.

Concluding, Professor Shaw said there were risks attached if a future independent Scotland permitted dual citizenship, and also no historical precedent for such a scenario.

PROFESSOR CHRISTINA BOSWELL,
PROFESSOR OF POLITICS, UNIVERSITY OF EDINBURGH

Professor Boswell focused on migration, asking what the policy would look like and what the main constraints would be – the pressure from neighbouring countries (the UK and Ireland), EU restrictions, issues arising from the unpredictable movements of immigrants, or the constraints imposed on government by public opinion, mobilised by the media and political extremists in response to changing economic and social conditions.

Her first premise was that Scotland would be keen to pursue a more liberal or more expansive policy on immigration than the current UK Government does. There are some demographic reasons for this, based on Scotland's population profile and the need to boost our "human capital," attracting people with the right skills to come here and work. The inability to have an autonomous policy to meet the different labour needs of Scotland has led to a certain amount of frustration. This more liberal stance is also "supported by the impulse to a more generous approach" in Scotland in general, and the evidence gathered in surveys of public opinion, which also indicates "a relatively higher tolerance or immigration and ethnic minority groups than the rest of the UK."

Professor Boswell said that she is not so much concerned with the "technical modalities" of the debate or the many examples of good and bad practice in Europe. She thinks it is more pertinent to look at the constraints on any future immigration policies, and focused on four sources of constraints:

1 The practical constraints imposed on any future Scottish government by its neighbours in England, Wales and Northern Ireland and Ireland, and by being part of the Common Travel Area.

2 The constraints emanating from the EU.

3 The constraints deriving from public opinion.

4 Unintended consequences as a result of the dynamics of migration flow.

How autonomous could Scotland's policy be? Professor Boswell "strongly assumes" that a future independent Scotland would continue to be part of the Common Travel Area, along with the rest of the UK and Ireland, and not be forced to sign up to Schengen. Contrary to some opinion, this would not lead to substantive constraints on Scotland's policies on who would be permitted to work here, but what may constrain future policy is how to address the issues of immigration control and asylum. A Common Travel Area has no internal borders and allows free circulation, and third-country nationals may have the right to work or be resident in one of the countries but not in the others, so this may lead to concerns about "irregular movements." For example, third-country nationals authorised to work in Scotland may seek unauthorised work south of the border, and illegal immigrants, over-stayers and asylum seekers who have had their request for asylum rejected may also move southwards, creating a potential problem for England. Scotland may therefore adopt a more restrictive approach to reduce the differences between the two countries, particularly with regard to asylum policy. Therefore, she suggested, although in principle there may be fewer restrictions in Scotland immediately after independence, issues may arise afterwards as a result of irregular movements, leading to more robust policies being imposed.

Borders, Immigration and Citizenship

Professor Boswell said there are many misconceptions regarding potential EU constraints on immigration policy, and suggested that the EU would not impose Schengen. She also suggested that if an independent Scotland did become part of the Common Travel Area, one can only assume that it would enjoy the same opt-out options as the UK and Ireland enjoy at the moment. Ireland is effectively "obliged" to opt out in the same way as the UK at present, and has very similar immigration and asylum policies – an area where the EU does not have such robust mechanisms. So if Scotland did become an EU member, this would have a "negligible" impact on its immigration policies.

When it comes to public opinion, however, Professor Boswell does anticipate problems. "It's one thing to design the policy and another to enlist the long-term support of the electorate," while running the country and policing the borders. Scotland today may have "a lower level of intolerance" or hostility towards immigration and ethnic minorities, but she cautioned that a future Government may not be able to sustain this, in the event of independence and a move to liberalise policy on immigration, especially if there was an increase in levels of immigration. No country since the 1970s has been able to sustain a "more explicitly" liberal policy towards immigration, with the possible exception of Spain. The UK and Germany have tried it, she said, but "the negative populist media and negative party mobilisation" turned people against this and encouraged anti-immigrant sentiment. It is important to "decouple your rhetoric from your action." To get around the problem of public opinion, some governments may let in lots of immigrants at one time then clamp down at regular intervals, or they may talk tough in public but then take advantage of complex and "opaque" legislation to quietly let in more people to meet the demand for skilled labour.

"Open and liberal rhetoric can be hard to sustain in face of rapidly changing realities," she added. There may be strong public support for more liberal policies in Scotland now, but as soon as any future government has to take responsibility for immigration and becomes accountable to the electorate, with the media and opposition parties quick to exploit any weakness, this could lead to less liberal policies. Countries in Europe have a long history of being susceptible to the mobilisation of "volatile and unpredictable" public opinion to articulate other concerns and blame minorities for various problems such as "unemployment, inequality and declining social cohesion," and it may also be hard to get any cross-party agreement or get the media on board, so public opinion may be the chief constraint on future policy makers. "A future government would have to be very careful about how they phased in reform."

Finally, Professor Boswell dealt with the possible constraints of immigration itself, because of unexpected movements or increases caused by new more liberal policies. Once immigration policies are liberalised, there can be unanticipated consequences, she said, which may undermine the whole system. For example, asylum seekers may appeal for citizenship on the grounds that they can meet the country's need for skilled labour, rather than on the grounds that they need asylum as a form of protection. So, if asylum then becomes a much more common mode of entry and a way to bypass the usual procedures, this may lead to a rise in the number of "asylum seekers," who may regard Scotland as an easy and much quicker option than neighbouring countries. A more liberal immigration policy may thus send the wrong signals to people, she added, and this could in turn lead to greater media and public hostility. It may be possible to support more asylum seekers joining the workforce, but the message would have to be carefully managed so asylum is not seen as an opportunity to move abroad for economic benefit rather than safety. If the public do become more hostile to immigrants because of these issues, this may also undermine the applications of bona fide refugees.

Professor Boswell concluded by saying that there is plenty of scope for an independent Scotland to pursue a more autonomous approach to immigration, "more suited to its demographic and economic context." Being part of the Common Travel Area and being a member of the EU would not place big constraints on future policies, but a future Scottish Government would have to be wary of public opinion, because whatever policies it did adopt might have unintended consequences, especially when it comes to asylum.

Ms Sarah Craig,
Lecturer in Public Law, University of Glasgow, and Co-Convenor, Gramnet (Glasgow Refugee Asylum and Migration Network)

Ms Craig discussed Scotland's protection-oriented national "vision" and the possible constraints on future policies on refugees and asylum seekers, explaining how Scotland has been able to use what limited powers it already has to act differently on immigration issues, and how an independent Scotland could aim even higher to set it apart from its neighbours.

Borders, Immigration and Citizenship

She began by saying that the Scottish Government's vision has been very "pro-protection" in relation to refugees and people seeking asylum – and to their rights to welfare and the rights of their children. This chimes very well with major international conventions, and Ms Craig does not anticipate any major problems for a future Scottish Government signing up to these instruments. Focusing on her own experience of policy, she said it would be easy to change the "culture of disbelief" that was generally applied to asylum seekers, and instead give people the benefit of the doubt. But there are also very complicated practical issues. She also criticised the UK Government's recent campaign to send mobile billboards to areas where illegal immigrants are reported to gather, bearing slogans which suggest they should "go home." This is a very negative attitude, she said, and it suggests the UK Government "doesn't mind being seen as the bad guys," partly because it faces no competition from another government sending out a contrary (more liberal) message. There is also a difference between having very pro-protection attitudes and building the complex structures we need to support these.

Ms Craig also described how some EU structures and laws are designed to protect refugees, while others may tend to deflect them from the EU's external borders or deflect them from one member state to another, particularly from countries in the north to the south and the east. The current Scottish Government appears to be enthusiastic about being part of the EU, but any future Government would have to make some difficult decisions concerning the common European asylum system, and decide whether it continues to be pro-protection or is forced to become more inclined to deflection, even though the latter may be hard to imagine.

If Scotland continues to be part of the Common Travel Area and negotiates the same Schengen opt-outs as the rest of the UK, it may take the same broadly conservative view as the UK and Ireland, much in the same way that Ireland has followed UK policy until now – for example, the length of time that migrants are detained. It may sound negative, Ms Craig said, but it must be acknowledged that whatever happens, there will be constraints, particularly because Scotland is keen to be part of the EU and would have little room for manoeuvre. An independent Scotland would need to work hard to develop more liberal policies, taking advantage of its own experience in dealing with asylum in the past. "Having little room for manoeuvre would test the Scottish Government's commitment to protection," she said. "Maintaining a pro-protection approach in these circumstances would require effort and commitment, but it could be done."

The dispersal policy introduced in the UK resulted in hundreds then thousands of asylum seekers heading from England to Scotland, but the devolved institutions in Scotland have still managed to do things differently, despite the fact that nationality, immigration and asylum are still reserved issues. For example, in Scotland there has been "an emphasis on policies and practices aimed at the integration of refugees from arrival as asylum seekers, and not from the later granting of status." In 2005, the Scottish Commissioner for Children and Young People, Kathleen Marshall, pointed out that "functions are reserved or devolved, not people," and this set the tone for framing Scotland's policy concerning the detention of refugees' families, and had set Scotland apart from its neighbours. In Scotland, there is also a strong recognition that the welfare of families and free access to education must be considered when assessing individual applications for asylum. The Scottish Government and the Scottish Executive have both tried to take a more "positive" view than their Westminster counterparts.

"Even though there would be constraints from Europe," she continued, "Scotland already has experience of finding solutions, even when there is little room for manoeuvre." After independence, the Government would have more responsibilities, and Ms Craig suggested it could change its approach from adversarial to investigative, and locate asylum in a different department – separate from the agency which looks after our borders. "We should look elsewhere for best practices. We should look at alternatives to detention, rather than using it as a policy tool, and seek out easier and fairer routes to naturalisation."

Finally, Ms Craig said that an independent Scotland would have little room for manoeuvre, but could draw on the experience of the devolved institutions to do things differently, sharing the burden and even offering help to its neighbours. "Scotland could decide to go higher," she said.

Borders, Immigration and Citizenship

DISCUSSION

Professor Curtice praised the speakers for their "brilliantly laid out policy options," and started the discussion by asking each of them to imagine that they were advisors to the First Minister, helping him write his White Paper on Borders, Immigration and Citizenship. "What should be the headlines of the policies on citizenship, immigration and asylum?" he asked. "And tell us what you think should happen rather than could happen."

Professor Ryan said that he would use the current UK system as his reference point, and said it is important to deal with the question of the Scottish diaspora – including second-generation Scots who may want to be citizens of a new Scotland. There is scope to be different, he said, and also to draw on the Irish experience.

Professor Shaw said "look at the numbers and tread carefully." About 850,000 people born in Scotland are not resident here, she explained, and that is a very large number. "It's not just about not making the offer too broad," she continued. If the doorways are opened to those who were born here and perhaps their children and grandchildren, there could also be consequences in electoral terms – including requests for external voting – so it may be wise to be more restrictive about the diaspora. Ireland has always been very restrictive and has gone against the trend in relation to external voting. The decision should be less about who should be citizens than who should be able to vote, and it would be good if only people who live here can vote. "I am not a fan of external voting," she added, because external voters do not have the same duties and loyalties to the state.

Professor Boswell's advice was: "Drop the obsession with demographics." Simply focus on attracting the people with the best skills and the best brains to improve our human capital; introduce measures to bring back fresh talent; encourage foreign graduates to stay here and seek employment; set up a points system to attract the best qualified people, along the lines of countries such as Canada; do an annual review of acute labour shortages and analyse where skills are needed, then recruit the right people.

Professor Curtice then asked if she was assuming there should be more migrants, and Professor Boswell said that demographics was "not a good selling point" for government in the global "race for skills." She also said it should be argued that highly skilled people create jobs and tend to increase productivity and levels of entrepreneurship.

Ms Craig advised the Government to "keep saying what you're saying about human rights and asylum but acknowledge there will be constraints, and learn from what you know." She also said asylum would not be "a problem" for Scotland, and that any future Government should say it is not a problem, right from the start, and "do things not say things" about it, in order to ensure that it stays that way.

QUESTIONS AND ANSWERS

Question 1: The first question was about the "notion of Scottishness," and how some people may have Scottishness "thrust upon them" while others may have Britishness taken away. If you were a UK citizen, resident in Scotland, and there was a relatively narrow win for the 'Yes' vote, would you have the opportunity to opt out of Scottish citizenship? And if you did so, how would that affect your voting rights?

Professor Shaw said there was a difference between being a citizen and exercising your rights as a citizen. It would be legitimate to legislate right from the start on citizenship, but people may not exercise their rights or register as voters. Current UK citizens would not cease to be British unless the Westminster Government legislated accordingly. Professor Shaw also repeated her view that the UK faces a unique situation of "secession by consent," not an attempt to establish a completely separate national identity, as happened when the Irish Free State was formed. "There is no will in Scotland to do so," she said. In 1922, there was no concept of British citizenship, as there is today. Ireland was devising a more modern notion of citizenship, while Britain was still thinking in Imperial terms. The current prospect is that two relatively modern states may go their separate ways, and possibly overlap in various areas. The details will be determined by what the two new states decide on their own, as well as what they both agree on. There is also the question of what will happen in the event of a narrow 'Yes' vote, with a possible overlap of voting rights. Professor Shaw also said that, like a lot of other people, she would not be happy to lose her UK citizenship. "There has been a peculiar gold-plating of voting rights under devolution," she continued, allowing EU citizens to vote in elections. "The complexities are legion," she added.

Borders, Immigration and Citizenship

Professor Ryan said a key issue is how to protect Scottish people with a strong British identity, post-independence. If people in Scotland automatically became citizens of Scotland, they may not automatically lose their UK citizenship, but a future Westminster Government could decide to change this. Professor Ryan said he had previously floated the idea of Scotland and what remained of the UK following the Irish model. Ireland has a different attitude towards the citizens of Northern Ireland who identify themselves with Ireland, and Scotland could also be treated as "a special case," allowing people with a strong British identity to be given a different status by the Westminster Government.

Professor Curtice summed up these responses by saying it was likely most people would therefore have two passports, post-independence, thus taking the "angst" out of the issue.

Question 2: Do individuals have a legal right to their citizenship? Could people's EU passports be easily taken away if Scotland did not automatically become a new member state of the EU? What constraints are there on the Westminster Government to take away people's UK citizenship?

Professor Shaw replied that in the case of Czechoslovakia, some issues were hard to disentangle, because of problems with registration of people, including ethnic minorities. If the UK did take away UK citizenship, it would not be a breach of international law because people would not be stateless – they would still be citizens of the new Scotland. "That is why the Scottish Government is taking a broad attitude towards dual citizenship," she said, and there is a tradition of this in the UK. It would be a "major departure" for Westminster to change its position.

Asked if we have individual rights as "EU citizens," Professor Shaw said that it was "a slippery argument" to suggest the EU would deny this to people, and that politicians would do all in their power to avoid testing EU laws in an international court.

Professor Ryan said he is "afraid" we don't have individual rights to be citizens of any state. Only states can decide issues of citizenship, not individuals, as long as their decisions are not "wholly arbitrary" and as long as they do not make people stateless.

Question 3: The next question came from the Chair, as Professor Curtice asked how long it should take for a professional coming from England to Scotland in order to work to claim the right to Scottish citizenship, and how long for a refugee from Afghanistan, seeking asylum.

Professor Boswell said there were lessons to learn from the European experience in the 1970s, when many people talked about the so-called "myth of return" – the idea that migration is a temporary status and that people will work in another country then go "home" later on. "This didn't happen and created a big headache for many countries," she said, leading to current debates about "failed" integration. If it is assumed that migration will be temporary, integration issues will have to be dealt with from Day One.

New countries need to establish appropriate paths and procedures for acquiring citizenship and think about appropriate incentives, but the number of years it will take to establish citizenship will tend to vary across different routes – with Professor Boswell suggesting five years as one likely figure. If Scotland became independent, then people who move here would not automatically become Scottish citizens. Professor Boswell also pointed out that Irish citizens can vote in a UK election, and suggested that passports are "largely symbolic." Ms Craig agreed with the figure of five years and said that an asylum seeker's indefinite "right to remain" in the country provides extensive rights without needing to become a citizen, and that citizenship is a matter of choice.

Question 4: Once someone achieved full citizenship in an independent Scotland, how long would it take for that person's extended family to get the same status?

Professor Boswell said it would be "more or less automatic" but Professor Shaw pointed out that this is not an automatic right in the UK today – for example, there are "very severe" income restrictions. Therefore, she added, it's "acutely interesting" to raise this issue in the context of the current debate. Ms Craig added that there is an important distinction to make between indefinite right to remain, and citizenship, and that refugees already have "family reunion" rights.

Question 5: Based on the experience of someone who has been involved in the past with Immigration Tribunals, immigration is a highly complex issue, but why would Scotland want to deviate after all these years – why take a more liberal approach? Open borders "would be lovely" but well-educated young people today find it hard to get jobs.

Borders, Immigration and Citizenship

A points system may help to decide on the right to remain for skilled people, but not citizenship. Asylum seekers are a very different issue, but "we can't be more liberal than we are now." We don't have the facilities to deal with the issues today.

Professor Boswell suggested that this question confirmed her earlier point that public opinion could be "problematic" when drawing up new immigration laws. She said that she is sceptical about the possibility of any government being able to sustain a more open and liberal policy on immigration, considering the full weight of public opinion and media pressures. The previous Labour Government has talked in the past about adopting a points system for immigration, because of concerns about a shortage of skills, but she strongly disagrees with the idea of awarding temporary rights to skilled workers, because you can't expect them to leave after putting down roots. It is also not a good idea to send out a message that immigrants will only have the right to remain for a period of five years, for example. "This won't appeal to potential candidates," she said, in the race for skills. Limiting residence to five years simply "won't fly."

Professor Ryan suggested that immediately after independence, immigration policy would be largely the same as today, then deviate thereafter. Ireland has adopted different policies and has a different electoral system and a different constitution, and future UK policy will also change as time goes by. Some "discredited" immigration rules will not survive, he added. Professor Shaw said Scottish universities are already "hobbled" by the regulations on recruiting people from overseas. Even employing our own graduates is difficult, she added.

Question 6: There is an assumption that an independent Scotland would remain in the Common Travel Area. Since the signing of the Maastricht Treaty, however, not one single country has been granted an opt-out, and if Scotland joins the EU, all the other member states could veto an opt-out. How sure are you that Scotland could rejoin the EU, and what about Schengen?

Professor Ryan replied that it was hard to say how this would work, whether in relation to an independent Scotland or an independent Catalonia, wishing to remain in the EU. "EU law doesn't provide for states seceding, but only for new states applying to join," he said. Scotland would not be a "new applicant" like other countries, so legally and politically, Scotland does have grounds to claim it should stay automatically in the EU, but the terms of this would still have to be negotiated.

Question 7: What are the practical issues of dealing with refugees in the event of independence? Who would staff the asylum system, the borders and the embassies? Would there be a Scottish Foreign Office? Would some responsibilities be passed on to a privatised body?

Ms Craig said a separate and independent agency – and not a privatised body – would be a good idea, as recommended by the Scottish Refugee Council.

Question 8: Where do you get this indication that Scotland would adopt a more liberal attitude to immigration? Many Scottish people living overseas were encouraged to come home to work but, when they did so, found that there were very few jobs. Forecasts of immigrant arrivals have also been inaccurate – for example, the numbers of Polish arrivals were closer to 400,000 than the 200,000 estimate. Housing is a related issue – for example, housing officers report they have not housed a Scottish family for years. "People in Scotland are not against migration, but there has to be a limit and, as a small country, we're reaching that limit." What constraints should there be on freedom of movement within the EU?

Professor Boswell said that "economic disparity does not always equate to migration." For example, despite its recent economic crisis, Greece has not experienced a mass outflow of Greek nationals. During a downturn, politicians also have to be sensitive to different issues. There can also be "a mismatch in skills and geography" in different regions and different countries, with people not always in the right place to fill employment vacancies. There can also be a labour shortage during periods of high unemployment. That's why there is always a case for migration, even during a downturn.

SUMMARY

The debate put the spotlight on several issues, including the rarely asked but fundamental question "Who are we?" It was also suggested that citizenship is a concept that does not develop fully until after a state is established, and that it is hard to "do everything new." Citizenship is also an issue in which "there are not many votes," because it presents so many difficult choices – for example, how to deal with residence and the Scottish diaspora. There is also the possibility that the UK would not "make things so easy," but it's also the case that the UK has always accepted dual citizenship. Unlike other situations when new states were created, the UK today faces the prospect of a "civilised separation" which would allow many people to enjoy the benefits of dual citizenship.

Science
and Higher
Education

Science and Higher Education

17 October 2013, at the University of Aberdeen

INTRODUCTION

This seminar on science and higher education was the eighth in the series. The speakers were asked to discuss the possible effects of Scottish independence upon the ability and ease with which students would be able to cross the border to take up higher education opportunities, and how this might affect the accessibility of higher education for people in the rest of the UK as well as people in Scotland. They were also asked to examine the future of research funding and how the UK Research Councils would decide to allocate funding in the event of Scotland leaving the UK.

Chair:

Ken Macdonald, Special Correspondent, News and Current Affairs, BBC

Speakers:

> **Professor Rick Rylance**, Chief Executive, Arts and Humanities Research Council;

> **Professor Lindsay Paterson FBA FRSE**, School of Social and Political Science, University of Edinburgh;

> **Professor Stephen Salter MBE FRSE**, Emeritus Professor of Engineering Design, School of Engineering, University of Edinburgh;

> **Professor Chris Hawkesworth FRS FRSE**, Deputy Principal and Vice-Principal for Research, University of St Andrews;

> **Mr Colin Macilwain**, Editor of *Research Europe* and Associate Editor of *Research Fortnight*.

The debate was conducted as an open, public discussion seminar.

PROFESSOR RICK RYLANCE,
CHIEF EXECUTIVE, ARTS AND HUMANITIES RESEARCH COUNCIL

Professor Rylance was concerned about disturbing "the delicate ecology" of funding systems which currently supports researchers in the UK and Scotland. How would independence affect the research infrastructure in terms of individuals and facilities, collaborative projects and the quality of assessment? Would Scotland lose the advantage it gains from being part of a wider scientific community?

He began by describing how the Research Councils UK (RCUK) is a UK-wide organisation that awards funds on the basis of excellence and open competition, decided through peer review by appropriate expert researchers on a project-specific basis. "They are thus not allocated on the basis of location, either geographic or political," he added, although the RCUK does keep an eye on "distribution of national capability."

Within the system, Scotland does exceptionally well when it comes to competing for funds, and this is a tribute to the quality of Scotland's higher education institutions as well as its research and researchers. The key point, he said, is that if we shifted to "a notional, normative distribution of research funds by research councils," Scotland would lose, because it currently enjoys some degree of advantage under the 'dual-support system' which underpins the Research Excellence Framework. Block grants go to individual researchers and there is also local control by the separate administrations, including Scotland, England and Wales. It is crucial, he said, that even though the income is distributed unevenly, consistent methods and standards are applied to the allocation of funds – something which is good for the image of the UK as a whole. In addition, there is some direct funding from government agencies (e.g. the Ministry of Defence, the Technology Strategy Board [TSB] and the UK Space Agency), as well as other bodies such as charities (e.g. the Royal Society of Edinburgh).

Professor Rylance described this as an interlocking system – "a delicate ecology of research funding," with a high degree of flexibility. And the proof of the pudding is the "good science" and the world-leadership of UK researchers in many areas, including the ground-breaking work done by our latest Nobel Prizewinner, Professor Peter Higgs of the University of Edinburgh.

Professor Rylance then quoted several figures to illustrate how the UK punches above its weight in international research. The country has 1% of the world's population, but spends 3% of the total research funds.

Science and Higher Education

The UK's commitment to research produces 7.9% of all papers published, 11.8% of all citations and 14.4% of the world's most-cited papers. And this means the UK is a "major world power" in terms of research, and highly productive in terms of original research and value for money.

It is tempting, he continued, to see a correlation between the flexibility and the variety of funding and the results we produce. It does set a benchmark against which to measure any future changes. The approach to funding includes judgement of excellence according to common standards and methods, and there are also "nuanced methods for distributing by volume at a devolved level."

Professor Rylance then addressed a number of issues which would have a major impact on the funding of research in the event of Scotland becoming independent, including critical mass, the quality of research and access to facilities.

Considering the excellent record of UK researchers, Professor Rylance cautioned that there were several issues and "risks to guard against" if the current system were changed, whatever the result of the Referendum. If Scotland became independent, administrators of research funds would have to be mindful of disturbing the system under which we apply common methods and standards to funding. It is not just about the mechanics of the system, he said, but the advantages we gain from peer review by a much larger pool of scientists. If this pool were reduced, it would be harder to reproduce the same level of expertise, as well as harder to refresh and distribute the workload. It would also be harder to maintain our "powerful UK-wide reputation," since every institution in Scotland and elsewhere profits from the international standing of the UK as a whole. "We all get a boost from the fact that the UK is generally good," he said. Professor Rylance also said that there were benefits to being part of a sizeable competitive system, and that a smaller system might put this in jeopardy.

The trend in the UK and around the world is towards a greater concentration of research and the creation of centres of excellence, pooling research and resources. "It's a big-player world," he said, and collaboration is increasingly seen as key to success.

Collaboration is also something that Scotland is good at, he added, and has pioneered a number of initiatives; but collaborative projects have not just been established within Scotland's borders but also operate cross-border – for example, out of the 1,100 grants awarded by the Engineering and Physical Sciences Research Council, about 400 involve collaboration between researchers in different areas of the UK.

In the Arts & Humanities sector, there are similar cross-border projects, such as the Copyright Centre in Glasgow, and the Hub for the Creative Economy in Dundee.

Access to advanced national facilities may also be affected if Scotland became independent. Most of the important facilities used by Scotland's researchers are in England, he said, and it would be "impossibly expensive" to duplicate these in an independent Scotland, while continued access to existing centres may not be so easy – for example, those funded by the Science and Technology Facilities Council (STFC) or the Natural Environment Research Council (NERC). There would also be an impact on the use of common facilities in other countries and international subscriptions – for example, the UK, not Scotland, is the partner in projects such as CERN. There are also implications regarding shared costs, and affordability. It would also be hard to reproduce the international networks of which the UK is a part – e.g. science and information – and build new relationships with international organisations in leading and emerging centres such as Delhi, Brussels, Washington and China, where RCUK has offices. We would need to "be mindful" of dismantling these networks if multiple systems were established, he added.

Professor Rylance then turned to the important questions raised in relation to research careers and training, and the flow of scientists across borders, sharing access to each other's facilities and developing their expertise. "I personally would worry if we started to chunk up the supply chain in terms of people's career development and the spread of talent across the UK research base," he said.

PROFESSOR LINDSAY PATERSON FBA FRSE,
UNIVERSITY OF EDINBURGH, SCHOOL OF SOCIAL & POLITICAL SCIENCE

Professor Paterson focused on four basic questions in the context of the current independence debate:

1 How good is Scotland's higher education?

2 How international is Scotland's higher education?

3 How 'Scottish' is Scotland's higher education?

4 What political conditions are needed to enable Scotland's higher education system to flourish?

Science and Higher Education

In terms of quality, Scotland currently has four or five universities in the world's Top 200, including one in the Top 20 and three in the Top 100. Scotland also currently competes very well for research funds, but the proportion of funds corresponds very closely to the number of academics who work here. Scotland's share of research funds in the current academic year is about 10.7%, and Scotland employs 10.4% of the UK's academics, slightly higher than our 8.5% share of the UK population.

Similar figures apply to medicine, the social sciences and environmental science, with funds more or less proportionate to the number of researchers. The healthy income earned by Scotland's universities comes via its success in open competition, rather than from institutional grants. And this suggests that it is driven by the "autonomous efforts of academics," competing on a level playing field with other academics in the UK. For example, medical researchers last year won 15.3% of the funds available from the Medical Research Council (MRC), up from 10.2% two years before, while their share of institutional grants fell from 9.9% to only 4.5%, over the same period.

To maintain the international quality of our research base, Professor Paterson added, we must maintain our access to international funding and maintain our international standards. To do so, it has been calculated that an independent Scotland would need to find an extra £300 million in funds per annum – double the amount currently distributed by the Scottish Funding Council.

How international are Scotland's universities? Professor Paterson said the great fear was that Scotland would become more parochial if it became independent, and drop down the international league table. Scotland's academic researchers do relatively well by UK and international standards, according to its GDP and number of researchers, but countries such as India and China are now on the rise. This is important, he said, because in our efforts to attract international academics and students, we should remember it is now a global market. Scotland has a high proportion of researchers relative to population, he added – 4.1 researchers per 1,000 people, compared to only 2.8 researchers per 1,000 in the UK as a whole. Scotland's researchers also produce 2.5 times the number of academic papers per head of population, compared to other countries of a similar size, "and our papers are noticed," he said, with a disproportionately large share of the most-cited papers.

Putting this in perspective, however, Professor Paterson pointed out that almost half of these papers, by 2008, were co-authored with researchers outside the UK, including small countries such as Israel, Switzerland, Belgium, Denmark and Finland.

Another major challenge is to attract leading academics from abroad. "The market for academics is global," he said, and half of our academics are from outside Scotland, with a quarter of those being from outside the UK. Scotland's universities are, therefore, "already on the world stage," he continued.

There are also major intellectual benefits from international student flow. Since 1975, there has been a fivefold increase in the worldwide number of students enrolled in universities outside their country of origin, especially students from developing countries. The EU also accounts for a large share (25%) of students moving abroad, and Scotland has a relatively large share of these compared to most OECD countries – currently about 14.6% of first-degree students. This is lower than the UK as whole, (18.3%) but more than four times the proportion in the USA, and also much higher than Sweden (7.5%), Ireland (5.9%) and Norway (1.4%). If Scotland became independent and students from England were included in this figure, the proportion would rise to almost 28%, very high by international standards.

Adding together Scotland's performance in research and its ability to attract international academics and students, Scotland has a good reputation, but in an independent Scotland, would this high proportion of "foreign" students be considered too high and sustainable from a political or cultural standpoint, even though most people agree there are cultural benefits? There are past precedents of high foreign intake of students or other academics becoming an issue in other countries in Europe (e.g. Austria and Belgium), particularly in individual departments, but the legal position today seems to be that restricting foreign intake would not be possible. What is not unusual, however, is the fact that half of the "foreign" students in Scotland come from its neighbour, and recruiting 28% of student intake from outside our borders is not unusual.

Professor Paterson put this in context by saying that although there was a period of "unusual parochialism" in Scotland from the 1960s to the 1980s, with regard to foreign students, we have a tradition of openness which dates back to the 18th Century, when many people came north from England to Scotland to study. Unlike other smaller, newly-independent states, Scotland also does not have a problem with language, and there is not "significant unmet demand" for university places among Scottish people, even during periods when the number of students from outside has grown.

Science and Higher Education

It is likely that, by international standards, there will always be a high level of students from outside, but this is not without precedent or parallel. It has been alleged in the past that taking in too many academics from outside may "undermine the Scottishness of Scottish university traditions," but according to the evidence, "academic activities, values and achievements are similar, regardless of origin." For example, the "incomers" also want our universities to be public institutions and they want them to play an active international role. Our allegiance to this international mobility is not just a "romantic attachment to the democratic intellect", but because this dual support of public good and international networks is the norm in the world's most influential academic market, the USA.

Professor Paterson then discussed what political conditions were needed to enable Scotland's universities to flourish, and focused on the issue of academic autonomy, and Government's traditional respect for this when it comes to funding. In Scotland and the UK as a whole, the level of autonomy is already high in terms of selection of students and staff, as well as in the design of the curriculum, and this helps to maintain the quality of our academic research base. "Since Scotland's academics are already autonomous, independence would not make much difference," he said, unless there were major shifts in economic, fiscal or social policy. Education policy is already devolved, he added. Student fees would not come under education policy, but would be an economic and social decision, and this is already devolved.

Finally, Professor Paterson defined the paradox at the heart of the constitutional debate, with arguments for and against independence, as regards the future of research and education. Our successes to date may encourage the belief that independence would enable us to achieve even more. On the other hand, these same successes may encourage the belief that things are good as they are, so we should stay that way. If Scotland were to become independent, academics would still need to argue for funds and compete to attract global talent. Issues such as academic freedom and autonomy would still be on the agenda, but there is no sign that these principles are seriously under threat from either side of the political divide. "Ensuring these things if Scotland became independent would require political goodwill, as much from politicians in the rest of the UK as from those who would be governing Scotland," he concluded.

PROFESSOR STEPHEN SALTER MBE FRSE,
EMERITUS PROFESSOR OF ENGINEERING, UNIVERSITY OF EDINBURGH

Professor Salter began by addressing the issues from a personal viewpoint, describing his own frustrating experience in applying for research funds. He then suggested that if the present SNP policy with regard to higher education continues after a 'yes' vote, scientists and academics have no cause for concern. Scottish universities could continue to punch above their weight, and the £300 million funding gap could be easily dealt with by cutting the defence budget.

Referring to a recent article in *The Independent*, Professor Salter said it was "deeply symbolic" with regard to per capita NHS spending. According to the article, the health of people in southeast Hampshire starts to decline at the age of 68 years, compared to only 58 years for people in Sunderland. However, spending in Hampshire is to be increased by 14%, while spending in Sunderland will go down by 11%. "That really hurts," said Salter, adding that it also makes him feel "ashamed." "The level of compassion in the NHS in England is somewhere wrong," he continued. "I want to be governed by people who have more compassion than that and I want them to exercise it efficiently."

Moving on to higher education and science, Professor Salter quoted the First Minister Alex Salmond, who declared (courtesy of Robert Burns) that "the rocks will melt wi' the sun" before Scottish students are required to pay university fees, like their counterparts in England. Professor Salter then said he would focus on his own experience, particularly in the field of renewable energy, even though other disciplines may lead to different conclusions. "Engineers can only stand in awe at the achievements in fields such as medicine in Dundee," he explained.

Most of the funding for Professor Salter's projects comes from Brussels, he said, including collaborations with people in the US, Australia and Norway. The Internet makes communication easy, and the world of science now is one big melting pot. "We don't worry about borders," he added. But his experience of seeking research funding from UK sources had been "miserable". In Professor Salter's experience, there is insufficient knowledge of Scotland in the UK research councils. As examples, he quoted the fact that assessments of proposals for research in wave energy are assessed by 'the nuclear people' at Harwell (the UK Atomic Energy Authority) and pointed out the lack of understanding, possibly wilful, of the conditions in the Pentland Firth.

Science and Higher Education

Professor Salter said that there is sometimes a different kind of problem when applying to UK research councils for funding. According to the current rules for EPSRC funds, an unsuccessful applicant can't re-apply for funding for the same project, and this applies even retrospectively (i.e. before the rules were changed). Professor Salter thinks that "this is punishing people who are thinking ahead."

Professor Salter said that "many people in universities are not happy" with the current funding system, he added, expressing concern that "hardly any people who apply for academic jobs today are from the UK." There are very good applicants from China, India and eastern Europe, he said, but no-one from the UK wants to apply to work in a UK university any more.

PROFESSOR CHRIS HAWKESWORTH FRS FRSE,
DEPUTY PRINCIPAL AND VICE-PRINCIPAL FOR RESEARCH, UNIVERSITY OF ST ANDREWS

Professor Hawkesworth said that he came to St Andrews in part because of Scotland's reputation for valuing research and education. One of the things that interests him is "to ensure that leading academics and students have good reasons for wanting to be in Scotland for their research and studies."

He is also concerned about the uncertainty caused by the Referendum debate, which he believes is holding back investment and making academics (both researchers and students) wary of coming to Scotland. In his view, "it is difficult to evaluate how funding structures and opportunities will operate, whatever the outcome" of the Referendum debate.

Professor Hawkesworth then focused on three areas: the future of Scotland's universities; their relationship with the UK Research Councils; and the challenges faced by universities in a small country seeking to play a big role in international research. These are challenging times for all universities in the UK, he continued. There are concerns that without adequate funding, our institutes of higher learning will begin to slip down the world rankings: capital funding was cut by £600 million in 2010–11. For universities in a smaller country such as an independent Scotland, this would be even more challenging.

To boost their income and "develop their positions," many universities in England have increased student intake, but because Scottish students don't need to pay fees, the number who can study here is capped, so increasing intake to secure their future would not be easy without increasing the proportion of students from the rest of the UK and elsewhere. This could lead to other problems.

The quality of the research done in Scotland is high, he continued, and our universities receive about 13% of the research funds available in the UK, compared to a UK population share of just 8.5%. This means Scottish academics generally get a bigger slice of the pie, but there is anecdotal evidence that smaller countries generally have smaller research communities and smaller budgets, which tends to lead to directing resources towards applied research rather than towards blue-sky research. He also questioned how a smaller community of researchers in an independent Scotland would be able to work under the Research Excellence Framework. "University departments have to be much more selective on what they prioritise than those in universities with higher-level strategies," he added. This would be a bigger problem if Scotland became independent, and the targeting of research into more selected areas would result in more low-quality, more narrowly-focused research being funded.

Much of the debate among academics so far has focused on the idea of an independent Scotland "buying-in" to a larger research fund, much like the current EU model, which invites researchers in member countries to compete for European Research Council (ERC) funds, but Professor Hawkesworth suggested that the dominant partner (i.e. England) would have more influence on how the funds were spent, and Scotland would thus lose its current advantage. Deciding how to fund industry-focused research would be even more challenging, since different governments would also have different priorities; for example, different policies on energy. Both sides may want to make the new relationship work but, as Andrew Marr wrote in his book *The Battle for Scotland*, "many initiatives on Home Rule crumbled in the face of Westminster resistance." There is no guarantee that any future government in Westminster would be disposed to help an independent Scotland.

Another key issue is scale, he suggested. Internationally-competitive researchers and students tend to prefer larger educational communities. There may be a diaspora effect, but most researchers would be attracted elsewhere, and Professor Hawkesworth described this by saying that given a choice between New Zealand and Australia, most researchers in his field would choose Australia.

Science and Higher Education

Scotland's universities are performing well at the moment, with three in the world's Top 100, but Professor Hawkesworth suggested that this may reflect its position within the larger unit of the UK, which is second only to the USA in terms of academic reputation. He said that in the future, Scotland's three institutions in the Top 100 might drop to just one institution, in line with other small countries such as Ireland, Denmark and Norway. The implication is that if Scotland became independent, he said, "it is hard not to conclude that fewer academics would want to come here."

Finally, Professor Hawkesworth said it may be helpful to frame the argument by evaluating the worst possible case and the best possible case that might follow from independence. "Even the best reasonable case would be no better than today, and the concern is that the worst reasonable case will be different and is likely to disadvantage researchers in Scotland," he said.

Mr Colin Macilwain,
Editor of *Research Europe* & Associate Editor of *Research Fortnight*

Mr Macilwain prefaced his remarks by describing himself as a journalist, not a scientist, who has written a lot about how research funds are distributed in different corners of the world. He then said he took exception to the idea that the UK funding system is "close to perfect" and that Scotland somehow couldn't do without it. He focused on four things which he feels are important in the context of the current debate:

1 the notion that many small countries perform very well on their own in terms of innovation;

2 the fact that the current research system in the UK has weaknesses of its own;

3 the neglect of R&D outside the remit of the UKRC;

4 the idea that sound research policy needs to involve "rapid and deft innovation, not self-congratulation," to succeed.

Why shouldn't a small nation deliver world-beating research? Some people argue that Scotland's universities gain from the UKRC system because the scientists are competing for funds from a large pot of money, but Mr Macilwain questioned whether Scotland really gains from the current arrangement.

When it comes to innovation, small countries generally do very well in international league tables – for example, Switzerland, Sweden, Singapore and Finland. "Small nations are the strongest scientific performers in Europe," he said, and in the 2012 round of ERC starting grants, the best performers per head were Switzerland, Holland, Israel and Denmark. Scotland has a very strong tradition in research, but is not competing as well it could, he suggested.

There are no concrete plans for any changes in policy yet and the current funding system could continue, he said. Scotland could participate in the system as it functions today and pay for the awards it wins, as non-EU members such as Switzerland and Israel now do in EU research programmes, but if Scotland became independent, it could set up its own funding structures. Academics in Scotland are used to dealing with the UK Research Councils, but – like many UK-wide institutions such as the intelligence services – these are "not as good as they keep telling us," said Mr Macilwain, and still suffer from "post-imperial hubris," as if they don't need to do anything except "exert their natural superiority." They are also not as accountable as they should be, and are overseen by a "supine" Westminster committee system.

The autonomy of some UK Research Councils has also been curtailed in recent times, he continued, citing the case of the Medical Research Council. Even though it is one of the strongest research councils, its headquarters were closed down and moved to Swindon, shedding half of its staff on the way. The Science and Technology Funding Council and EPSRC have also had management problems. Mr Macilwain also cited the example of a recent announcement by NERC that it was opening up a new doctoral centre for oil and gas, but not in other energy sectors. "There is no way of getting to the bottom of the politics" of that decision, he added.

"It was just something that happened." So, are the research councils "state of the art?" Some aspects of their work are opaque and not accountable enough, and someone once described them as being staffed by "a strange mixture of gifted enthusiasts and disaffected bureaucrats."

Whilst the UK Research Councils have a somewhat "old-fashioned take on innovation," and their interaction with the public tends to be paternalistic, the Scottish Government has been "reinvigorated by devolution," he continued. An independent Scotland would have to devise its own policies in applied areas such as agriculture, fisheries, forestry and energy, where its needs are perceived to be different, but the UK Research Councils have "slashed and burned capacity" for these areas.

Science and Higher Education

Energy, for example, has been a victim of cuts, and this is a "major flaw" in UK policy. While David Willetts, the Minister for Universities and Science, has praised policy makers in the USA for their strong support of NASA and the Department of Energy, these are the very same areas where the UK Government has cut support in recent times.

Mr Macilwain then turned his attention to innovation, saying that today it was "less about patents, spin-outs and venture capital and more about openness and collaboration." But the UK tends to cling to the old model, he said, unlike global leaders such as California, Denmark, Sweden and the Netherlands. He cited the computer games industry in Dundee as a good example of a more relevant approach to innovation in Scotland, but thought the TSB "had not yet got its head around that."

After a tentative start, the Scottish Government has also proved itself an innovative policy maker – e.g. with regard to alcohol pricing and cigarette packaging. He then challenged opponents of independence to name a single policy area where the UK Government has really innovated in the last 20 years. The Government has recently invited China to help build new nuclear power stations in the UK, and Mr Macilwain wondered if this is an example of being "innovative."

"Why should we believe that science and innovation – of all things – are best served by a system of government at Westminster which is effectively a closed cabal of special interests, incapable of innovating in itself?" he asked. Whatever the result of the Referendum, further constitutional change is coming and research and education in Scotland are heading down a distinctly Scottish path. We should consider our options carefully and openly, he said, especially when it comes to deciding our research priorities in areas of special interest such as public health, alleviation of poverty, energy, the natural environment, fisheries and agriculture. Mr Macilwain doubts that the UK could adapt or modernise enough to deliver for Scotland in these areas, and said that if Scotland became independent, "at least there is a chance it could" build structures of its own to promote science and innovation more effectively.

DISCUSSION

1 The first comment came from a representative of the James Hutton Institute, "a world- leading research institute for land, crops, water and the environment," based in Dundee and Aberdeen. The Institute is not eligible for UKRC funding; but because of an agreement between the Scottish Government and BBSRC, it has access to some funds. It has been so successful, however, that the Institute can no longer apply. Researchers should therefore "be careful what sort of agreement is made" with the UKRC in the event of independence. Because of where you are and the history of your relationship with the Scottish government, you may not be able to apply for the same funds in future, even though you can demonstrate excellence. "We demonstrate excellence and we are punished for it."

The Chair, Mr Macdonald, commented that this did not sound like an argument for the constitutional status quo, and the questioner responded that researchers have to "face the challenges." Collaboration and engagement are the way forward, with institutions working together. The isolation of institutions – as a result of independence – could create problems. "Science is about innovation and this means collaboration between institutions and across disciplines, and we have to find ways to support this through the funding mechanisms that there are."

Professor Hawkesworth said that these issues would be all up for negotiation if Scotland became independent, and said he is wary of the "asymmetry" that might result.

Professor Rylance said that he doesn't want to defend the status quo, but agreed that the future of science is all about collaboration and organisations working together. There are protocols which govern allocation of funds, and such issues are currently being debated. Professor Salter said that the best way to stop collaboration is to have more researchers competing for funds under the current research assessment system. Nowadays, people don't want to release ideas outside their own "charmed circles." In the 1960s, he said, all academics helped each other, rather than being forced to compete, and he would like a return to those days. Professor Paterson suggested that the current investment in research networks shows this is not true, citing the example of collaborative networks in Scotland. There are lots of ways to measure success, he continued, but partnerships across universities do pay off. Things are not perfect, but Scotland's autonomous policies have also been a success. Mr Macilwain agreed that these networks have been a success but thought that this does not rebut Professor Salter's point about research assessment stifling innovation.

Science and Higher Education

2 The next comment focused on the £300 million funding gap identified by many commentators. Either Scotland finds the extra money, or it partners with the rest of the UK and has "almost no say" over distribution of funds. Scotland has specific needs and striking a deal with the UK "is not a very good plan." The funding gap has not yet been remotely addressed. In addition, "collaboration" is not "a replacement for cash." This is merely a red herring that distracts attention from the funding gap. Would the residual UK disproportionately fund Scotland's researchers in the event of independence? That would require a lot of good will on the part of those dispensing the money.

Professor Paterson suggested that competing for funds is the best way to raise the overall standards of research, but some principles would have to be established. Scotland would have to negotiate the terms of its contribution to a larger research fund, without expecting to get a fair return on its money, and be willing to compete fair and square with other partners. Good will may prevail, but that is not the way international collaboration tends to happen, he added. Professor Salter said £300 million could be saved from defence straight away, by ending the quest for a "more expensive ways of killing people." Mr Macdonald commented that there are only so many times you can cancel Trident, and said that funding one thing always means reducing the budget for something else – a challenge when considering that Scotland currently receives 13% of UK research funds but only contributes 9% of total UK taxation.

3 The next comment focused on the numbers, and the different figures different speakers quoted in the course of the debate, including the figure of "9%" for Scotland's total tax contribution. According to the speaker, the more accurate figure for "what we put in" is actually 9.8%, and this makes a big difference when you compare it with the figure for "what we get back" – 9.3%.

In other words, if we need cash, look no further. These figures were in turn questioned by another member of the audience, who pointed out that "what we get back" is not calculated on the same basis as "what we put in", because even though "what we get back" may be 9.3% of total UK spending, the actual sum is higher than the money raised in taxes. These figures are also not representative, the first speaker countered, because they do not take account of revenues from oil.

4 Describing his vision for research funds in a future Scotland, another speaker cited the example of the oil and gas doctoral centre set up by NERC and suggested that Scotland could go its own way, with funding organised along the lines of the "well-costed" US model. He also questioned the "need for size," saying that in the 21st Century, it is more important to be nimble and focused on needs. "It's agility that matters."

Apologising for using journalese when describing the figures, Mr Macdonald said that one of the most common complaints about the current Referendum debate is that "we don't want more men in suits arguing about the figures – we want good solid facts." Professor Paterson added that there are many ways of interpreting the figures for research council spending. For example, when it comes to medical research, where the money received appears to be significantly higher than for most other disciplines, you have to disentangle NHS funds from the rest of the budget, which includes pharmaceutical research. "There can't be a settled position on statistics," Professor Paterson continued. That would be Utopia. The argument over the figures will continue to be ideological. Professor Rylance echoed this by saying "it depends what you count." He then said there is an ongoing debate about the nature of postgraduate research, pointing out the "intriguing" fact that the number of UK-wide postgraduate students is at an all-time high, with 46% of them from overseas. Asked to comment on the "small is beautiful" argument, Professor Hawkesworth said that when any small country becomes independent, it has to find more money for research, but it also has to be wary of a small community of researchers assessing applications for funds. He also cited the example of Ireland, where central government has focused on two or three things, and sometimes "over-targeted" some areas.

5 If Scotland became independent, would some institutions drop down the world rankings and would Scotland lose out in the "innovation stakes?" Mr Macilwain said that some small nations do extremely well, citing the example of Switzerland and Singapore – both prime locations for postgraduate students. "We won't disappear from the international map," he added. Professor Hawkesworth asked what Scotland aspires to and pointed out that Switzerland allocates much larger funds than Scotland would be able to afford.

Science and Higher Education

6 There appear to be advantages on both sides of the argument. On the one hand, we gain from the critical mass of the larger UK, and on the other hand we gain from the idea that "small is beautiful." Scale isn't everything, however, and the debate needs to go beyond these issues. Too many people take the positives and turn them into negatives.

Scotland is successful at the moment in winning research funds, and if it continues to be properly funded, we'll continue to compete, whether we become independent or not. The critical question is to argue about the positive attributes of the UK, instead of painting a picture of Scotland in trouble. The evidence does not support that. The UK has value and the various parts of it working together have value, and Scotland should be seen as a valuable player in that system.

The emphasis on positives continued, with another comment highlighting the "invigorating effect of devolution" and the "positive benefits" of being part of the UK, suggesting the invigoration could continue, with Scotland enjoying the best of both worlds. Scotland should promote itself internationally in terms of its distinctiveness and as "a back door to the UK and Europe." Devolution is "a process which is still going on," and was also a solution to over-centralisation in the UK, which was bad for all its individual parts. To walk away from that and centralise everything again within an independent Scotland would be a backward step. This led to a later comment describing the benefits of centralisation in certain areas such as public health, with different agencies working together for the common good in one central organisation. Perhaps this should encourage more links with England, rather than the opposite.

7 The debate should be about outcomes and evidence. In higher education, Scotland has done well per head of population and we should focus on what made us successful and will keep us successful. The key issue is what we would gain from independence and what we would lose. We could sort out the funding, but what about the process? There may be "wishful thinking" on the part of some people who believe that going it alone is a better idea. Could Scotland really run a funding council of its own? Some researchers argue for a separate funding council for Scotland simply because their applications are rejected by a UK national body, but that is not a good basis on which to proceed.

8 What Scotland needs does not depend on independence or not. "More analytically," what's needed either way – in education, industry and research – is to move to the next stage. What aspects of the current system are most useful? What are the critical factors we need to consider, independence or not? Professor Rylance said the positives are "glaringly obvious" – e.g. the imagination and collaborative spirit of Scottish researchers. And all of these things would persist, independence or not. There would always be an argument for focusing on areas of special interest, as well as some degree of "local" control.

9 What changes would there be if there is a 'no' vote and more devolved powers? Mr Macilwain commented that the UK has concentrated all of its resources into the UKRC and "decimated" the rest of publicly-funded R&D funding. He also doubts that centralisation – e.g. to address public health issues – would ever happen at the UK level. Professor Paterson said that academics have a responsibility to point out how to avoid the worst effects of different political outcomes, as well as how to take advantage of potential benefits. He also said that since the 1970s, there has been a lack of self-confidence among academics in relation to the prospect of independence, as if we would suddenly throw away 300 years of tradition and not be able to survive on our own. In the event of independence, collaborations will continue and there will be cross-border traffic in both directions. That's the way it is in the international market of ideas, he added. It is possible to avoid parochialism and continue to operate internationally. Will the inter-networks of researchers survive? "You need the good will of academics, not other governments," he said. "We should stop talking down Scotland's academia," he said. We should talk about the positives and explore the possible scenarios, to realise the benefits of small-country innovation, whether we like independence or not. Professor Hawkesworth suggested there may be a "technical question" about scale, strategy and focus. If you "shrink your country," would you become more focused, and would that be something you wanted? And if you bought into another country's funding system, would you be able to influence how it is managed?

Science and Higher Education

10   The next comment questioned the criteria for judging research, suggesting that it is not always innovation, but also personal glory and money, that motivates people. Maybe researchers should "ask what they can do for their country, not what their country can do for them." Social deprivation, for example, is one area where Scotland's academics could influence policy and help to deliver better services via more focused research. It would be useful to hear more about how we value research and "useful knowledge." Mr Macdonald asked: "Is localism parochialism?" The speaker replied that we also have to use international resources to solve local problems.

11   Another speaker commented that NHS funding in the UK has been steady for a number of years, and is currently worth £1 billion a year, with Scotland doing very well out of the total. "We have an ambivalent attitude," he added. We pay into some of the UK schemes and get something back, but in other areas, we don't have access to the larger funds available to researchers in England. To fund a clinical trial, however, we need access to larger funds simply because of the large sums of money required, and independence would make matters worse.

Welfare and
Public Services

Welfare and Public Services

20 November 2013, at Barony Hall, the University of Strathclyde, Glasgow

Introduction

This seminar on welfare and public services was the ninth in the series.

Most aspects of welfare policy and spending are currently the responsibility of the United Kingdom Parliament. This discussion seminar was not designed to identify or advocate any policies relating to the welfare agenda. It was intended to provide information and expert commentary about the welfare-related issues which the people of Scotland may wish to consider when deciding on 18 September 2014 if Scotland should be an independent country.

Social security spending is set to continue rising as a proportion of all public spending, with pensioners being protected in relative terms and the pressures being most keenly felt by those in the working-age groups and those with children. Attitudes to welfare reform in Scotland and the rest of the UK were explored in this discussion seminar, including whether there would be options for further devolution of welfare powers if Scotland remained part of the United Kingdom, and the significant issues which would arise should Scotland become an independent country. The seminar also took account of some international comparators which may be relevant for Scotland.

The welfare system and public services are inextricably linked, and responsibility for many of Scotland's public services is already devolved to the Scottish Parliament – such as education, the National Health Service, housing and policing. The seminar did not cover these matters in any great depth, but inevitably touched upon them within a wider welfare context.

The debate was conducted as an open, public discussion seminar.

Chair:

> **Ms Shereen Nanjiani**, Journalist and Broadcaster

Speakers:

> **Mr Chris Goulden**, Head of Poverty Team, Joseph Rowntree Foundation;

> **Professor David Bell FRSE**, Professor of Economics, University of Stirling;

> **Professor Ailsa McKay**, Professor of Economics,
  Glasgow Caledonian University;

> **Professor Jochen Clasen**, Professor of Comparative Social Policy,
  University of Edinburgh;

  and

> **Professor Michael Keating FBA FRSE**, Professor of Politics,
  University of Aberdeen.

MR CHRIS GOULDEN,
HEAD OF POVERTY TEAM, JOSEPH ROWNTREE FOUNDATION

Mr Goulden opened with the observation that welfare is not the answer to poverty, and stated his intention to speak about poverty rather than about welfare. He explained that his discussion would focus on poverty across the UK and how it can be prevented and reduced. He observed that while all parts of the UK have anti-poverty strategies, previous and current strategies seem to have consistently failed. This is true at both the local and national levels.

Mr Goulden observed that there is a tendency to believe that poverty is something which will always exist. He disagreed with this assumption. He observed that in the UK there are high levels of relative income poverty, and that the percentage of people living below the poverty line has not been lower than 20% since the late 1980s. He indicated that this flatline hides a huge amount of movement; however, pointing out, for example, that pension credit and better pensions for older people have improved their circumstances. He observed that for many single pensioners and lone parents, their prospects have been improved, and pointed out that as both groups tend to be predominantly women, this has gone some way towards addressing gender imbalances in poverty.

Welfare and Public Services

He said that poverty is not a single-issue problem, and observed that the lack of breadth taken in policy approaches to tackling poverty is problematic. He added that there is no compelling vision of what a poverty-free Scotland would look like, and argued that a clear destination is essential in designing strategies to address poverty. Legislation such as the Child Poverty Act does not meet this need, and provides only an abstract set of quantitative targets, rather than a clearly defined destination. A further flaw in current strategy to address poverty was thought to be the fact that there is no long-term, cross-party support for anti-poverty policy. This means that each time there is a new Government, they try to reinvent the wheel, and do not take forward the good work of the previous administration. What is more, interactions between policy areas are not good. Policies with relevance for poverty are not coordinated, because they are managed by different Government departments, and a dynamic lifecourse approach does not feature at the heart of current policy strategy. Finally, Mr Goulden observed that whilst all places experience poverty, and Scotland has established the Poverty Alliance and the Poverty Truth Commission, there still remains little participation by those most affected by poverty in guiding and informing policy. There needs to be greater inclusion of and consultation with these people.

Referring to these problems, Mr Goulden stated that the Joseph Rowntree Foundation aims to show how these problems can be tackled, and is developing its own strategy for addressing poverty. The strategy for Scotland is due to be published in 2015, and will be based on what has been demonstrated to work, across 30 policy areas. He explained that the Joseph Rowntree Foundation has so far set out 20 visions of what a poverty-free UK would look like, and next year plans to build a new model which takes a lifecourse approach to tackling poverty. The Joseph Rowntree Foundation has brought together a panel of people experiencing poverty, in order to test the strength and relevance of the Foundation's thinking on the issue. The aim of this work is to change the debate about poverty and to reduce the fatalism which sees poverty as a constant feature of human society.

PROFESSOR DAVID BELL FRSE,
PROFESSOR OF ECONOMICS, UNIVERSITY OF STIRLING

Professor Bell's presentation focused mainly on welfare, and he set out to address the question on what the size and distribution of welfare spend would be, in the event of constitutional change. He observed that whilst in the long term, radical change to the welfare system in an independent Scotland may be possible, in the short to medium term we must begin from the starting point we have.

Professor Bell observed that in 2012, Scotland's total Gross Value Added (GVA) was £112 billion, and defined this as the value of goods and services produced in Scotland, excluding the contribution from North Sea Oil. Spend on social protection was £21.3 billion, which represented one sixth of the value of production. He pointed out that most of this (£15.9 billion) was paid for by the Department for Work and Pensions (DWP), which is focused on benefits and the state pension.

The rest was paid for by local government; for example childcare costs, housing and social care for the elderly. In 2012, Scottish income from its two largest revenue sources – income tax receipts (£10.7 billion) and petroleum revenue tax and corporation tax levied on North Sea Oil and Gas fields (£9.3 billion) – did not, together, cover the total costs of social protection in Scotland. Total receipts from all forms of revenue, including North Sea Oil and Gas, totalled £42.4 billion. This leaves around £21 billion to spend on everything else, if the budget is to be balanced.

Referring to Scotland's macroeconomic issues, Professor Bell pointed out that it is difficult to envisage the prospect of a significant expansion to Scotland's welfare budget in the short to medium term, due to constraints imposed by Scotland's share of the national debt. Had Scotland chosen independence in 2004, it would have had fewer issues to deal with; at that time debt was only around 40% of GDP.

The per capita share of Scotland's debt is likely to peak at around £106 billion in 2016/17, assuming the same kind of trajectory as the UK as a whole. That figure would represent around 86% of Scotland's GDP at that time. Significant reform is difficult if there is not an expanding budget, as the 'gainers' cannot compensate the 'losers'.

Welfare and Public Services

Professor Bell observed that Scotland currently spends around £300 more per person, per year, on welfare, than the rest of the UK, but this has been decreasing. Spending is higher on older people than it is on children, due to the fact that Scotland has a greater number of older people and fewer children. Spending on social housing is lower in Scotland, but spending on disability is higher. In the UK, benefit spending is increasingly focused on the elderly. Professor Bell made the point that the welfare budget has moved much more towards means testing, and observed that many households face high marginal effective tax rates, because as they increase their income from work, they experience a significant loss of benefits. This constitutes an effective tax rate of over 70% amongst the poorest households.

The intention of Universal Credit is to ensure that this does not exceed 65%. However, Professor Bell pointed out that those in the highest income bracket face a marginal tax rate of 45%, meaning that low-income families face a higher marginal tax rate than the wealthiest families in the UK.

If significant reform were a possibility, Professor Bell suggested, a key consideration would be political support. There is substantial support in Scotland for welfare decisions being taken in Holyrood. However, it may be that what is desired as an outcome of this decision making may not be much different from what is desired by the rest of the UK. Professor Bell observed that Scots do not hold out much hope that more would be spent on welfare if Scotland did become independent. He also indicated that there is no evidence to suggest that Scotland as a country is more disposed to the welfare state than is the rest of the UK; recent survey evidence indicates that 55% of Scots are in favour of unemployed people being made to work for their benefits. Professor Bell pointed out that there has been greater hostility towards the welfare state in the UK in recent times, and suggested that this disenchantment is greatest amongst young people.

Professor Bell suggested that a possible way of restoring confidence in the welfare state would be to strengthen the contributory principle. The link between National Insurance payments and benefits received has been lost in the UK, although politicians continue to maintain the fiction that National Insurance is meaningful, rather than just representing an extension of income tax.

Professor Bell referred to a paper by Demos, in which the conclusion was drawn that Job Seeker's Allowance (JSA) should be greater for those with a stronger contributory record; this would mean that work incentives for disabled and non-disabled people would be equalised. Professor Bell pointed out that the welfare budget would be larger through a contributory approach.

Turning to the question of how Scotland might manage its welfare system under a devo-max arrangement, Professor Bell discussed whether Scotland would be able to operate a separate welfare system within the UK. He observed that not many countries have a devolved welfare system, because this creates a risk of welfare migration. This could lead to a competitive benefit-cutting process, whereby sub-national authorities pay lower benefits to encourage recipients to move across the border. However, Professor Bell pointed out that evidence of this type of competitive benefit cutting is not very strong. He referred to recent evidence from the US, which demonstrates that whilst there are some differences in welfare payments administered in different states, and therefore potentially some incentive for people to move, there is little evidence of this having a strong effect. A devolved welfare system may be a possibility then, and could be a way of addressing some anomalies in the welfare system as it exists at present, without substantially redesigning it. One such possibility suggested by Professor Bell was for Scotland to take over some of the DWP's employability budget. Professor Bell pointed out that employability is a part of the agenda for Skills Development Scotland, and that there is therefore scope for this organisation to work more closely with the DWP.

Another opportunity exists in the care of older people. Professor Bell observed that there are currently two non-means-tested benefits, attendance allowance and disability living allowance, which are paid to pensioners as benefits expressly targeted at personal care issues. The budget of each exceeds the budget for free personal care in Scotland, which Professor Bell indicated is frequently cited in the media as the budget which will 'break Scotland'. Professor Bell suggested that there must be an opportunity for managing the outcomes for older, disabled people better, by rationalising these budgets and giving Holyrood control of them.

Welfare and Public Services

PROFESSOR AILSA MCKAY,
PROFESSOR OF ECONOMICS, GLASGOW CALEDONIAN UNIVERSITY

Professor McKay suggested that the constitutional debate offers an opportunity for thinking about the radical changes that we might wish to make to the welfare system; an opportunity for 'thinking outside the box.'

She proposed to begin by thinking about what sort of welfare system Scotland might want, and suggested that the Referendum provides an opportunity for us to consider welfare reform more compassionately. This includes placing greater focus on preventative spend and taking an anticipatory approach to welfare, rather than a reactive approach. With this opportunity in mind, Professor McKay proposed to address two questions: (1) what makes a good society? And (2) what kind of welfare system would support this?

Professor McKay indicated that she would not discuss the option of reforming what we already have, but would instead focus her discussion on what values and principles should guide spending and policy on welfare. She referred to the proposal for a Citizens Basic Income (CBI); a payment made to every citizen as a minimum income guarantee. This would replace all income benefits, and the amount paid would be tax free. The CBI ensures that the financial gains of working are always positive, and successfully addresses the high marginal tax rates of lower-income families, referred to by Professor Bell. Professor McKay argued that the CBI would create a more secure basis for individuals to opt in and out of the labour market, and suggested that its universality would protect against discrimination. She acknowledged that the CBI requires accepting an entirely new way of thinking about welfare and the functions it can and should perform, but recommended that we stop thinking only about long-term change and start thinking in the short to medium term. She argued that the current 'crisis in capitalism' provides an opportunity to reshape our thinking on society and how its structures can be tailored to the needs of all citizens across Scotland's communities.

The current system is argued to be failing, particularly from a gender perspective, because formal social security arrangements have traditionally served men more favourably than women.

This is in part due to the direct relationship between insurance-based benefits and the labour market, but is also due to the failure of policy to recognise the diverse role of women as wives, mothers, carers and workers. Professor McKay suggested that the constitutional debate provides a platform for discussing these failings, and argued that gender concerns should be central to this debate.

Professor McKay indicated that the CBI should not be viewed as a panacea for all ills, nor as a stand-alone measure. It should instead be viewed as a framework for building a welfare system that allows us to consider the totality of women's contributions. She asked whether there is a desire for this in Scotland, and pointed out that the current Scottish Government has demonstrated its commitment to gender equality, indicating that there might be support for something like CBI in the current political climate. Professor McKay suggested that the door is open for creating a space for new thinking that more accurately accounts for a whole range of economic activity that is currently invisible within a policy framework focused on paid work.

Professor McKay posed the question: 'What kind of welfare system would support a good society?' She responded by explaining that the CBI does not link income provision with work, and so is emancipatory; she suggested that this model is not so much an alternative to the current welfare framework, but a philosophy aimed at enhancing individual freedom. She acknowledged that, given the value we attach to work, it is unlikely that we will reach a stage where we give payments to people for 'doing nothing'. She suggested that this reveals the narrow consideration we have of what we consider as work, and who and what we value in society. Professor McKay suggested that policies which encourage private sector investment, by boosting aggregate demand, might be best achieved by targeting resources towards meeting the needs of women and their families. This would require a fundamental shift in thinking, and an acceptance of the centrality of public sector expenditure and the care sector in supporting economic and human development. She closed with the suggestion that the CBI provides the platform for achieving this in a more gender-equal Scotland.

Welfare and Public Services

Professor Jochen Clasen,
Professor of Comparative Social Policy, University of Edinburgh

Professor Clasen agreed that the forthcoming Referendum on Scotland's future provides an opportunity to think about welfare in terms of first principles. His discussion reflected upon the British benefit system, and compared it with those of other countries.

He began by pointing out that social surveys tell us the welfare state is still very popular in the UK, but that looking into these surveys in more detail reveals that this applies more in some areas than in others. Pensions and the NHS are still considered the most deserving areas of the British welfare system, but the public image of Britain's attitude towards people in poverty is rather harsh. He indicated that similar divisions do apply in other European countries. He referred to a study done by Danish academics, comparing articles on 'poverty' in thousands of broadsheet and tabloid newspapers in the UK, Sweden and Denmark over a five-year period. This study demonstrated that poverty is a far more prominent issue in the UK than elsewhere, and that negative images of poverty, which associate it with crime, benefit abuse, illegal immigrants and unwillingness to work, feature almost twice as much in the UK as in Sweden and Denmark. He added that the notion of single parents 'defrauding' the system is still a theme in the British press, but is entirely absent from the press in Denmark and Sweden.

Professor Clasen speculated that the negative public image of welfare benefit claimants may simply be a reflection of current political discourse, and pointed out that recent policy has reinforced this mentality. He observed, by way of example, that the latest budget speech by George Osborne justified decisions to make jobseekers sign on weekly rather than fortnightly, and to extend the waiting period before benefits actually become payable. By contrast, improvements to public pensions were justified with the argument that people have paid into the system all their lives. There is evidence of a division between how taxpayers and benefits claimants are viewed.

Acknowledging that similar divisions might be found in other countries, Professor Clasen nevertheless suggested that the strength of this division in the UK can be linked to the architecture of the British benefits system. He observed that everywhere in the world there are three underlying notions of social justice:

1. **Universal benefits:** these are the kind of benefits that we should strive for, but they are not being advanced. In the UK, universal benefits such as child benefits and some disability benefits have been cut back. They have also become less prominent elsewhere;

2. **Means-tested benefits:** these are found in all European countries, but their use is a very significant part of the social security system in the UK, and has become more significant in recent decades;

3. **Social insurance contributory benefits:** these types of benefits are received for contributions made during employment. The use of this type of benefit is still considerable in the UK, with close to half of all cash spending on benefits coming out of the National Insurance fund. However, almost all of this goes towards pensions. In Nordic countries, by comparison, social insurance benefits remain highly relevant not only for pensioners, but also for those below pension age.

Professor Clasen suggested that there is a big difference between the UK and other European countries with regard to welfare policy and practice, and that this difference could be used as a foundation for debate about first principles. In particular, there might be opportunity to consider the advantages and limitations of the idea of reciprocity in relation to social welfare, i.e. the notion of getting 'something for something' and not 'something for nothing'. Professor Clasen indicated that this type of debate would serve three purposes. First, it would shift the debate away from primarily looking at poverty and towards the notion of insurance as a way of creating confidence that there is support available for all people paying into the welfare system. Secondly, it could create the opportunity to look to other countries and the way they do things. The governance of social security can look very different in other European countries, for example in France and Germany there is not one single NI fund, but several different funds run for different risks. These are not always run by the state, but by intermediary organisations.

Finally, shifting the debate towards a consideration of reciprocity would better engage higher income groups with the system. This notion of reciprocity is currently very alien in the UK, where the focus is frequently on benefit payments being 'too high'. Professor Clasen pointed out that in the rest of Europe, benefits are understood as necessary to maintain the living standards of people who find themselves out of work through no fault of their own.

Welfare and Public Services

Professor Michael Keating FBA FRSE,
Professor of Politics, University of Aberdeen

Professor Keating started his contribution with the proposition that the current division of competencies with regard to welfare in Scotland is very much like that in other devolved countries around the world, and is based upon the principle that redistributive matters should be dealt with at the highest level; i.e., at the level of national Government, with service delivery matters dealt with at the local level. He observed that this assumption arises partly from the notion that social solidarity is best expressed through the nation state, and partly from the fact that a larger area is required to mobilise the resources effectively for redistribution. This notion was articulated by the Calman Commission, ahead of the Scotland Act 2012. The Scotland Act, Professor Keating observed, did not noticeably shift the balance of responsibilities with regard to welfare. However, he proposed to argue that this notion is one which can no longer be held, because the whole concept of the welfare state is restructuring; so that in the future we will not have anything which looks like the present welfare state. Making projections about the future costs of welfare in the UK on the basis of the welfare state we have at present is therefore very misleading. Professor Keating suggested that the assumption that redistributive matters must be dealt with at the level of the nation state has two dimensions, a functional one and a territorial/spatial one. These two dimensions, he suggested, come together in the case of Scotland.

Professor Keating observed that welfare has typically been understood as entailing redistributive cash benefits, and argued that it is not the case that only cash payments are redistributive. We need to look at welfare in a much broader sense; it is increasingly apparent that all public services are redistributive. In Scotland, investments in health and education, for example, are highly redistributive, because they affect different populations in different ways. He pointed out that where Scotland has had the option to take redistributive decisions, it has done so; for example with regard to student fees and health charges. Professor Keating made the point that the old model of the welfare state is based upon the 'old' social risks posed by the traditional model of the labour market, a model which is now out of date.

There is now acknowledgement of a set of new social risks, and the whole vocabulary of talking about need and benefits has evolved to address the complexity of the new social risks which are being insured against. He pointed out that there is a general consensus that it does not make sense to pay people to remain out of work, and suggested that linking welfare into the work of labour markets is a broad international trend that has consensus from left to right. The controversy lies in the political disagreements about how this should be delivered.

Professor Keating observed that this broad international trend has a territorial dimension, and that the welfare state is changing its territorial scale, with combinations of social risks and problems occurring differently in different places. Many anti-poverty initiatives are therefore territorial, and often the best place to link welfare and labour markets is at the local and regional scale, because that is where problems arise. The problem is that if you detach this from the national welfare system, you lose the coherent approach to tackling these issues. Professor Keating suggested that the scale of approaches to welfare is shifting and becoming more territorialised, and argued that it is no longer adequate to suggest that the nation state is the sole locus of social solidarity, or even the most appropriate. He added that smaller countries tend to be better at social solidarity.

Asking how these factors affect Scotland, Professor Keating observed that the two dimensions discussed, the functional and the territorial, intercept in Scotland. He added that the constitutional debate in Scotland is increasingly turning towards these questions about welfare. Whether we are talking about independence, enhanced devolution or the status quo, these policy issues and the challenges of bringing power and resources together in the right place, are going to be present. Professor Keating suggested that the present allocation of responsibilities under the devolution settlement does not adequately address these issues.

Thinking about what will happen next, Professor Keating predicted that the welfare state as we know it will not exist in 20 years' time because the money will run out. He observed that there has been a certain tendency in Scotland towards greater universalism, and suggested that the balance of policy instruments is changing. The implication of this is that an independent Scotland would end up with a welfare settlement somewhat different to the rest of the UK. Welfare, he suggested, will not be exclusively Scottish or British; it will operate at multiple levels, but there will emerge a Scottish space of social solidarity, which has enormous implications for the division of powers, which Professor Keating suggested needs to be looked at again. It also has huge implications for taxation and the amount of money we are prepared to pay. He suggested that we are heading for a different welfare settlement to what we currently have, and observed that the resources for this are very limited. He suggested that we use the constitutional debate to think about how we can use social solidarity to address the new issues in the welfare debate, not to focus on the old issues.

Welfare and Public Services

QUESTIONS AND ANSWERS

The first question from the audience asked what economic benefits there would be, to an independent Scotland, of helping to get people who are disabled back into work. Responding to this question, the panel suggested that this was a relevant question, and one that applied not just to Scotland but to the whole of the UK. Mr Goulden indicated that it is unclear how constitutional change in Scotland might affect this, but suggested that assisting people back into work would be one of the most important strands of a welfare system in an independent Scotland, and would have to be at the heart of it.

A point was made by an audience member that although the speakers' presentations had addressed many important issues, they had missed some fundamentals, including the idea that in order to have viable welfare and public services we need first to have a widespread and responsible attitude to each person contributing what they can to the country's wealth. Given that the scenario in 2004 would have led to a Scotland which sought independence then being encumbered by the failure of Scottish banks, it was asked in what way an independent Scotland without a viable policy for wealth improvement could have the basis for radical change.

Professor Keating responded that, when looking at small, independent states, there is a notion that social investment can be used to achieve economic development; for example investments in childcare. It is therefore useful to link the social and the economic; you don't have to be an independent state to do this. It does involve thinking in the long term, however, and political cycles do not readily facilitate this.

Professor Clasen observed that social insurance is founded on the notion of getting something for something, and suggested that instead of starting with the broad question of what an independent Scotland should do with regard to welfare, we should start empirically by looking at what works in other countries. Denmark, for example, has a different welfare system, and incorporates childcare that allows more parents into work. This model could be used as an empirical example of what Scotland might do. In thinking about what sort of system Scotland might want, Professor Clasen acknowledged that we would need to raise the tax question, and to look at social justice within the tax question.

Professor Keating responded that, when looking at small, independent states, there is a notion that social investment can be used to achieve economic development; for example investments in childcare. It is therefore useful to link the social and the economic; you don't have to be an independent state to do this. It does involve thinking in the long term, however, and political cycles do not readily facilitate this.

Professor Clasen observed that social insurance is founded on the notion of getting something for something, and suggested that instead of starting with the broad question of what an independent Scotland should do with regard to welfare, we should start empirically by looking at what works in other countries. Denmark, for example, has a different welfare system, and incorporates childcare that allows more parents into work. This model could be used as an empirical example of what Scotland might do. In thinking about what sort of system Scotland might want, Professor Clasen acknowledged that we would need to raise the tax question, and to look at social justice within the tax question.

Professor McKay referred to the social investment model, and suggested that the relationship between the social and the economic is currently missing. She questioned what we mean by gainful employment, and suggested that we should in fact remove the focus on employment and instead refer to gainful work, adding that some of the work that people are engaged is in very useful, but currently invisible. Professor Bell suggested that the Scottish Government has a lot of control over the levers of economic development, and noted that Scotland spends three times as much per head on economic development as the rest of the UK. However, it is difficult to know what works and what does not work. Economic development in Scotland currently touches on areas of social policy and early intervention, and is starting to get the message that these interventions have to be focused on the very young. Careful consideration is required, however, of the impact this will have upon taxes. He pointed out that Scotland has a very unequal distribution of income which, although not quite as unequal as in London, still represents a challenge in that Scotland relies upon a very small number of people for economic development. Professor Bell suggested that there are lots of ways of thinking about income distribution that rely less heavily on such a small proportion of the population. He observed that a big increase in Scotland's income inequality began in the 1980s, and suggested that this will take a long time to reverse.

Welfare and Public Services

The Chair, Ms Nanjiani put the question to the panel, *"do you agree with the Institute of Fiscal Studies that Scots would have to pay higher tax in an independent Scotland?"* Professor Bell responded that this belief is based upon an assumption about what an independent Scotland would do, and it is based upon the understanding that Scotland has a larger deficit than the rest of the UK, although this understanding does not take into consideration Scotland's oil revenues. Professor Bell indicated that Scotland will still have a larger deficit than the UK in the long run, and added that there would be long-run pressure on budgets. He observed that most small countries have low levels of debt relative to their GDPs, but indicated that Scotland's GDP is much higher. Debt in itself is not necessarily bad, but it becomes a problem if it means that markets lose confidence in you.

Looking to other countries, Ms Nanjiani asked the panel which model, in a country closest in size and population to Scotland, is the best for Scotland to try and follow.

Professor Clasen suggested that the process of change is evolutionary, and that it is therefore not possible to look at another country and simply make the decision to introduce something similar in Scotland right away. He observed that Denmark is famous for its flex-security model, whereby job protection is quite weak but there are strong benefits and active labour market policies. He pointed out that this model is not something that was invented, but that it was almost an historical accident. He suggested that if we agree that having people in work and raising the employment rate makes sense, then it is a good idea to look to countries such as Denmark. For this, Denmark is very close to the sort of country that Scotland could become, although in other respects it is very far away. There is no one best country for Scotland to emulate, but we can look at different aspects that work in different countries.

A point was made by a member of the audience, that in Scotland there is a tradition of designing policy to protect the weak, but that with regard to the comments made on the gender gap, there is a gender-specific vulnerability that has not been adequately addressed. This audience member commented that in his professional capacity as a GP, he sees lots of disenfranchised young men who are unemployable, and who are more vulnerable than the women their age who are apparently more ready for work. He pointed out that there are no services to refer these men on to, and suggested that society currently leaves young men entirely behind.

Professor McKay responded by suggesting that a shift in attitudes will only be achieved by evolution, not by revolution. She added that we cannot only focus on the supply side of the labour market, but indicated that we must also look at the demand side and the role of employers. She suggested that this focus has been lost in the UK, and argued that we need to move towards a new partnership of working. She pointed out that the public sector is not the enemy of economic growth, and can be very productive in driving economic development. She also pointed to the role of households in driving economic development, and suggested that resources are depleting from households and being directed into the labour market instead, meaning there is a gap in many households between resources going in and resources going out. An independent Scotland, she suggested, would give space for considering this issue, but whether there would be the political will to address this is not known.

Mr Goulden responded to the issue around gender by pointing out that New Labour's policies on poverty accidentally addressed many gender gaps as a side effect of other aims. He provided the example of pension credits and observed that although this benefit was introduced for all pensioners, single female pensioners benefited most from these, because they had fallen so far behind. The same phenomenon applies to lone parents, because so much extra was put into child tax credits, and lone parents had fallen behind so badly, they were helped proportionately more by the policy. When you look at national minimum wage, the same story applies again; rates of low pay amongst women went down quite dramatically, because they had experienced higher rates of low pay to begin with. Conversely, the rate of low pay amongst men was not nearly as heavily affected by the introduction of a national minimum wage. Mr Goulden went on to suggest that poverty amongst young people, and their living standards, is a real concern. He observed that the Institute of Fiscal Studies' analysis of the poverty figures focused on intergenerational poverty, and highlighted this as representing a big challenge.

Professor Bell added that there have been stories in the media in recent years about graduates not being able to get graduate-type jobs, and observed that the statistics tell us that this difficulty applies to all young people, not only to young graduates. Lower wages are a feature of young people's early employment, whether they are graduates or not; so that over the last ten years, people in the 16–24 age bracket are now getting around 50% of an average adult's wage, compared with around 58% ten years ago. He pointed out that the types of jobs young men would have done 40 or 50 years ago simply do not exist anymore. He added that the challenge for young men also applies in the United States, where recent statistics have shown that the life expectancy of poor white men is actually falling.

Welfare and Public Services

A member of the audience asked the panel to comment on the idea that, if Scotland were to become independent, this would offer the opportunity for a quiet revolution, whereby Scotland could look at what poverty means and set up an effective strategy for dealing with it.

Responding to this question, Mr Goulden suggested that this is probably the closest to a revolution that Scotland will get. Professor Keating observed that the Referendum debate comes to life when it is looking at substantive issues such as poverty and welfare, and added that these questions and issues should have been debated after the devolution settlement, but that at that time there was more money available and the hard choices which now have to be made were not seen to be necessary. He suggested that if we are going to sustain the sort of long-term policies that we probably all think of as desirable, then we have to get the institutions right. The institutions don't simply concern Scotland's relationship with the UK or Europe, but institutions within Scotland. He suggested that we have not got this right so far, and have not been very good at taking the hard, long-term decisions. Referring to social partnership, Professor Keating suggested that what marks the UK out from the rest of Europe is the notion that social partnership is dead, and has been for 30 years. By way of example, he indicated the proposition in the UK that it is acceptable to cut corporation tax for the whole of business without asking for anything in return, pointing out that other European countries do not work like that.

A comment was raised by a member of the audience that the forthcoming Referendum does provide opportunity for debate about public services, but that it is not clear that this debate is actually being had. Referring to intergenerational issues, he suggested that there are profound choices between universal approaches to welfare and more targeted ones, which are evident in the discussions being had around interventions in child poverty and the types of support that are being given. It was suggested that in the constitutional debate, a lot of focus has been on the principles and very little has been on the actual practicalities of welfare and public spending. The question was raised as to whether the constitutional debate actually gets in the way of discussing these practicalities and of addressing the difficult choices that might have to be made. The point was made that poverty statistics are worse in Scotland than they are south of the Border, and it was suggested that the debate about Scotland's future is characterised by comfortable delusions about the choices Scotland faces.

Responding to this comment, Professor Bell echoed the earlier sentiment that in the short term, nothing much in the way of radical change can occur, and that change will be evolutionary rather than radical. He observed that there have been lots of opportunities for Scotland, since Devolution, to do more radical things. Some things have happened south of the Border which we may not like, but decisions have been made and policies have been put into place.

By way of example, Professor Bell pointed to the reluctance by Scotland in giving out direct payments to individuals rather than providing services to them, observing that England has progressed much further than Scotland in relation to giving people cash benefits. Scotland has been very tentative about experimenting with that type of provision. The budget for that type of provision in Scotland was £59 million, out of a £12 billion total Scottish Government budget. In this sense, Professor Bell suggested that devolution has been a bit of a disappointment.

A member of the audience expressed frustration that opportunities have been identified for doing things differently, but have not been grasped. It was suggested that this is because of what is happening in our society. The observation was made that even in the speaker and audience contributions of the evening, there was an implicit assumption that an ageing population is a bad thing, for example. It was suggested that there has also been too much focus on problems with the benefit system. Referring to the discussion on direct payments, it was observed that there is a consequence of those direct payments on the worker who is providing the service for the person using direct payments, including a series of issues around irregular work patterns for that person, lack of training, access to maternity pay and a number of other conditions of employment which are quite threatened by the direct payment model.

Child tax credit was referred to by speakers as being a good and redistributive benefit. However, it was observed that what child tax credit has done is to shift a large amount of money into the private sector by paying high fees to private sector nurseries. The point was made that there is currently no cap on the private rented sector, which causes people to really struggle when there are cuts in their wages. We need to look at how we are going to address these issues. This involves ensuring there is access to regular work and good working conditions. The point was also made that an ageing population can still see older people in work, and that there are very good models for this.

Welfare and Public Services

Professor McKay stated her agreement with the points raised, but pointed out that addressing these points means going back to looking at institutions. The current model is still built around a male-breadwinner model, which is out of date. We need to look at our institutions and to see the welfare state as an institution that is built around a gender and labour market bias that is very outdated.

A final question was raised by an audience member, who suggested that the constitutional debate has so far focused on the big ideas, but that better decisions by voters might be possible if the political debate was more up front and addressed the practical issues more directly. Professor Keating agreed, and suggested that the debate so far has been guilty of dishonesty. He added that in the Western world, it is impossible to talk about taxation, as this is seen as a taboo by politicians. He observed that no economist would design the UK taxation system from scratch, and suggested that the constitutional debate is not currently getting the political leadership it needs. This is because politics does not reward politicians who take risks. Professor Bell remarked that politicians need to address how policy is designed and delivered, but they do not do this.

CLOSING REMARKS AND SUMMING UP

Bringing the discussion to a close, Ms Nanjiani asked the panel to reflect briefly upon what issues and questions the public should keep in mind when deciding how to vote in the forthcoming Referendum. Mr Goulden acknowledged a consensus in the audience's questions that the Referendum represents an opportunity, but that there is, as yet, no one who is putting the vision out there of what Scotland will look like in the future; either as an independent country or as part of the UK.

He suggested that both sides of the debate should try to put forward their vision more clearly. Professor Bell echoed the sentiment that the Referendum certainly represents a big opportunity, and cautioned that people should not expect immediate change.

He encouraged people to think about the political leadership that will be necessary to drive change and to bring about a better overall welfare distribution. Professor McKay agreed that the Referendum would be about political leadership, and advised people to think about who would deliver, and who has the commitment to deliver, on both the gender equality agenda and on the welfare and public services reform agenda. She suggested that these agendas should be delivered in a compassionate and anticipatory way.

Professor Clasen felt that there are big issues to address in the debate about Scotland's future, and noted that talking about benefits necessarily entails talking about taxation. He suggested that in some respects there is a big debate taking place, but that this is not being led by the politicians, as it should be. He added that political parties should set out their intentions with regard to welfare and public services, and provide a clear indication of what they would need to do to achieve these intentions. He suggested that this would be essential for a proper debate about welfare.

Professor Keating concluded by suggesting that it is heartening that citizens are now starting to take the debate out of the hands of the politicians. He added that rather than asking themselves what they would like to happen, people should begin pushing the politicians as to what the consequences of a 'Yes' or a 'No' vote in the Referendum would be. It is not clear that a 'Yes' or a 'No' vote alone would bring about change, there needs to be an indication of how this change would be achieved by each side of the debate.

Scotland's Referendum and Britain's Future

Scotland's Referendum and Britain's Future

5 March 2014, at the British Academy

INTRODUCTION

The Chair, **Sally Magnusson,** Reporter for BBC Scotland, opened the eleventh seminar in the series with the observation that Scotland has been talking about constitutional matters for a long time, but with less than 200 days to go until the Referendum on Scotland's future, England has only just begun to acknowledge and refer to the fact that the Scots will soon be making a decision which will affect them also. She added that nuance and subtlety have not been regular visitors to the independence debate, and welcomed the Enlightening the Constitutional Debate series as providing a more nuanced discussion of Scotland's constitutional future. She then introduced the panel of speakers who would be addressing the topic. These speakers were invited by the British Academy and the Royal Society of Edinburgh to discuss aspects of the Referendum debate, including the legal and constitutional issues relevant to the debate, and the key factors influencing public opinion on what Scotland's future could and should be. Closing remarks were provided by **Professor Neil Walker FBA FRSE**, Regius Professor of Public Law and the Law of Nature and Nations, University of Edinburgh.

Speakers:

> **Professor Vernon Bogdanor CBE FBA**, Research Professor, Institute for Contemporary British History, King's College, London

> **Professor Michael Keating FBA FRSE**, Professor of Politics, University of Aberdeen

> **Professor Adam Tomkins FRSE**, Professor of Public Law, University of Glasgow

> **Professor John Curtice FRSA FRSE**, Professor of Politics, Strathclyde University

The debate was conducted as an open, public discussion seminar.

Professor Vernon Bogdanor CBE FBA
Research Professor, Institute for Contemporary British History, King's College, London

Professor Bogdanor began with the question *can the union survive?*, and suggested that this is a question which only the Scots can answer. He added that this is a momentous question, and pointed out that those in favour of independence do not see themselves as seeking sovereignty, but rather as wishing to renegotiate the union. Under the current Referendum debate, the Scottish Government is not seeking sovereignty, but rather a shared monarchy, a shared currency, and a shared social union with the rest of the UK. Opponents of independence often highlight the constraints that would face an independent Scotland, in particular those that would follow from continuing to use the pound, which would probably also involve banking and fiscal union. Professor Bognador observed that the arguments which are raised by the unionist camp are, paradoxically, not that different from the arguments raised in the nationalist camp. The nationalists in the Scottish independence debate have frequently argued that independence is not a radical step, but rather an adjustment. At the same time, the unionists argue that an independent Scotland will not be able to make as many changes as it might wish to, so there is little gain to be made from Scotland becoming independent. Within the Eurozone, for example, there is little scope for sovereignty. In matters such as competition, trade, agriculture and fisheries, members of the Eurozone are constrained. An independent Scotland joining the Eurozone would be similarly constrained. Both unionists and nationalists therefore argue the same point; that we live in a world where sovereignty matters much less than it used to. We live in a global and interconnected world in which borders are no longer so important.

Professor Bogdanor expressed the view that both sides of the debate take this point too far. He pointed out that despite the rhetoric, the European Union (EU) has not succeeded in establishing a common foreign or security policy, and on all foreign policy issues in the last 25 years the EU has been divided. It would therefore be open to an independent Scottish Government to choose its own foreign and defence policy. He referred to the example of the Republic of Ireland, which has chosen its own foreign defence policy and which remained neutral throughout WWII and the Iraq war. Independence, therefore, is not just a further step along the path to devolution; devolution is a question of degree, whereas independence is absolute. Independence, he indicated, has two implications. The first is that Scottish representatives would become the representatives of an independent state, meeting in Edinburgh.

The second, as a necessary corollary of this, is that Scotland would no longer send MPs to Westminster. Instead, Scotland would be represented in London by its own High Commissioner. This means that Scotland would no longer enjoy any leverage over decisions being made in Westminster.

Scottish nationalists have various aspirations for an independent Scotland, such as a shared currency and social union. However, Professor Bogdanor observed that an independent Scotland would have no right to these things. It could only propose them and see if the rest of the UK would agree to them in negotiations. A 'Yes' vote in the Referendum, he observed, is a vote to become a citizen of another country, distinct from the UK, after which it would not be possible for Scotland to pick and choose which aspects of the union it wished to enjoy. An independent Scotland would have to negotiate for those things it now enjoys as a right.

Professor Bogdanor concluded with the suggestion that there is an argument for saying that his opening question – *can the union survive?* – has already been answered. This is because the debate is often thought to centre on economics; and, in particular, on the question of whether independence would make the Scots richer or poorer. He suggested there has been at least one poll which has indicated that people's views would change if they could be persuaded that Scotland would be better off under independence. However, he expressed the opinion that questions about independence are not actually questions about economics, but about identity. He pointed out that the Irish did not seek home rule because they thought it would make them richer, nor did the British colonies, and nor did Slovakia when separating from the Czech Republic. In these cases, these countries are making a statement about identity. Arguments about economics cannot be used to persuade people that they are British, or that they are not. When an entity no longer wishes to be identified along with another entity, independence is the logical conclusion. The question, therefore, is whether Scottish identity is compatible with membership of the UK, as in the case of Northern Ireland, or is it entirely incompatible, as in the case of the Republic of Ireland?

Professor Bogdanor closed with the remark that in the debate so far, there has been a lot of analysis of the forces seeking to break up the union, but insufficient analysis of the forces trying to keep it together.

Professor Michael Keating FBA FRSE
Professor of Politics, University of Aberdeen

Professor Keating proposed to speak about the 'middle-ground' options available to Scotland, and began with the observation that independence does not mean what it used to mean in the old days of the nation state. He suggested that the Referendum question is clear in words but not in meaning, and provided two reasons for why independence and sovereignty no longer mean what they used to:

1 The functional meaning of independence no longer exists. This is the understanding of independence as macroeconomic management and the control of fiscal levels. Independence does not provide this anymore, but it does provide choices, for example about which unions to join and which opportunities to negotiate.

2 At a deeper level, the question of sovereignty is not straightforward, and this is particularly the case in the UK. Professor Keating suggested that the issue of sovereignty has never been resolved in the UK, nor has the relationship between England and Scotland. Sovereignty, and the relationship of nationhood to sovereignty, has taken different forms in the UK, which is why the UK has worked as well as it has as a state, up until now – except for the problem of Ireland. Professor Keating referred to the work of the late Professor Sir Neil MacCormick, who argued that there are at least two doctrines of sovereignty: either Westminster is absolutely sovereign and this is the sole condition of sovereignty; or there are other conditions of sovereignty. In the Scottish example, sovereignty has historically been divided between Parliament and the Crown, so there is no clear, absolute sovereignty as there is in England. Scotland is part of the UK and the EU, but it does not have absolute sovereignty. Therefore, unionists who argue that Westminster is sovereign and nations are either in or out, are arguing across others in the debate who have a different understanding of sovereignty. Professor Keating observed that multiple meanings of sovereignty can and have coexisted, until a crisis point is reached, and then there has to be a Referendum. He added that it would be a pity if the UK lost its notion of constitutional pluralism within the debate on Scotland's constitutional future. He reiterated the point that the union is understood differently in different parts of the UK, and suggested that this has been forgotten by some of the unionists in the Scottish Referendum debate.

Scotland's Referendum and Britain's Future

Having identified the theoretical framework for discussing sovereignty, Professor Keating went on to observe that the question of a middle ground is not only about devolution, but about the rights of nations within a complex union. The critical issue on which this discussion often centres is the issue of the welfare state. In Scotland, the welfare state is a big issue, and taxation is clearly a further issue which directly corresponds with that. The nationalist argument is that welfare can be delivered better at the Scottish level. However, this does not pay attention to the way the welfare state looks now. The general feeling in debates about the welfare state is that the current welfare settlement in the UK is not sustainable. There is no clear consensus as to what should be done about this, other than the general agreement that employment policy is the best way to address the issue, on the basis that it is better to pay people to work than to pay them not to work. Professor Keating's discussion of the welfare state and its relationship to the Referendum debate raised points discussed by him in more detail at the series event on Welfare and Public Services. This discussion is summarised under the chapter heading of that name.

Professor Keating observed that there is a territorial dimension also, and pointed out that many of the instruments of the welfare state are best handled at local, regional and sub-state levels. If we look at the political arena in Scotland, Scots don't have different preferences with regard to social welfare, compared with the rest of the UK, but the social compromises in Scotland are struck differently. Scotland may not wish to have exactly the same welfare settlements as England; i.e. those determined by marginal constituencies in the south of England. Desire for a different kind of welfare reform in Scotland necessarily implies taxation powers, which in turn may imply people in Scotland paying more in taxation. Professor Keating predicted that in ten years' time we will have a Scotland which is more autonomous, and which has its own welfare settlement, not radically different from that in the rest of the UK, but significantly different. He suggested that these changes would probably take place without Scotland becoming fully independent. Concluding his section of the discussion, Professor Keating suggested that the 'third way' does not need to represent a compromise between Scotland being independent and Scotland being a member of the UK, but that there is a foundation upon which we can build a broader consensus about where Scotland is going.

PROFESSOR ADAM TOMKINS
PROFESSOR OF PUBLIC LAW, UNIVERSITY OF GLASGOW

Professor Tomkins focused his discussion on the legal and constitutional implications of a 'Yes' outcome in the Scottish Referendum in consideration of public international law. He made the point that in the event of a 'Yes' outcome, Scotland would become a new state and the rest of the UK would be the 'continuator' state. He observed that this position is the one set out in the very first of the UK Government's *Scotland Analysis* series of reports, and is based upon published legal opinion. He added that this view is not generally contested, but is fairly widely accepted. What is less well understood are the consequences of this essential distinction. The consequences are that, in the event of Scotland becoming independent, the institutions of the UK would automatically become the institutions of the rest of the UK. These institutions include, for example, security and intelligence services, the Bank of England and the BBC. Scotland, Professor Tomkins suggested, would not have any claim over these institutions.

The legal position with regard to assets and liabilities has slightly different implications to that regarding institutions, and the assets and liabilities of the UK would, in the event of Scottish independence, be apportioned equitably between the two states. This would constitute a large part of the negotiations which would take place between Scotland and the rest of the UK in the event of a 'Yes' outcome in the Referendum. Any settlements would take place within the broad framework of international law principles, meaning that UK fixed property located in Scotland would become the property of the new Scottish state, and conversely Scotland would have no claim over the UK's fixed property in the rest of the UK, or overseas. The UK's moveable property in Scotland would become the property of the new Scottish state where it was specifically for local use. Other assets and liabilities would be apportioned equitably; this could be determined by a population share, or in the case of national debt, by a GDP share. Historical contributions would have no relevance to this process, so it would not matter, for example, if UK fixed assets in Scotland had been paid for by the rest of the UK; they would still pass to the new Scottish state.

Scotland's Referendum and Britain's Future

Dividing the assets and liabilities of the union is a hugely complex task, and Professor Tomkins observed that the UK Government, in its *Scotland Analysis* series, has given an indication of some of the key aspects of this complexity. In the *Scotland Analysis* paper on defence, for example, it was noted that an independent Scottish state could not simply co-opt existing units that are primarily recruited or based in Scotland, because these are an integral part of the UK armed forces. While many military bases are located in Scotland, these do not operate in isolation; they depend upon close integration with other capabilities, services and infrastructure spread across the UK. Moveable military and defence assets located in Scotland would not therefore pass automatically to an independent Scotland, because if they are integral to the UK as a whole then they are not specifically for local use.

Professor Tomkins observed that the Scottish Government White Paper on Independence has been written without regard for the legal distinction between assets and institutions. The White Paper makes the claim, for example, that the pound is as much Scotland's as it is the UK's; but this statement is legally incorrect. The pound is Scotland's currency now, precisely because Scotland is part of the UK now. If Scotland leaves the UK it also leaves all UK institutions, of which the pound is one. This does not mean that Scotland cannot use the pound unilaterally, but that it cannot do so as part of a monetary union with the rest of the UK, unless the rest of the United Kingdom agree to this. If Scotland were to choose to use the pound unilaterally, it would have no control over interest rates and would therefore lose some of its autonomy, rather than gaining any.

With regard to UK embassies, the White Paper claims that Scotland is entitled to UK embassies overseas. Again, this is legally incorrect. These embassies would remain in the possession of the rest of the UK in the event of Scottish independence, unless they were based in Scotland. If the Scottish Government wanted to use these institutions, it would therefore have to negotiate their terms of use. Professor Tomkins observed that many of the core elements of the Scottish Government's approach to independence are based on assumptions that are highly questionable in law.

PROFESSOR JOHN CURTICE FRSA FRSE
PROFESSOR OF POLITICS, STRATHCLYDE UNIVERSITY

Professor Curtice discussed public opinion in Scotland and England and, in particular, the implications of public opinion, on both sides of the border, for Scotland's relationships with the rest of the UK in the future. He began with the suggestion that the Referendum in itself may be taken as evidence enough that Anglo–Scottish relations are not very rosy. He added that there tends to be a presumption that after 15 years of devolution, Scotland feels less closely tied to the UK than it previously has. He suggested that this is not the case, however. There is no clear evidence in the polls that Scotland is any keener on independence now, following this period of devolution, than it was before. What we have seen is the SNP succeeding in exploiting devolution in a way that has proved to be much more in tune with the preferences of the Scottish public.

In addition, Professor Curtice suggested that 'accidents of history' have played a part in bringing Scotland and the UK to the point that they are at now. He referred to 'Black Wednesday' of September 1992 and the fall in popularity of the Conservative Party across the whole of the UK. This ultimately led to the Conservative Party losing all of their representation in Scotland, and the SNP emerging as the Labour Party's biggest rivals in Scotland. Following this, it was discovered that people were more willing to vote for the SNP in a devolved election that in a Westminster one. Proportional representation in Scotland ensured that this voting was translated into parliamentary seats. The SNP played this hand well, Professor Curtice suggested, and the Labour Party made the error of assuming that what the Scots wanted out of devolution was a partnership with England. This is not what Scotland is looking for. The evidence suggests that what Scotland is looking for are representatives in Edinburgh who are capable of defending and advocating Scotland's interests in London. This is what the SNP proved to be extremely effective at doing and is at least part of the reason they won in 2011. The SNP was successful because of its perceived competence and its programme of devolution, not for its commitment to independence.

Professor Curtice suggested that in terms of independence, the Scottish case is not the same as the Irish case. He argued that the Irish probably would have voted for independence come what may, because they were strongly committed to it. The situation in Scotland is different. The crucial thing about Scotland is that it is a nation with a dual identity, so the Referendum is not about how Scottish the Scots feel, but about how British they feel. Do the Scots wish to hang on to the 'British' aspects of their identities? Professor Curtice observed that, according to polling evidence, even of those who state that they are Scottish and not British, not all want independence as a natural consequence of that view.

Scotland's Referendum and Britain's Future

This is why economics becomes crucial, because a lot of people in Scotland begin to say that unless there are clear, economic benefits to Scotland becoming independent, they would rather hang on to their 'Britishness'. The implication of this is that if there is a 'No' outcome in the Referendum, it will be an unconditional outcome; given what is on offer, the Scots would prefer to hang onto what they have within the Union. At the present, Scotland does not appear to want independence, but the instinct of the Scots does appear to be that taxation should be decided in Edinburgh. Only when it comes to defence and international affairs do they tend to be of the opinion that these are not matters about which Scotland should make independent decisions. What is more, according to polls, only half of Scots think that Scottish public services should be locally funded.

Referring to England, Professor Curtice observed that while the Scots want more and more devolution, England still expects to be run by the House of Commons and is not looking for further devolution for itself. If Scotland does move towards funding more of its own public spending though, it will be reliant on taxation in Scotland rather than on the largesse of England. On this basis, England is likely to be happy for Scotland to adopt further devolution. England and Wales are currently three to one against Scotland leaving the union completely, and are beginning to accept that this outcome would not be good for them economically. England, he suggested, is increasingly keen to hang on to Scotland.

At this stage in the discussions, Sally Magnusson (the Chair) put some questions to the whole panel, for brief discussion before the open Question and Answer session.

Sally Magnusson referred to the evidence that women in Scotland are apparently less keen on independence than men, and asked the panel why they thought that was the case. She suggested the interpretation that this is because women tend to be more pragmatic than men with regard to things such as the household budget, and less directly concerned with identity.

Professor Tomkins responded that the gender gap is not to do with identity but with certainty and uncertainty, and observed that women tend to be more sceptical than men that Scotland would be better off under independence. This scepticism makes them less certain of Scottish independence and therefore less likely to favour it. Professor Bogdanor argued that the key question is not about Scottish identity, but whether Scottish identity is felt to be compatible with British identity. He added that the status quo is likely to benefit the closer we get to the Referendum.

Sally Magnusson then opened the floor for questions from the audience.

QUESTION & ANSWER SESSION

A member of the audience asked the panel to speak a little more about what is meant by 'Scottish identity' and how this manifests itself in the debate about Scotland's constitutional future. He also asked the panel to discuss how 'Scottish identity' differs from 'British identity'. Professor Tomkins responded by stating that he disagrees profoundly with the SNP's constitutional policy; however, he added that the SNP deserves considerable credit for shifting the nature of Scottish nationalism away from ethnic nationalism and towards civic nationalism. He made the point that people born outside Scotland but living there will have a vote in the Referendum, but Scottish-born people living outside Scotland will not. This supports the civic dimension to the Scottish nationalist position. The debate is not really about identity, he suggested, but about the nature of Scottish nationalism.

Professor Curtice made the point that there is no difference between Scottish and British identity, in the sense that they are both forms of psychological identity. They both represent an emotional attachment which helps people to distinguish whom they regard as 'us' and whom they regard as 'other'. He suggested that one of the fascinating things about Scotland is that a lot of people feel both Scottish and British, although for many the Scottish identity is the stronger of the two. These are all social identities, which are created by people's sense of emotional attachment. Professor Bogdanor restated that the question is not really about which identity – Scottish or British – is stronger, but rather whether Scottish identity is compatible with British identity.

Professor Keating argued that if you have to define identity, then you have lost it. Identity is a complex set of relationships. Referring to the unionist position, he suggested that unionists in Scotland used to be very good at playing on Scottish identity; if you are a patriotic Scot then you are a unionist. Being a unionist in Scotland and being a unionist in Ireland therefore meant very different things. The unionists have lost that, Professor Keating argued, because they have tried to pin down what Scottish identity is. Scottish identity, he suggested, is very politicised, although it does not map very well with politics. Scottish nationalism made that connection between identity and politics, which was not there in the past. In practice, Professor Keating suggested that people have multiple identities, and often refuse to be put in boxes.

Scotland's Referendum and Britain's Future

A member of the audience asked the panel what the political implication of a 'Yes' outcome in the Referendum would be for the rest of the UK, and made the observation that this would presumably result in the loss of 39 or 40 Labour MPs in Westminster. Professor Curtice responded that moving Scottish MPs would be nowhere near as significant for the Labour Party as moving boundaries in England and Wales. He made the point that if we go through historical records, we discover that Labour usually end up with a majority in England and Wales, and added that Scotland is not really a Labour fiefdom anymore. However, he observed that if Scottish Labour MPs were taken out of Westminster, the boundaries in England redrawn and Wales' overrepresentation reduced, then things would become much more difficult for the Labour Party. He concluded that the removal of Scottish MPs alone would not have a very significant an impact, because Labour does not typically rely on Scottish seats. Professor Bogdanor agreed, observing that there have only been two occasions when a Labour Government has depended on a Scottish vote. He acknowledged that there is more of a disparity now than has previously been the case, but suggested that the Labour party would simply need to adapt to that. Professor Tomkins observed that all MPs elected in 2015 will be elected for the duration of that Parliament. If, during that time, Scotland did become independent the House of Commons would have to resolve what to do about Scottish representation there. He added that it is not at all clear what the correct constitutional position would be, but much would depend on the position that the political parties take in the general election campaign in 2015. By the time we get to that campaign, the outcome of the Referendum will be known, and if there has been a 'Yes' outcome, negotiations will probably be already underway. One of the big political themes in the 2015 election campaign will therefore be precisely the question of what each party would try to do with regard to representing the interests of the rest of the UK during the completion of the independence negotiations. He therefore concluded that the question will be resolved by the political parties during the 2015 election campaign.

A member of the audience observed that Professor Curtice had mentioned the possibility of a conditional 'No' outcome and asked if there could be a conditional aspect to a 'Yes' outcome. She also raised a question about the envisaged timeline for independence of March 2016, suggesting that this timeline seems quite short.

Professor Curtice said that a conditional 'Yes' outcome was not likely. The UK Government was concerned that if there was the prospect of a second Referendum, then voters might be more likely to vote 'Yes' in the first instance; and the SNP were concerned that if there was a second Referendum, voters would vote 'Yes' in the first, but then vote 'No' in the second. This means that whatever the outcome of the Referendum, this is the final outcome. Professor Tomkins observed that the Referendum is taking place on the basis of the Edinburgh Agreement, which requires the Referendum to be fair, legal and decisive. This means that in constitutional terms, this Referendum must determine the outcome, even if this is determined on a small turnout or a narrow majority. In the event of a 'No' outcome, how long Scotland continued to remain in the Union is another question, and one which would depend on the size of the margin and also on the political mood in Scotland. He suggested that immediately following the Referendum, Scotland might feel completely exhausted and want anything but another round of constitutional arguments. Alternatively, Scotland might feel that nothing had been resolved, and the big question around what a 'No' outcome actually meant might still be to play for. He suggested that the beginnings of that political argument are already playing out amongst the Scottish political parties.

On the question of the SNP's proposed timeline for independence, Professor Keating suggested that the timeframe depends upon the negotiations and the attitude of the two parties. If there is goodwill on both sides, then the March 2016 deadline could be realised. However, he added that in the event of a 'No' outcome, the issue would not go away. Territorial tensions would remain, and the issue would return in later generations. Professor Bogdanor argued that the rejection of the proposal for a further Referendum is precisely due to the fact that the debate is not about economics. The vote is not conditional upon the terms of a negotiated settlement, but is absolute. He observed that originally, referenda were binding on Government, but not on Parliament, and asked whether the Scottish people count as a third chamber of Parliament for this purpose.

A member of the audience asked the panel why all of the 'disenfranchised' Scots, who live outside Scotland and cannot vote in the Referendum, have not made more of a fuss. He also asked; *if the third way were to take place, what will happen with regard to the West Lothian Question?*[1]

---

1 The question in the UK as to whether devolved regions of the UK – Northern Ireland, Scotland and Wales – can vote in the Commons on issues affecting only England.

Scotland's Referendum and Britain's Future

Responding to the first part of the question, Professor Curtice suggested that the Referendum is a residential franchise, so any disenfranchised Scot wishing to vote in the Referendum can do so simply by becoming resident in Scotland for the period leading up to the Referendum, and getting themselves on the electoral register. On the West Lothian Question, he suggested that something probably is going to have to be done with regard to Commons procedures. He referred to the Commission, chaired by Sir William McKay, established to examine this question. This Commission came up with a sensible principle that somewhere along the line there should be a vote limited to English MPs. However, Professor Curtice indicated that this Commission had suggested too many options for how that proposal might be implemented. He suggested that as a result of this, the proposal may be at risk of running into the sand. To a degree, he observed, the West Lothian Question is going to keep on dogging this issue, but so long as England continues to want to be ruled by the House of Commons there is not going to be any neat solution. Professor Bogdanor suggested that a 'dog which hasn't barked' yet is the role of the cities in the North and Midlands, which lack the leverage of either Scotland or London. He suggested that these are the areas where UKIP – which is essentially an English nationalist party – will make gains.

A question was raised about the role of Europe in the Referendum debate. The point was made that the prospect of a Referendum on the UK's membership of the EU could reopen the whole business of Scotland's place in Europe. The panel were also asked, in the event of a 'No' outcome in the Referendum on Scotland's future, what would happen to the Barnett Formula? This Formula benefits Scotland at present, but this may unravel in the event of a 'No' outcome. Professor Bogdanor responded that both supporters and opponents of the EU tend to exaggerate the degree of power sharing that is brought forward. He suggested that the EU is moving in an intergovernmental direction, and that the economic crisis of the Eurozone has been resolved broadly through intergovernmental actions. Countries within the EU are now resisting further extensions of sovereignty; for example Germany, which in many ways appears to be the most Federal of all EU countries, does not want a sharing of economic burdens with the poverty-stricken countries of the Mediterranean. He therefore argued that both sides are using the European argument irrelevantly, because it is not going to develop into the integrated Europe that its founding fathers perhaps hoped it would.

Responding to the question on the Barnett Formula, Professor Keating suggested that this Formula has survived simply because we cannot think of an alternative to it. He observed, however, that the UK is not unique in having this problem; all European countries in recent years have had debates about the regional distribution of Government spending. None has come up with an answer to this issue. Professor Curtice suggested that one of the implications of the 2012 Scotland Act and further devolution with regard to taxation in Scotland is that resources coming to Scotland under the Barnett Formula will cover a lower proportion of Scotland's spending. He suggested that this creates the potential for a win-win situation, with further devolution actually solving the Barnett problem. Professor Keating suggested that we cannot address Barnett without addressing the concerns of the Welsh, who are being seriously disadvantaged by it. Professor Tomkins agreed that further fiscal devolution makes the Barnett problem less important, however he added that further fiscal devolution also makes answering the West Lothian Question mandatory.

A question was put to the panel about the players in the Referendum debate. It was suggested that the debate so far has appeared to assume that the only players are England and Scotland, with Wales on the sidelines. The suggestion was made that this is not the case, and that in Ireland there is a great deal of awareness that the outcome of the Referendum will break the St Andrews Agreement and the Irish Settlement. A further question was put to the panel about who the negotiating body should be in the event of 'Yes' outcome in the Referendum. The observation was made that the Government of the UK has been referred to as taking on this role; however it was argued that this makes little sense. Professor Tomkins responded that it may be the case that the SNP are the players on the Scottish side between now and March 2016, but that Scotland will then have its own election, meaning that the SNP may not be the ones conducting the negotiations on the future of an independent Scotland. Professor Keating raised the concept of a 'pluri-national' state, and suggested that within the UK it is less significant that the nations of the UK are different, but more significant that the meanings of nationality in each nation are different. This is an additional complication; a multi-national state is a mosaic of separate nations living under a common roof, but the very meaning of nationality in England is distinct. In Scotland, nationality is, almost by necessity, a dual nationality, and in England it is not. This additional layer of complexity needs to be faced. This ties in with the point about the other parts of the UK, and who is a player in the debate. It is not just England as a nation versus Scotland as a nation; there is a very complex set of relationships to consider.

Scotland's Referendum and Britain's Future

Professor Tomkins added that the serious mistake of Scottish politics has been to treat the Referendum debate as though it is a question about the relationship between Edinburgh and London. He pointed out that we hear a lot about the idea of the Union, but suggested that nobody in the UK is taking a pan-Union approach to this question. He suggested that in the event of a 'No' outcome, what needs to happen is for the future of Scotland's constitutional position to be put in the context of the whole of the UK, including relationships between Edinburgh and other cities in the UK and in Scotland. He argued that the voices of governments and peoples in Northern Ireland, Wales and the north of England have to be brought to the table. At the moment, he observed, there is no table for these voices to be heard; one has to be built. He argued that we have reached the end of the road in terms of delivering devolution in the way it has traditionally been delivered. Devolution has never been imposed on anyone, it has been voted for after a coherent demand has been made in the relevant place. The process is therefore one of local demand followed by state delivery. Professor Tomkins expressed doubt that we can continue with this pattern. Whatever happens with regard to Scotland's future cannot be dictated by Scots alone.

A member of the audience asked a question about the role of identity in the Referendum debate, and suggested that making the Referendum on Scotland's future a question about identity, rather than a question about economics, was dangerous for Scotland. She argued that the arguments made about national identity tend to be very emotive, and expressed concern that now that 16 and 17 year-olds are to be allowed a vote in the Referendum, they will be particularly vulnerable to nationalist propaganda, which is being advanced in the absence of rational argument. Addressing the issue of 16 and 17 year-olds being allowed to vote in this Referendum, Professor Curtice suggested that he has reservations about this, simply because 16 and 17 year-olds are less likely to vote. However, he added that it is not necessarily the case that an older person should have a vote when a younger person does not, given that the younger person will have to live with the outcome for longer.

A member of the audience questioned some of the points raised by the panel during the discussion. He observed that several of the panel have implied that we shouldn't be asking this question, about Scottish independence, at all; it is the wrong question to ask, or it is not a sensible question. However, he suggested that we have been forced to ask this question, by the outcome of a political process.

In this respect, the Referendum perhaps represents an opportunity for the UK to explain itself more fully. He suggested an understanding of the UK not as a union state, but as a multi-national state, and asked if the panel would accept that description, and in particular if they would accept the proposition that, by the very act of agreeing that there will be a decisive Referendum, the UK has acknowledged that the Scottish people are, apparently, sovereign. Professor Curtice agreed with this position, and likened the Scotland example to when the UK acknowledged Northern Ireland as sovereign. He observed that the UK has been here before, and suggested that there is consensus that Scotland and Ireland do have the right to leave the UK, if they choose to. He agreed with the view of the UK as a multi-national state.

Sally Magnusson (the Chair) brought the discussion to a conclusion by putting the question to the panel; *how will the Referendum outcome go?* Professor Bogdanor suggested that Scottish independence will be heavily rejected, but that the political problem which will be faced will be that of the English cities in the Midlands and the North. Professor Tomkins agreed that Scotland will reject independence, but suggested that the interesting question will be what happens next; what will 'No' mean? He added that there is a further question around how unionists can ensure that the union is strengthened robustly enough that the issue of Scottish independence does not have to be revisited again. Professor Curtice indicated his view that this is a Referendum that the unionists would have to make a mess of their campaign to lose. He advised that the audience follow the debate about what might happen with regard to further devolution, which is not a debate which is going to stop following a 'No' outcome in the Referendum. He predicted that the 'victor' will end up being the option that is not on the ballot paper, i.e. significantly increased devolution. Professor Keating agreed with Professor Curtice and added that he was impressed with the way people in Scotland are taking the debate out of the hands of the politicians and asking questions about pensions and the economy. He suggested that this is very healthy, and observed that associated with the Referendum question is a question about the future of the country and the future of society. He expressed a hope that this type of discussion remains open following the Referendum.

Scotland's Referendum and Britain's Future

Closing remarks

Professor Neil Walker said that the debate had been very enlightening, and he suggested that although the discussion may not have thrown up any firm answers to the key questions surrounding the Referendum debate, it had certainly brought increased clarity to the analysis of the key issues. He then provided a brief summary of the key issues which had come to light during the discussion:

The role of identity: Professor Walker suggested that the discussion about the role of identity in the Referendum debate had been very interesting, and added that when we speak about national identity it is an umbrella term for two different types of identity. There is a cultural identity, and also a political identity. We should not necessarily take the view that there is a dichotomy between reason and identity; sometimes reason is built into identity.

The question of spectrum: Professor Walker expressed interest in the question of whether the Referendum represents an either/or choice, or whether it occurs along a spectrum. He referred to Professor Bogdanor's point that neither side of the debate is taking sovereignty seriously enough, and suggested that there is a genuine set of questions about the extent to which this is a debate which is on a spectrum. He added that this question is not just one about the here and now, but is one about what happens over the next ten to fifteen years, and observed a general consensus that the debate will not be over after the Referendum. This is consistent, he suggested, with the view that this is a debate on a spectrum.

The role of legal arguments: Professor Walker referred to the arguments presented by Professor Tomkins, which he regarded as largely correct. He suggested that the Scottish Government has made a strategic mistake in trying to base their arguments on legal grounds. He added that an interesting issue is not so much what the legal positions are, but the extent to which this is a legal question. He asked at what point this becomes a mixture between a legal and a diplomatic question, and observed that on both sides of the debate it has been treated very much as a legal question. This has polarised the debate, but has also diverted attention from what would be reasonable compromises.

Multilateral vs unilateral debate: Professor Walker questioned the extent to which this is a multilateral rather than a unilateral debate, and suggested that in Scotland the debate feels very unilateral. He argued that the debate is not, in fact, a unilateral debate. This is the case for pragmatic reasons; for example, negative feeling in the rest of the UK may affect Scotland's ability to negotiate a desired outcome for itself. What is more, there is a more creative debate to be had about the Union, which would be more successful if more people participated in it.

Appendix 1 Contributors

This contains short biographies of the speakers who contributed to the series. These are listed alphabetically. It also contains brief biographies of the Royal Society of Edinburgh (RSE) and British Academy (BA) Fellows who wrote the introductory chapter.

Introduction

PROFESSOR ALAN ALEXANDER OBE FRSE

Alan Alexander is General Secretary of the Royal Society of Edinburgh and Emeritus Professor of Public Sector Management at the University of Strathclyde. He is a former Chair of Scottish Water and has been a member of the Economic and Social Research Council, the Accounts Commission for Scotland and Postwatch.

PROFESSOR IAIN MCLEAN FBA FRSE

Iain McLean is Professor of Politics and Fellow of Nuffield College, University of Oxford. His areas of expertise are public policy, public choice, party systems and electoral systems, devolution, public finance and fiscal policy. He is a Fellow of the Royal Society of Edinburgh and of the British Academy, where he is Vice-President of Public Policy.

Speakers

DR ANGUS ARMSTRONG

Angus Armstrong is the Director of Macroeconomic Research at the National Institute for Economic and Social Research (NIESR) and also visiting Professor at Imperial College London. He holds an ESRC Senior Scotland Fellowship to assess currency and fiscal arrangements for Scotland and the UK.

MS JO ARMSTRONG

Jo Armstrong is an independent economist. She is Honorary Professor in the Business School at Glasgow University and researcher with the Centre for Public Policy for the Regions (CPPR). She has been Budget Advisor to the Scottish Parliament's Economy, Energy and Tourism Committee and its Local Government Committee. She is currently Chair of Enable Scotland and a Trustee of Social Investment Scotland.

MR GRAHAM AVERY

Graham Avery is Senior Member of St. Antony's College, Oxford University; Senior Adviser at the European Policy Centre, Brussels; and Honorary Director-General of the European Commission. His last post with the European Commission was as Director for Strategy, Coordination and Analysis in the Directorate General for External Relations.

PROFESSOR DAVID BELL FRSE

David Bell is a Professor of Economics at the University of Stirling. His specialisms are labour economics, health economics and fiscal federalism. He has advised various governmental and international bodies and was until recently the Budget Adviser to the Finance Committee of the Scottish Parliament.

VERNON BOGDANOR CBE FBA

Vernon Bogdanor is a Research Professor at the Institute for Contemporary British History at King's College, London. He has been an adviser to government and parliamentary bodies on many occasions. He is also Editor of, amongst other books, *The British Constitution in the 20th Century; Joined-Up Government*; and *From the New Jerusalem to New Labour.*

PROFESSOR CHRISTINA BOSWELL

Christina Boswell is Professor of Politics and Deputy Dean of Research, College of Humanities and Social Science at the University of Edinburgh. She specialises in European immigration and asylum policy. She has acted as consultant to the UN High Commission for Refugees, the UN Global Commission on International Migration, the British Foreign Office and the European Commission.

Contributors

MR STEPHEN BOYD

Stephen Boyd is STUC Assistant Secretary, with responsibility for economic and industrial policy, the environment, utilities, transport and arts and culture. He is a member of the First Minister's Energy Advisory Board for Scotland and of many other advisory bodies.

MR JAMES BOYLE

James Boyle was head of BBC Radio Scotland when it was named UK Radio Station of the Year. As Controller of BBC Radio 4, he reformed the network. His public service posts include Chair of the Scottish Arts Council and Chair of the Scottish Cultural Commission, and he is currently Chair of the National Library of Scotland and of the British Council Advisory Committee in Scotland.

PROFESSOR JOCHEN CLASEN

Jochen Clasen became Professor of Comparative Social Policy at Edinburgh University in 2007. He is co-founder and honorary chairman of the European Social Policy Analysis network (ESPAnet) and co-editor of the *Journal of European Social Policy*.

SARAH CRAIG

Sarah Craig, Public Law Lecturer at the University of Glasgow, is co-convenor of the Glasgow Refugee Asylum and Migration Network. Sarah has conducted research for UNHCR and the Scottish Executive and she was a member of the Scottish Refugee Council's expert group "Improving the Lives of Refugees in Scotland after the Referendum".

LIEUTENANT COLONEL STUART CRAWFORD

Stuart Crawford was a career army officer for 20 years. He attended both the British Army and US Army staff colleges, instructed at the British Army Staff College, and undertook a Defence Fellowship at Glasgow University. He now runs his own political, media and defence and security consultancy in Edinburgh.

Professor John Curtice FRSE FRSA

John Curtice is Professor of Politics and Director of the Social Statistics Laboratory at Strathclyde University and Research Consultant to NatCen/ScotCen Social Research. He is co-director of ScotCen's annual Scottish Social Attitudes surveys and an editor of NatCen's annual *British Social Attitudes* reports series.

Mr Paul Doyle

Paul Doyle is the Deputy Director of the Devolved Countries unit at HM Treasury, with responsibility for monitoring the spending of the Devolved Administrations and Territorial Offices; the Government's approach to fiscal devolution; and heading up work across the UK Government on the Scotland analysis programme.

Mr David Elstein

David Elstein has been a BBC director/producer (*Panorama, The Money Programme*); an ITV director/producer (*This Week, The World at War, Weekend World*); an independent producer (*A Week In Politics, Concealed Enemies*); Director of Programmes, Thames TV; Head of Programming, BSkyB; Chief Executive, Channel 5. He has held many other senior posts in the arts and broadcasting sectors.

Dr Jan Fidrmuc

Jan Fidrmuc is Senior Lecturer in Economics at Brunel University and Research Fellow at CESifo Institute, University of Munich, at the Institute of Economic Studies, Charles University and at the Centre for Economic Development and Institutions, Brunel. He was also a Member of the Accreditation Commission of the Slovak Republic.

Dr Gary Gillespie

Gary Gillespie was appointed Scottish Government Director and Chief Economist in September 2011. Gary joined the Scottish Government in 2000 from the Fraser of Allander Institute at the University of Strathclyde. He was appointed an Honorary Professor at Glasgow Caledonian University in January 2011.

Contributors

Emeritus Professor Charles Goodhart CBE FBA

Charles Goodhart is Emeritus Professor in the Financial Markets Group at the London School of Economics. He worked at the Bank of England for seventeen years as a monetary adviser, becoming a Chief Adviser in 1980. He served as an outside independent member of the Bank of England's new Monetary Policy Committee, 1997–2000.

Mr Chris Goulden

Chris Goulden leads the Anti-poverty strategy research programme at the Joseph Rowntree Foundation. He joined JRF in 2003. He used to manage and conduct social research on drugs and crime at the Home Office and helped develop the alcohol harm reduction strategy at the Prime Minister's Strategy Unit in the Cabinet Office.

Professor Chris Hawkesworth FRS FRSE

Chris Hawkesworth is Deputy Principal and Vice-Principal for Research at the University of St Andrews. He was appointed a Wardlaw Chair in Earth Sciences at St Andrews in 2009. He is an isotope geochemist interested in how to constrain the rates of natural processes from the geological record, and more specifically when and how the continental crust was generated and its subsequent evolution.

Professor Gerald Holtham

Gerald Holtham is Visiting Professor at Cardiff Business School and Managing Partner of Cadwyn Capital LLP, a fund management boutique. He is a former Chief Investment Officer of Morley Fund Management (now Aviva Investors), former Chair of the Independent Commission on Funding and Finance for Wales and Chief Economist at Lehman Brothers, London.

Professor Gordon Hughes

Gordon Hughes is a part-time Professor of Economics at the University of Edinburgh. From 1991 to 2001 he was Senior Adviser on energy and environmental policy at the World Bank in Washington DC, dealing with energy and infrastructure in Europe, Latin America and Asia.

MR PAUL JOHNSON

Paul Johnson is Director of the Institute for Fiscal Studies. From 2004 to 2007 he was Director of the Public Services and Growth Directorate and Chief Micro-economist at HM Treasury, as well as deputy head of the Government Economic Service.

PROFESSOR JOHN KAY CBE FBA FRSE

John Kay chaired the Review of UK Equity Markets and Long-Term Decision Making which reported to the Secretary of State for Business, Innovation and Skills in July 2012. He is a visiting Professor of Economics at the London School of Economics, and a Fellow of St John's College, Oxford.

PROFESSOR MICHAEL KEATING FBA FRSE

Michael Keating is Professor of Politics at the University of Aberdeen and Director of the Scottish Centre for Constitutional Change, an inter-university consortium based at the University of Edinburgh. He has published widely on Scottish politics, European politics and public policy.

MR COLIN MACILWAIN

Colin Macilwain is Editor of the science policy newsletter *Research Europe*, Associate Editor of *Research Fortnight*, a columnist for *Nature*, and writes news and commentary on global research policy for *Science, Cell* and other publications. He trained as an engineer and has extensive experience in writing and editing on technology, business, science and research policy.

MR BRANDON MALONE

Brandon Malone is a solicitor advocate, and a partner in a commercial law practice. He is the Chairman of the Scottish Arbitration Centre and a Co-Director of the International Centre for Energy Arbitration. He is a member of the Law Society of Scotland's Constitutional Law Sub-committee.

Contributors

PROFESSOR GAVIN McCRONE CB FRSE

Gavin McCrone has studied, written and lectured about the Scottish economy for many years. He was a Fellow and Tutor in Economics at Brasenose College, Oxford in the 1960s. He then spent two decades as Chief Economic Adviser to successive Secretaries of State for Scotland. He was successively head of two Scottish Government Departments – the Industry Department for Scotland and the Scottish Development Department.

PROFESSOR AILSA McKAY

Ailsa McKay was, until her death in March 2014, Professor in Economics at Glasgow Caledonian University. Her teaching and research interests were in the economics of the welfare state, the reform of current social security measures and the economics of gender inequalities. She was a founding member of the Scottish Women's Budget Group and a member of the Scottish Government's Equality and Budgets Advisory Group.

DR PHILLIPS O'BRIEN

Phillips O'Brien is a Reader in History at the University of Glasgow, where he also directs the University's Global Security Network. He has published very widely on British and American defence policy in the 20th and 21st centuries, with a particular emphasis on naval questions.

MS DIANA PANKE

Diana Panke is Professor of Governance in Multi-level systems at Albert-Ludwigs-Universität Freiburg. She was previously Associate Professor at University College Dublin. Her research interests include international negotiations, European integration, comparative European Union politics and Europeanisation.

PROFESSOR LINDSAY PATERSON FBA FRSE

Lindsay Paterson is Professor of Educational Policy in the School of Social and Political Science, University of Edinburgh. He has published widely on the expansion and purposes of higher education, on social mobility, on the relationship between education and civic values, on the 20th-Century history of Scottish education, and on Scottish politics.

Professor Jeremy Peat OBE FRSE

Jeremy Peat has been a member of the Competition Commission for over eight years. He was Director of the David Hume Institute until April 2014, a member of the board of Scottish Enterprise and Chair of the Board of Trustees of the Royal Zoological Society of Edinburgh. He has been Senior Economic Advisor at the Scottish Office, Group Chief Economist at RBS and BBC Scotland National Governor.

Rt Hon Lord Robertson
of Port Ellen KT GCMG PC HonFRSE

Lord Robertson of Port Ellen was United Kingdom Secretary of State for Defence from 1997 to 1999, Secretary General of NATO and Chairman of the North Atlantic Council (1999–2003) and Shadow Secretary of State for Scotland (1992–97). Amongst other roles, he is also Special Adviser to the CEOs of BP plc and Cable and Wireless Communications plc.

Professor Frances Ruane

Frances Ruane has been Director of the Economic and Social Research Institute (Ireland) since December 2006. She is a member of the Commission of the National Pensions Reserve Fund, the Economic Advisory Group in Northern Ireland, the Council of Economic Advisors in Scotland and a Research Associate of the Institute of International Integration Studies.

Professor Bernard Ryan

Bernard Ryan became Professor of Migration Law at the University of Leicester in September 2013, having previously been Professor of Law at the University of Kent. His teaching and research covers various aspects of migration law and policy. He is the co-chair of the Migration and Law Network, which aims to promote the field of migration law in British universities.

Professor Rick Rylance

Rick Rylance is CEO of the Arts and Humanities Research Council (AHRC) and Chair of the Research Councils UK (RCUK) Executive. He is Honorary Professor of English at the University of Exeter.

Contributors

PROFESSOR STEPHEN SALTER MBE FRSE

Stephen Salter is Emeritus Professor of Engineering Design at Edinburgh University. He has worked, *inter alia* on robots, energy from waves and tidal streams, desalination, traffic congestion, computer-controlled hydraulic pumps and motors, flood prevention, mine clearance, and the suppression of explosions.

PROFESSOR JO SHAW

Jo Shaw holds the Salvesen Chair of European Institutions at the University of Edinburgh, and until December 2013 was Dean of Research and Deputy Head of the College of Humanities and Social Sciences at the University of Edinburgh. She has worked in recent years on citizenship and constitutionalism from a European perspective and is co-Director of the EUDO Citizenship Observatory at the European University Institute in Florence.

PROFESSOR ADAM TOMKINS FRSE

Adam Tomkins is a constitutional lawyer. He has held the John Millar Chair of Public Law at the University of Glasgow since 2003 and since 2009 has been a legal adviser to the House of Lords Constitution Committee. He is also a member of the Advocate General's Legal Forum (advising HM Government on aspects of Scottish devolution and the independence Referendum).

PROFESSOR NEIL WALKER FBA FRSE

Neil Walker is Regius Professor of Public Law and the Law of Nature and Nations at the University of Edinburgh. Previously he was Professor of European Law at the European University Institute in Florence. He is an expert in constitutional law and constitutional theory, both in the Scottish and UK context and in the context of the European Union.

PROFESSOR WILLIAM WALKER

William Walker has been Professor of International Relations at the University of St Andrews since 1996. He is author, with Malcolm Chalmers, of *Uncharted Waters: The UK, Nuclear Weapons and the Scottish Question* (2001); and *A Perpetual Menace: Nuclear Weapons and International Order* (2012).

RT HON. BRIAN WILSON

Brian Wilson is a former Labour MP who held five Ministerial posts, including UK Trade Minister and Energy Minister, prior to his retirement from politics in 2005. He was the Founding Editor of the *West Highland Free Press* and continues to write extensively on current affairs.

MS RUTH WISHART

Ruth Wishart is a journalist and broadcaster who has worked extensively in both print and broadcast media. She has been Assistant Editor at a number of titles, including the *Sunday Mail, Sunday Standard* and *The Scotsman*, and is a columnist for *The Scotsman* and *The Herald*. She is a Board Member of Creative Scotland, and Chairs the Dewar Arts Awards.